THE

GENERAL AHIMAN REZON

AND

FREEMASON'S GUIDE:

CONTAINING

MONITORIAL INSTRUCTIONS

IN THE DEGREES OF

ENTERED APPRENTICE, FELLOW-CRAFT AND MASTER MASON,

WITH EXPLANATORY NOTES, EMENDATIONS AND LECTURES.

TOGETHER WITH THE

CEREMONIES OF CONSECRATION AND DEDICATION OF NEW LODGES,
INSTALLATION OF GRAND AND SUBORDINATE OFFICERS, LAYING
FOUNDATION STONES, DEDICATION OF MASONIC HALLS,
GRAND VISITATIONS, BURIAL SERVICES, REGULATIONS
FOR PROCESSIONS, MASONIC CALENDAR, ETC.

TO WHICH ARE ADDED A RITUAL FOR A

LODGE OF SORROW,
AND THE CEREMONIES OF

CONSECRATING MASONIC CEMETERIES.

ALSO, AN APPENDIX, WITH THE

forms of Masonic Documents, Masonic Trials, etc.

BY DANIEL SICKELS, 33°.,
AUTHOR OF "THE FREEMASON'S MONITOR," SECRETARY GENERAL OF THE
SUPREME COUNCIL, NORTHERN JURISDICTION, ETC.

NEW YORK:

MASONIC PUBLISHING AND MANUFACTURING CO.,
482 BROOME STREET.
[1868]

"I should say much more if I were not afraid of being heard by those who are uninitiated; because men are apt to deride what they do not understand; and the ignorant, not being aware of the weakness of their minds, condemn what they ought most to Venerate."—CYRIL, OF ALEXANDRIA.

ENTERED according to act of Congress, in the year 1865, by THE MASONIC PUBLISHING AND MANUFACTURING CO., In the Clerk's Office of the District Court of the United States for the Southern District of New York.

ISBN: 1493736388
ISBN-13: 978-1493736386

TO

JOHN W. SIMONS,

PAST GRAND MASTER OF MASONS AND KNIGHTS TEMPLAR OF NEW YORK;

GRAND TREASURER OF THE GRAND ENCAMPMENT OF THE UNITED STATES;

GRAND TREASURER OF THE GRAND LODGE OF NEW YORK;

SOVEREIGN GRAND INSPECTOR GENERAL, ETC., ETC.,

THIS BOOK IS RESPECTFULLY

Dedicated

AS AN APPRECIATION OF HIS INDEFATIGABLE LABORS IN

THE CAUSE OF THE

SCIENCE OF FREEMASONRY,

AND AS A

SLIGHT TESTIMONIAL OF THE ESTEEM AND FRIENDSHIP ENTERTAINED

FOR HIM BY THE

AUTHOR.

AHIMAN REZON.

SIGNIFICATION OF THE TERM.

BY WILLIAM S. ROCKWELL,

GRAND MASTER OF GEORGIA.

THESE two words have acquired a wide Masonic celebrity. They constituted the title of the Book of Constitutions, used by the division of Freemasons, which separated from the Grand Lodge of England in 1736, and have since become the usual designation of such works in this country. DERMOTT, in 1772, styled his book the TRUE *Ahiman Rezon*, and he claimed for his portion of the Order the practice of Ancient Masonry. The inference is obvious that there was a spurious work under this title then extant. An inquiry into their meaning is, therefore, not irrelevant.

I have met with no exposition of the signification of this phrase, except in the edition first published in South Carolina by Dr. DALCHO, in 1807, and reprinted, with additions, in 1822; and afterward re-arranged and edited by Dr. MACKEY in 1852; and, also, in the "*Lexicon of Freemasonry*," by the last-mentioned distinguished author.

The following is Dr. DALCHO'S definition in the edition of 1822: "The Book of Constitutions is usually denominated AHIMAN REZON. The literal translation of *ahiman* is a *prepared brother*, from *manah, to prepare*; and that of *rezon, secret*. So that Ahiman Rezon literally means *the secrets* of *a prepared brother*. It is likewise supposed to be a corruption of *achi man ratzon*, the thoughts or opinions of a true and faithful brother."

There are several difficulties which seem to render this definition inadmissible. The derivations do not appear to be in accordance with the structure of the Hebrew language (if the words be Hebrew); and the phrase, with this view of its derivation, has no grammatical construction. The Hebrews were accustomed to a species of inversion, which in our language has no parallel: for example, *the great work of Jehovah* would be in Hebrew הנדול יהוי מעשה, literally, *work of Jehovah the great*. Now, if the phrase under consideration was intended to import "the secrets of a prepared brother," the construction would have been, according to the example just quoted, *ahi rezon man*. But there are further objections to this rendering of the phrase into English. True, מנה *MNE*, to divide, *to number*, in its piel form, signifies to appoint, to constitute, and, in that sense, to prepare; yet, in accordance with the genius of the Hebrew tongue, it undergoes a change in its vocalization. Its stem-letter is doubled, and the vowel sound softened; it is pronounced *minnah*, and its derivative should be *ahiminnah*. In Chaldee, רז *RZ* signifies a secret, and might be imported into the Hebrew, but its plural is *razin*; besides, it is something of a misnomer to call a published book "*Secrets* of a prepared brother."

The last suggestion of Dr. DALCHO would seem more plausible, if it were not open to the same grammatical objection. *MAN* can not signify *true* or *faithful*, unless derived from אמן *AMN*, and then the compound word would be *achiamon*; and if the א *A* of *AMN* suffered elision, it would indicate a different radical, and if no elision took place, the two letters י *I* and א *A* would not coalesce, but the י *I* resumes its consonant sound as in בנימין *BNIMIN* (which we sound Benjamin), the vocalization would then be *Abhjamon*.

Dr. MACKEY thus renders it:—"This title is derived from three Hebrew words—*ahim*, brothers; *manah*, to select or appoint; and *ratzon*, the will or law—and it, consequently, signifies "the law of appointed or selected brothers."

It is true, that this definition more nearly accords with what the book contains, than that proposed by DALCHO; yet, there would seem to be no less formidable objections to this view of its signification. The verb מנה *MNE*, above referred to by DALCHO, in Kal, (i.e., its active form) means to appoint, but its radical meaning is to number; it was one of the prophetic words written by the spectral hand on the wall of Belshazzar's banqueting-room. It is itself a derivative, and will not rid us of the final ה *E*, and if it be any part of the root of the word, we must read *ahimanah*. It is just to notice, that the radical of this verb, signifying something divided מן *MN*, from the obsolete root מנן *MNN*, when in composition, conveys the idea of a *law*, *rule* or *precept*, in conformity with which something is done; as, for example, יהוה מפי *MPhI IHOH* by command of JEHOVAH (II. Chron. xxxvi. 12), but then the grammatical construction would require some other signification of *rezon*, and it should be construed as an adjective, in conformity with the example above quoted, and it might read *ahi*, being the genitive singular (אהי *AHI*,) the "*Supreme Law of a Brother.*"

EXPLANATION OF THE FRONTISPIECE.

THE Tracing-Board, or Floor-Cloth of an Entered Apprentice, here described, is a copy of a reproduction of Bro. GEORGE OLIVER, D. D., in his *Historical Landmarks of Freemasonry*, as follows " This was used in the early part of the last century. It varies considerably from our improved system, although we observe with pleasure, that it contains the Ancient Landmarks of the Order. It is an oblong square, between the cardinal points; the Master is placed in the East, with en altar before him, and the Wardens both in the West, as was the custom in many of our Lodges up to the time of the union in 1813. The three lights are placed in the N. E., S. E., and S. W. The two pillars, J. and B., are in the West, inscribed 'Strength and Wisdom,' and are both of the Corinthian Order; while the center of the Tracing-Board is occupied by a Blazing Star of five points, inclosing the letter G, and inscribed Beauty. Between the two pillars ascending from the west, are seven steps upon a Mosaic Pavement; but the Tesselated Border, or Indented Tessel, as it was called, is omitted. In the East, West, and South, are portrayed three windows. The W. Master's Tracing-Board is near the Blazing Star, while the corresponding Immovable Jewels are considerably higher up toward the East—the one called the Brute Stone,[1] the other the pointed Cubical Stone.[2] In the apex of the latter, an ax is inserted. The East is distinguished by a square, the South by a level, and the North by a plumb-rule, or perpendicular. The whole is surmounted by a cable-tow, or towline, as then called, with a tassel at each end."

---

[1] This was also called the Broached Thurnel, one of the original immovable Jewels, (according to the English system,) and was used as symbol for the Entered Apprentice to learn to work upon. It was subsequently called the Brute Stone, or Rough Ashlar.

[2] Now better known as the Perfect Ashlar.

"How far any will be guided by me I hope I shall always know myself so well as to leave that to their own choice. As to the inutility of my inquiries, and also the impartiality of them, here I confess myself to wish (as I think what I wish) they may be good, not absolutely terminating upon myself, that the reader will consider them with as unbiassed a freedom as I have written."—SHUCKFORD.

PREFACE.

"IN the present state of Freemasonry, dispersed as it is over the whole face of the habitable globe, and distinguished by an anxious inquiry, whether its reputed origin be well founded, and whether its philosophy and the evidences on which its claims to public notice are entitled to the implicit credence of mankind, it is the duty of every Brother, so far as his influence may extend, to furnish the means of satisfying this ardent curiosity."—OLIVER.

AMONG the many beautiful and appropriate definitions given to Freemasonry none is more comprehensive than the one to be found in the English lectures: "Freemasonry is a science of morality, vailed in allegory and illustrated by symbols."

Freemasonry, then, most prominently presents itself to our view as a science of symbolism. In the teachings of the ancient priesthood this science was first developed. Among them it was organized into a beautiful and impressive system, in which the most profound lessons of Divine Truth were taught in images of poetical form. It was thus that the ancient philosophers communicated all their instructions to their disciples. Having these views of the purposes of the institution, the undersigned has labored in the vineyard of Masonic symbolism for the advancement to a higher knowledge and an easier elucidation of its beautiful mysteries by the aid of symbols and moral illustrations.

The great object sought to be attained in the present volume is to give a more ample scope and a freer use of terms, whereby the Masonic student may become familiar with the great truths taught in the science of Freemasonry. The frequent applications of emendations and explanatory remarks to the ritualistic text may be easily understood by those who have been admitted into its temples, while the profane will have a better appreciation of its claims to something more than a name.

The usual forms and explanations incident to a complete monitor have been carefully revised, and are, it is believed, correct.

A new feature, in compliance with a very generally expressed want of the Fraternity, has been added in the Ritual for a Lodge of Sorrow, prepared by a well-known and distinguished Masonic writer, which, it is thought, will be welcomed as a most appropriate form for celebrating the memory of the fraternal dead.

To those brethren who have, with uniform kindness, favored me with their valuable aid I acknowledge with thanks my indebtedness.

DANIEL SICKELS.

NEW YORK, Dec., 1865.

CONTENTS

INTRODUCTORY.

REEMASONRY is a moral institution, established by virtuous men, with the praiseworthy design of recalling to our remembrance the most sublime TRUTHS in the midst of innocent and social pleasures,—founded On LIBERALITY, BROTHERLY LOVE, and CHARITY. "It is a beautiful system of MORALITY, vailed in allegory and illustrated by symbols." TRUTH is its center—the point whence its radii diverge, direct its disciples to a correct knowledge of the Great Architect of the Universe, and the moral laws which he has ordained for their government.[1]

A proper administration of the various ceremonies connected with the Ritual of Freemasonry is of the highest importance, as these form the distinctive peculiarity of the institution. In their nature, they are simple; in their end, moral and instructive. They naturally excite a high degree of curiosity in a newly-initiated Brother, and create an earnest desire to investigate their meaning, and to become acquainted with their object and design. It requires, however, close application and untiring diligence to ascertain the precise nature of every ceremony which our ancient brethren saw reason to adopt in the formation of an exclusive system, which was to pass through the world unconnected with the religion and politics of all times, and of every people among whom it should flourish and increase. In order to preserve our ceremonies from the hand of innovation, it is essentially necessary that every officer should be thoroughly acquainted with them, and that a firm determination should exist among the Craft to admit no change. A few words here or there may not in themselves appear of much consequence; yet, by frequent allowance, we become habituated to them, and thus open the door to evils of more serious magnitude. There is, there can be, no safety but in a rigid adherence to the ancient ceremonies of the Order. These ceremonies and regulations are fixed by rules similar to those. governing affairs in social life. Every Freemason is required to bring his portion of good ideas, and contribute to the perfecting of the ceremonies and symbols, and to the edification of TRUTH, the universal and eternal temple, which will one day inclose all humanity within its precincts.

---

[1] To use the words of an elegant writer, "Freemasonry is an institution, not, as the ignorant and uninstructed vainly suppose, founded on unmeaning mystery, for the encouragement of bacchanalian festivity and support of mere good. fellowship; but an institution founded on eternal reason and truth, whose deer basis is the civilization of mankind, and whose everlasting glory is supported by those two mighty pillars—SCIENCE and MORALITY."

ORIGIN OF MASONRY, AND ITS ADVANTAGES.

FROM the commencement of the world, we may trace the foundation of Masonry. Ever since symmetry began, and harmony displayed her charms, our Order has had a being. During many ages, and in many different countries, it has flourished. No art, no science, preceded it. In the dark periods of antiquity, when literature was in a low state, and the rude manners of our forefathers withheld from them that knowledge we now so amply share, Masonry diffused its influence. This science unvailed, arts arose, civilization took place, and the progress of knowledge and philosophy gradually dispelled the gloom of ignorance and barbarism. Government being settled, authority was given to laws, and the assemblies of the Fraternity acquired the patronage of the great and the good, while the tenets of the profession diffused unbounded philanthropy.

Abstracted from the pure pleasures which arise from friendship so wisely constituted as that which subsists among Masons, and which it is scarcely possible that any circumstance or occurrence can erase, Masonry is a science confined to no particular country, but extends over the whole terrestrial globe. Wherever the arts flourish, there it flourishes too. Add to this, that by secret and inviolable signs, carefully preserved among the fraternity, it becomes an universal language. Hence, many advantages are gained: the distant Chinese, the wild Arab, and the American savage, will embrace a brother Briton, and know that, besides the common ties of humanity, there is still a stronger obligation to induce him to kind and friendly offices. The spirit of the fulminating priest will be tamed, and a moral brother, though of a different persuasion, engage his esteem: for mutual toleration in religious opinions is one of the most distinguishing and valuable characteristics of the Craft. As all religions teach morality, if a brother be found to act the part of a truly honest man, his private speculative opinions are left to God and himself. Thus, through the influence of Masonry, which is reconcilable to the best policy, all those disputes which embitter life and sour the tempers of men, are avoided; while the common good, the general object, is zealously pursued.

From this view of our system, its utility must be sufficiently obvious. The universal principles of the Art unite, in one indissoluble bond of affection, men of the most opposite tenets, of the most distant countries, and of the most contradictory opinions; so that in every nation a Mason may find a friend, and in every climate a home.[1]

Such is the nature of our institution, that, in the Lodge, which is confined to no particular spot, union is cemented by sincere attachment, and pleasure reciprocally communicated in the cheerful observance of every obliging office. Virtue, the grand object in view, luminous as the meridian sun, shines refulgent on the mind, enlivens the heart, and heightens cool approbation into warm sympathy and cordial attention.—PRESTON.

---

[1] On this principle, unfortunate captives in war, and sojourners, accident. ally east on a distant shore, are particular objects of attention, and seldom fail to experience indulgence from Masons; and it is very remarkable that there is not an instance on record of a breach of fidelity, or of ingratitude, where that indulgence has been liberally extended.

GOVERNMENT OF THE FRATERNITY.

THE mode of government observed by the Fraternity will give the best idea of the nature and design of the Masonic Institution.

Three classes are established among Masons, under different appellations. The privileges of each class are distinct; and particular means are adopted to preserve those privileges to the just and meritorious. Honor and probity are recommendations to the First Class; in which the practice of virtue is enforced, and the duties of morality are inculcated; while the mind is prepared for a regular progress in the principles of knowledge and philosophy. Diligence, assiduity, and application, are qualifications for the Second Class; in which is given an accurate elucidation of science, both in theory end practice. Here human reason is cultivated by a due exertion of the intellectual powers and faculties; nice and difficult theories are explained; new discoveries are produced, and those already known beautifully embellished. The Third Class is restricted to a selected few, whom truth and fidelity have distinguished, whom years and experience have improved, and whom merit and abilities have entitled to preferment. With them the ancient landmarks of the Order are preserved; and from them we learn the necessary instructive lessons which dignify the Art, and qualify the professors to illustrate its excellence and utility.

Such is the established plan of the Masonic System. By this judicious arrangement, true Friendship is cultivated among different ranks of men, Hospitality promoted, Industry rewarded, and Ingenuity encouraged.—PRESTON.

THE LODGE AND ITS GOVERNMENT.

1. THE room in which a certain number of Freemasons assemble, for
    business connected with the institution, is called a LODGE. The assembly,
    or organized body of Freemasons, is also called a Lodge, just as the word
    CHURCH is expressive both of the congregation and the place in which
    they meet to worship. A Lodge of Freemasons, to be legally constituted,
    must be in possession of an unreclaimed charter, granted by the Grand
    Lodge in whose jurisdiction it is situated; the Book of the Law; Square and
    Compasses; the Book of Constitutions; a code of By-Laws; its Officers, and
    a sufficient number of members (not less than seven) to perform the
    ceremonies pertaining to the Order.

2. The constitutional officers of a Lodge are the Worshipful Master, Senior
    Warden, Junior Warden, Treasurer, Secretary, senior Deacon, Junior
    Deacon, and Tiler. To which may be added, two Stewards, (sometimes
    called Masters of Ceremonies) a Marshal, a Chaplain, and an Organist.

3. A Lodge ought to assemble at least once a month for work and instruction.

4. A Lodge has the right to do all the work of Ancient Craft Masonry; to be
    represented at all the communications of the Grand Lodge; to elect and
    install its officers; to increase its numbers by the admission of new
    members, and no member can be forced upon a Lodge without its consent;
    to make by-laws for its government; to exclude a member, on cause shown,
    temporarily or permanently; to levy tax on its members; to appeal to the
    Grand Lodge or Grand Master from the decision of its Master; to exercise
    penal authority over its own members, and over all unaffiliated Masons
    living within the limits of its jurisdiction, and to change its time and place of
    meeting within the town or city designated in its warrant.

5. A Lodge under dispensation is a temporary and inchoate organization of
    Freemasons, acting under authority from the Grand or Deputy Grand
    Master; is not entitled to representation in the Grand Lodge; cannot elect or
    install officers; is without power to frame by-laws, or adopt a seal.

QUALIFICATIONS OF CANDIDATES.

THE qualifications which are essential in those who apply for initiation into the mysteries of Freemasonry, are of two kinds, *Internal* and *External*.[1]

The Internal qualifications of a candidate are those which lie within his own bosom, and are not known to the world. They refer to his peculiar dispositions toward the institution: his motives and design in seeking an entrance into it. Hence they are known to himself alone; and a knowledge of them can only be acquired from his own solemn declarations.

The External qualifications are those which refer to his outward fitness for initiation, and are based on his moral and religious character, the frame of his body, the constitution of his mind, and his social position. A knowledge of these is to be acquired from a careful examination by a committee appointed for that purpose.

The person who desires to be made a Mason must be a man, believing in the existence of a Supreme Being and of a future existence; at least twenty-one years of age; of good moral character, temperate, industrious, and capable of earning an honest livelihood; he must come of his own free-will and accord, uninfluenced by mercenary or other improper motives; be of sound mind and body; capable of reading and writing; not deformed or dismembered, but hale and sound in his physical conformation, having his right limbs, as a man ought to have.

---

[1] It is true that the ritual of the first degree says, that "it is the internal and not the external qualifications which recommend a man to be made a Mason;" but the context of the sentence shows that the external qualifications there referred to are "worldly wealth and honors." The ritual, therefore, has of course no allusion to the sort of external qualifications which are here to he discussed.

ADMISSION OF CANDIDATES.

BY the regulations of the Fraternity, a candidate for the mysteries of Masonry cannot be initiated in any regular Lodge, without having stood proposed one regular meeting, unless a dispensation be obtained in his favor. All applications for initiation should be made in writing, at a regular meeting of the Lodge, giving name, residence, age, occupation, and references, in the following form:

To the Worshipful Master, Officers and Brethren of . . . . . . *Lodge, No.* . . . . , *Free and Accepted Masons.*

THE undersigned, unbiassed by the improper solicitation of friends, and uninfluenced by mercenary or other unworthy motives—prompted by a favorable opinion of your ancient and honorable institution, and a desire for knowledge— freely and voluntarily offers himself a candidate for initiation into the mysteries of Freemasonry, and respectfully prays that he may be admitted and become a member of your Lodge, promising a cheerful conformity to the ancient usages and established customs of the Order.

Was born in . . . ., is . . . years of age; occupation . . . . ., and resides . . . . . .

A. B.

Recommended by . . . . . .

The petition, having been read in open Lodge; is placed on file. A committee is then appointed to investigate the character and qualifications of the petitioner. If, at the next regular meeting of the Lodge, the report of the committee be favorable, the necessary preparations are made for his admission.

OPENING AND CLOSING THE LODGE.

IN all regular assemblies of men who are convened for wise and useful purposes, the commencement and conclusion of business are accompanied with some form. In every country in the world the practice prevails, and is deemed essential. From the most remote periods of antiquity, it may be traced, and the refined improvements of modern times have not totally abolished it.

Ceremonies, when simply considered, it is true, are little more than visionary delusions; but their effects are sometimes important. When they impress awe and reverence on the mind, and engage the attention by external attraction to solemn rites, they are interesting objects. These purposes are effected by judicious ceremonies, when regularly conducted and properly arranged. On this ground, they have received the sanction of the wisest men in all ages, and consequently could not escape the notice of Masons. To begin well, is the most likely means to end well; and it has been properly remarked, that when order and method are neglected at the beginning, they will be seldom found to take place at the end.

The ceremonies of OPENING and CLOSING a Lodge with solemnity and decorum is, therefore, universally admitted among Masons, and which differ in each of the degrees; but differ so slightly as not to affect their general character. They must, therefore, be considered in reference to the several purposes which they are designed to accomplish.

To conduct these ceremonies with propriety, ought to be the peculiar study of every Mason, especially of those who have the honor to rule in our assemblies. To persons who are dignified, every eye is naturally directed for propriety of conduct and behavior; and from them other brethren, who are less informed, will naturally expect to derive an example worthy of imitation. From a share in these ceremonies no Mason can be exempted. This is the first request of the Master, and the prelude to all business. No sooner has it been signified that the Lodge is about to be opened, than every officer repairs to his station, and the intent of the meeting becomes the sole object of attention.

A Lodge must always be opened on the Third Degree, and in due form, for the transaction of any business, except that of initiating or passing a candidate into the mysteries of the first and second degrees. The first business after opening, if it be a regular communication, is the reading of the minutes of the preceding communication, for the information of the brethren. The minutes of the proceedings of the evening should, also, always be read before the Lodge is closed, that the brethren may know that they have been properly recorded, and then duly approved.

The Lodge should always be opened and closed with prayer.

PRAYER,
TO BE USED AT OPENING.

MOST holy and glorious Lord God, the Great Architect of the Universe, the Giver of all good gifts and graces! Thou hast promised that, "where two or three are gathered together in thy name, thou wilt be in their midst, and bless them." In thy name we have assembled, and in thy name we desire to proceed in all our doings. Grant that the sublime principles of Freemasonry may so subdue every discordant passion within us—so harmonize and enrich our hearts with thine own love and goodness—that the Lodge at this time may humbly reflect that order and beauty which reign for ever before thy throne.—Amen.

Response by the brethren.—So mote it be.

ANOTHER PRAYER,
WHICH MAY BE USED AT OPENING.

GREAT Architect of the Universe! in thy name we have assembled, and in thy name we desire to proceed in all our doings. Grant that the sublime principles of Freemasonry may so subdue every discordant passion within us—so harmonize and enrich our hearts with thine own love and goodness—that the Lodge at this time may reflect that order and beauty which reigns for ever before thy throne.—Amen.

Response.—So mote it be.

In addition to the Prayer, the following CHARGE may be given:

The ways of virtue are beautiful. Knowledge is attained by degrees. Wisdom dwells with contemplation; there we must seek her. Let us then, brethren, apply ourselves with becoming zeal to the practice of the excellent principles inculcated by our Order. Let us ever remember that the great objects of our association are, the restraint of improper desires and passions, the cultivation of an active benevolence, and the promotion of a correct knowledge of the duties we owe to God, our neighbor, and ourselves. Let us be united, and practice with assiduity the sacred tenets of our Order. Let all private animosities, if any unhappily exist, give place to affection and brotherly love. It is useless parade to talk of the subjection of irregular passions within the walls of the Lodge, if we permit them to triumph in our intercourse with each other. Uniting in the grand design, let us be happy ourselves, and endeavor to promote the happiness of others. Let us cultivate the great moral virtues which are laid down on our Masonic Trestle-board, and improve in every thing that is good, amiable, and useful. Let the benign Genius of the Mystic Art preside over our councils, and under her sway let us act with a dignity becoming the high moral character of our venerable institution.

Or the following ODE may be sung:

AIR—*Dundee.*

Within our temple met again,
　With hearts and purpose strong,
We'll raise our notes of grateful praise,
　With union in our song.

Around our altar's sacred shrine
　May Love's pure incense rise,
Bearing upon its mystic flame
　Our music to the skies!

PRAYER,
TO BE USED AT CLOSING.

SUPREME Architect of the Universe, accept our humble thanks for the many mercies and blessings which thy bounty has conferred on us, and especially for this friendly and social intercourse. Pardon, we beseech thee, whatever thou hast seen amiss in us since we have been together; and continue to us thy presence, protection, and blessing. Make us sensible of the renewed obligations we are under to love thee, and as we are about to separate, and return to our respective places of abode, wilt thou be pleased so to influence our hearts and minds, that we may each one of us practice, out of the Lodge, those great moral duties which are inculcated in it, and with reverence study and obey the laws which thou hast given us in thy Holy Word.—Amen.

Response.—So mote it be.

CHARGE,
TO BE USED AT CLOSING.

BRETHREN: You are now to quit this sacred retreat of friendship and virtue, to mix again with the world. Amidst its concerns and employments, forget not the duties you have heard so frequently inculcated and forcibly recommended in this Lodge. Be diligent, prudent, temperate, discreet. Remember that around this altar you have promised to befriend and relieve every brother who shall need your assistance. Remember that you have promised to remind him, in the most tender manner, of his failings, and aid his reformation; to vindicate his character, when wrongfully traduced; suggest, in his behalf, the most candid and favorable circumstances. Is he justly reprehended? Let the world observe how Masons love one another.

These generous principles are to extend further. Every human being has a claim upon your kind offices. Do good unto all. Recommend it more especially to the household of the faithful.

By diligence in the duties of your respective callings; by liberal benevolence and diffusive charity; by constancy and fidelity in your friendships, discover the beneficial and happy effects of this ancient and honorable institution. Let it not be supposed that you have here labored in vain, and spent your strength for naught; for your work is with the LORD and your recompense with your GOD.

Finally, brethren, be ye all of one mind; live in peace, and may the God of love and peace delight to dwell with and bless you!

The following ODE may be sung at closing:

AIR—*Sicilian Hymn.*

Now our social labors closing,
  Homage of the heart we pay;
Each in confidence reposing,
  Kindest thoughts that ne'er decay.

Let us each, in Time's commotion,
  Heav'nly light and truth implore:
Thus we'll pass life's stormy ocean,
  Landing on a happier shore.

CLOSING BENEDICTION.

MAY the blessing of Heaven rest upon us and all regular Masons! May brotherly love prevail, and every moral and social virtue cement us!—Amen. *Res.*—So mote it be.

FIRST DEGREE.
ENTERED APPRENTICE.

"There are many prominent emblems in this degree, teaching, first, the propriety of maintaining regularity of life, and attending to the due improvement of time, by conforming to the prescribed rules, for which eight hours are allotted to repose, eight to labor, and eight to the service of GOD. Secondly, the cleansing of our hearts and minds from every vice, is inculcated, thereby fitting our bodies as living stones for that spiritual edifice built by the Grand Architect of the Universe. There are many other emblems in this First Step, representing human life as being chequered with good and evil; pointing to the comforts and blessings that surround us, and impressing upon our minds the necessity of a reliance on Divine Providence. Our imperfect condition by nature is likewise adverted to, and the state of perfection to which we hope to arrive by virtuous education, aided by the blessing of GOD upon our own endeavors, and a due observance of the Holy Scriptures, as pointing out the whole duty of man. Indeed, everything in this degree is adapted to impress upon the mind of the candidate the necessity of maintaining purity of life and conduct, in order to ensure a happy immortality."—STONE.

DEGREE OF ENTERED APPRENTICE.
SYMBOLISM OF THE DEGREE.

THE first, or Entered Apprentice degree of Masonry, is intended, symbolically, to represent the entrance of man into the world, in which he is afterwards to become a living and thinking actor. Coming from the ignorance and darkness of the outer world, his first craving is for light—not that physical light which springs from the great orb of day as its fountain, but that moral and intellectual light which emanates from the primal Source of all things—from the Grand Architect of the Universe—the Creator of the sun and of alt that it illuminates. Hence the great, the primary object of the first degree, is to symbolize that birth of intellectual light into the mind; and the Entered Apprentice is the type of unregenerate man, groping in moral and mental darkness, and seeking for the light which is to guide his steps and point him to the path which leads to duty and to Him who gives to duty its reward.

FIRST LECTURE.

THE first step taken by a candidate, on entering a Lodge of Freemasons, teaches him the pernicious tendency of infidelity, and shows him that the foundation on which Masonry rests is the belief and acknowledgment of a Supreme Being; that in Him alone a sure confidence can be safely placed, to protect his steps in all the dangers and difficulties he may be called to encounter in his progress through life; it assures him that, if his faith be well founded in that Being, he may confidently pursue his course without fear and without danger.

Every candidate, previous to his reception, is required to give his free and full assent to the following interrogatories, in a room adjacent to the Lodge:

1. Do you seriously declare, upon your honor, that, unbiased by the improper solicitation of friends, and uninfluenced by mercenary motives, you freely and voluntarily offer yourself a can-date for the mysteries of Freemasonry?

2. Do you seriously declare, upon your honor, that you are prompted to solicit the privileges of Freemasonry by a favorable opinion conceived of the institution, a desire of knowledge, and a sincere wish of being serviceable to your fellow-creatures?

3. Do you seriously declare, upon your honor, that you will cheerfully conform to all the ancient usages and established customs of the Fraternity?

SECTION I.

MASONRY was originally an operative society, and in that form those who worked as ENTERED APPRENTICES were styled the *first class*; but in Speculative or Freemasonry, the degree of which we are now treating is regarded as the first of the Order. Its reception places the novitiate in possession of the Masonic alphabet, and discloses to him the fundamental principles of this time-honored institution. This section is sub-divided under three heads, viz:

1st. THE CEREMONY;

2d. ITS MORAL; and

3d. ITS NECESSITY and CONSISTENCY.

A full and perfect knowledge of this section is indispensably necessary to every Mason who would be serviceable to the institution, and would avail himself of its privileges and its enjoyments.

THE ENTRANCE.—The preparations to which the candidate must submit, before entering the Lodge, serve allegorically to teach him, as well as to remind the brethren who are present, that it is the man alone, divested of all the outward recommendations of rank, state, or of riches, which Masonry accepts, and that it is his spiritual, or moral worth alone, which can open for him the door of the temple.

As Masons, we are taught never to commence any great or important undertaking, without first invoking the blessing of Deity.

The trust of a Mason is in God, as a basis which can never fail, and a rock which can never be shaken. Nor is it a mere empty profession; for it is borne out and illustrated by our practice. We open and close our Lodges with prayer; the same formula is used at the initiation of candidates; and no business of any importance is conducted without invoking the Divine assistance on our labors; and the blessing of God cannot be expected to follow any man's profession, unless it be verified by a good and virtuous life.

THE RITE OF INDUCTION.

WE are convinced by long and extensive observation that Masons need a truer and deeper insight into the nature of our esoteric work. We do not think our beautiful and truth-glowing ritual and our sublime symbolism are quite understood by the mass of the Brotherhood. It is true all are affected, in a certain degree, by them; it could not be otherwise: but many fail to discover the grand truths which are inculcated therein. Symbols are of no practical importance, if we have lost the sense they were intended to convey; and rites are puerile, if they do not immediately lead the mind to the consideration of tangible ideas and immortal verities. Our ceremonies are moral and philosophical lessons; and, earnestly studied and rightly understood, will be seen to be pregnant with mighty meanings.

Thus expressive and full of significance is the RITE or INDUCTION.

The induction of the Neophyte into the Order of Freemasonry, his first entrance into the sanctuary of the illuminated, is for him a step of momentous importance and solemnity. There are few candidates, we believe, who can approach the portals of the mystery-shrouded Lodge without much trepidation of heart, and a feeling of mingled awe and fear. Consequently, the induction is effected by the performance of certain appropriate symbolical ceremonies, all of which are remarkably and eloquently suggestive of the new life, duties, and obligations he is about to assume, and to which he is on the point of binding himself voluntarily, absolutely, and without reservation, for ever.

In ancient Egypt, the Neophyte was presented with a cup of water, and addressed in these words:—"Aspirant to the honor of a divine companionship! seeker after celestial truth! this is the water of forgetfulness. Drink!—drink to the oblivion of all your vices—the forgetfulness of all your imperfections; and thus be prepared for the reception of the new revelations of Truth, with which you are soon to be honored." Although modern Freemasonry does not retain this particular ceremony, it preserves the spirit of it, by other forms, not less expressive and instructive. The candidate is directed to close his eyes on the Past—to lay aside the trappings and vestures of the outward world—the symbols of traffic and war—all that reminds one of the selfishness and discords of life—and turn his face towards the dread unknown—the mysterious Future.

The RITE OF INDUCTION, therefore, signifies the end of a profane and vicious life—the *palingenesia* (new birth) of corrupted human nature—the death of vice and all bad passions, and the introduction to a new life of purity and virtue. It also prepares the candidate, by prayer and meditation, for that mystic pilgrimage, where he must wander through night and darkness, before he can behold the golden splendors of the ORIENT, and stand in unfettered freedom among the Sons of Light.

The Rite is intended, still further, to represent man in his primitive condition of helplessness, ignorance, and moral blindness, seeking after that mental and moral enlightenment which alone can deliver his mind from all thralldoms, and make him master of the material world. The Neophyte, in darkness and with tremblings, knocks at the portals of the Lodge, and demands admission, instruction, and light. So man, born ignorant, and helpless, and blind, yet feeling stirring within him unappeasable longings for knowledge, knocks at the doors of the temple of science. He interrogates Nature, demands her secrets, and at length becomes the proud possessor of her mysteries.

Finally, the RITE of INDUCTION refers to the supreme hour of man's worldly life, when, laying aside all earthly wealth, and pomp, and rank, and glory, and divested of his mortal vesture, he passes alone through the grim darkness of the tomb, to stand before the GRAND ORIENT of the immortal Land.

> "Through death to life I and through this vale of tears,
>   And thistle-world of mortal life, ascend
> To the great Banquet, in that world whose years
>   Of bliss unclouded, fadeless, know no end."

PRAYER,
AT THE INITIATION OF A CANDIDATE.

VOUCHSAFE thine aid, Almighty Father of the Universe, to this our present convention; and grant that this candidate for Masonry may dedicate and devote his life to thy service, and become a true and faithful brother among us. Endue him with a competency of thy divine Wisdom, that by the influence of the pure principles of our art he may be better enabled to display the beauties of holiness, to the honor of thy holy name.—Amen.

Response.—So mote it be.

THE SYMBOLIC PILGRIMAGE.

THE institution of Freemasonry—reaching backward until it loses itself among the mythological shadows of the past, its grand ritual and eloquent language of signs and symbols, originating in those distant ages—offers a field for exploration which can never be thoroughly traversed. Transmitted to us by remote generations, it is plain that, before we can, in any degree, appreciate Freemasonry, or understand the significance of its mysteries, we must go back to the Past, and question the founders of the Order. We must learn in what necessities of human nature, and for what purpose it was created. We must discover the true genesis of our rites, and become familiar with the ideas which the Fathers intended to shadow forth through them, and impress upon the mind. It is not enough for us to accept the *letter* of the ceremonial, and perform it blindly, interpreting its meaning in whatever way fancy or imagination or convenience may dictate. We should know what the Ancients meant to say through it: what truth each rite and each symbol represented to *their* minds.

From age to age, through countless generations, these Rites have read their sublime lessons of wisdom and hope, and peace and warning, to the "Sons of Light." These same lessons, in the same language, they read to us to-day. But do we see in them what they did? Do they impress us as they impressed them? Or do they pass before our eyes like a panorama of some unknown land, which has no delineator to tell us what or where it is, or give us any intelligible notion regarding it? Accepting the symbol, have we lost its sense? Our Rites will be of little value to us if this be the case. It is our duty, then, to make Freemasonry the object of a profound study. We must consult the Past. We must stand by the sarcophagus of the murdered, but restored Osiris, in Egypt; enter the caverns of Phrygia, and hold communion with the Cabiri; penetrate the "Collegia Fabrorum" of ancient Rome, and work in the mystic circles of Sidon. In a word, we must pursue our researches until we find the THOUGHT that lay in the minds of those who created the institution and founded our mysteries. Then we shall know precisely what they mean. We shall see in them a grand series of moral and philosophical dramas, most eloquent and instructive, gleaming with sublime ideas, as the heavens glow with stars. And, finally, we shall discover that our Rites embrace all the possible circumstances of man—moral, spiritual, and social—and have a meaning high as the heavens, broad as the universe, and profound as eternity,

The Rite of the Wanderer, or the Symbolic Pilgrimage, is entirely puerile and unmeaning, unless we have learned in what ideas it originated, and what its authors intended to represent by it. Happily, this is not a difficult task. In Egypt, Greece, and among other ancient nations, Freemasonry was one of the earliest agencies employed to effect the improvement and enlightenment of man. CICERO tells us that "the establishment of these Rites among the Athenians, conferred upon them a supreme benefit. *Their effect was to civilize men, reform their wild and ferocious manners, and make them comprehend the true principles of morality, which initiate man into a new order of life, more worthy of a being destined to imortality.*"—Consequently, the mystic journey primarily represented the toilsome progress of Humanity, from its primitive condition of ignorance and barbarism to a state of civilization and mental enlightenment. The Neophyte, therefore, wandering in darkness over his winding way, meeting with various obstructions and delays, was a typo of the human race, struggling onward and upward by devious stages, from the gloom and darkness of the savage state to the light, intelligence, and comforts of civilized life.

This symbolic journey is also emblematical of the pilgrimage of life, which, man soon enough discovers, is often dark and gloomy, surrounded by sorrow, and fear, and doubt. It teaches him that over this dark, perplexed, and fearful course lays the way to a glorious destiny; that through night to *light* must the earth-pilgrim work his way; that by struggle, and toil, and earnest endeavor, he must advance with courage and hope until, free of every fetter, and in the full light of virtue and knowledge, he stands face to face with the mighty secrets of the universe, and attains that lofty height, whence he can look backward over the night-shrouded and tortuous path in which he had been wandering, and forward to sublimer elevation—to more glorious ideals, which seem to say to him, "On, on for ever!"

Such, then, is the grand and inspiring lesson which this Symbolic Pilgrimage is perpetualy repeating to the brethren. Let them study it well, and labor with faith; for it announces a progress in science and virtue, which will reach through eternity.

The Lodge, when revealed to an entering Mason, discovers to him a representation of the world; in which, from the wonders of Nature, we are led to contemplate the great Original, and worship him for his mighty works; and we are, thereby, also moved to exercise those moral and social virtues, which become mankind to observe, as the servants of the Great Architect of the world, in whose image we were formed from the beginning.

The following passage of Scripture is rehearsed during the ceremony:

Behold, how good and how pleasant it is for brethren to dwell together in unity.

It is like the precious ointment upon the head, that ran down upon the beard, even Aaron's beard; that went down to the skirts of his garment.

As the dew of Hermon, and as the dew that descended upon the mountains of Zion; for there the Lord commanded the blessing, even life for evermore.

"The great teaching of this Psalm is Brotherly Love, that virtue which forms the most prominent tenet of the Masonic Order. And it teaches the lesson, too, precisely as we do, by a symbol, comparing it to the precious ointment used in the consecration of the High-Priest, whose delightful perfume filled the whole place with its odor. The ointment was poured upon the head in such quantity, that, being directed by the anointer in different ways in the form of a cross, it flowed at length down the beard, and finally dropped from the flowing skirts of the priestly garment.

"The fifteen Psalms, from the 120th to the 134th, inclusive, of which this, of course, is one, are called by the Hebrews 'songs of degrees,' because they were sung on the fifteen steps ascending from the court of Israel to the court of the women in the Temple."

Or the following ODE may be sung:

Music—*Auld Lang Syne.*

Be - hold! how pleas-ant and how good, For brethren such as we, Of the Ac-cept-ed broth-er-hood To dwell in u - ni - ty! 'Tis like the oil on Aa-ron's head Which

3

Behold! how pleasant and how good,
  For brethren such as we,
Of the Accepted brotherhood
  To dwell in unity!
'Tis like the oil on Aaron's head
  Which to his feet distills;
Like Hermon's dew so richly shed
  On Zion's sacred hills!

For there the Lord of light and love
  A blessing sent with power;
Oh, may we all this blessing prove,
  E'en life for evermore!
On Friendship's altar, rising here,
  Our hands now plighted be,
To live in love, with hearts sincere,
  In peace and unity.

It is the duty of the Master of the Lodge, as one of the precautionary measures of initiation, to explain to the candidate the nature and design of the institution; and while he informs him that it is founded on the purest principles of virtue; that it possesses great and invaluable privileges; and that, in order to secure those privileges to worthy men, and worthy men alone, voluntary pledges of fidelity are required; he will at the same time assure him that nothing will be expected of him incompatible with his civil, moral, or religions duties.

THE OBLIGATION OF SECRECY.

ONE of the most notable features of Freemasonry—one, certainly, which attracts, more than any thing else, the attention of the profane world—is that vail of mystery—that awful secrecy—behind which it moves and acts. From the earliest periods, this has invariably been a distinctive characteristic of the institution; and to-day, as of old, the first obligation of a Mason—his supreme duty—is that of silence and secrecy. Why is this? Why did Freemasonry, in the beginning, adopt the principle of secrecy, as a vital one? and why has it so persistently adhered to it, through all the changes that have swept over the earth, and transformed all things else?

The enemies of Freemasonry, like THOMAS PAINE and others, pretend that they have found the origin of Masonic secrecy in the fact that the esoteric doctrines of the Order were antagonistic to the prevailing opinions, and therefore could not safely be professed before the world. Hence, according to them, the retiring into silence and secrecy was simply an act of cowardice, to escape the danger that might follow the open and honest promulgation of an unpopular doctrine! Some distinguished Masonic writers have also—strange as it may appear—professed the same theory. We must nevertheless pronounce it an exceedingly shallow and unphilosophical one. The obligation of secrecy does not owe its origin to any such cause. That origin must be found, and can only be found, in the *intrinsic value and divine excellence of the principle of secrecy itself.* Among the ancients, silence and secrecy were considered virtues of the highest order. The Egyptians worshiped Harpocrates, the god of secrecy, raised altars in his name, and wreathed them with garlands of flowers. Among the ancient Romans, too, these virtues were not less esteemed; and a distinguished Latin poet tells us, "*Est et fideli tuta silentio merces:*"— "for faithful silence, also, there is a sure reward."

Mystery has charms for all men, and is closely allied to the spiritual part of man's nature. The entire fabric of the universe is founded on secrecy; and the great Life-force which vivifies, moves, and beautifies the whole, is the profoundest of all mysteries. We cannot, indeed, fix our eyes on a single point in creation which does not shade off into mystery, and touch the realms of Eternal Silence. As the fathers of Freemasonry discovered that all life and beauty were elaborated in Night and Mystery, they made the Institution, in this respect, conform to the divine order of Nature. In the Pythagorean Freemasonry, silence and secrecy were religious duties, and held to be the most fruitful sources of intellectual and moral improvement. A distinguished modern writer[1] repeats the same idea in quaint but forcible language:—"Thoughts will not work, except in silence; neither will virtue work, except in secrecy: Like other plants, virtue will not grow, unless its roots be hidden, buried from the light of the sun. Let the sun shine on it—nay, do but look at it privily thyself—the root withers, and no flowers will glad thee."

In the grand mythology of ancient Scandinavia, there is a remarkable myth, called the Yggdrasil-Tree, or Ever-blooming Ash, whose top rose to the highest heavens, and whose roots struck down through the regions of everlasting gloom and night. From age to age, its branches, loaded with benedictions, spread out over all worlds, the delight of gods and men, diffusing life and beauty and fragrance through the universe. And all this glory, and these capabilities to bless, were the fruit of the mysterious and secret labors of the sacred Nornas, who perpetually watered its roots from the deep-hidden wells, and thus preserved its vigor and vitality.

The Yggdrasil-Tree is a beautiful symbolical representation of Freemasonry, and illustrates well the character of Masonic secrecy. Like that tree, in the youth of Humanity, the Mystic Order arose among the nations of the earth, and its ever-green branches spread over the world; and, by the vital power of its secret ministry, it diffused order, and beauty, and virtue, and civilization over all lands.

Another reason why Freemasonry regards secrecy as a fundamental principle is, because a unity, harmony, and strength can be secured thereby, which cannot be obtained in any other way. Secrecy has a mystic, binding, almost supernatural force, and unites men more closely together than all other means combined. The common possession of a secret by a considerable number of people, produces a family-feeling. There is something profoundly mystical in this, no doubt; but it is, nevertheless, a fact. Suppose two men, strangers, traveling in a distant country, should by some accident be brought together for a few brief moments, during which they happen to be the involuntary witnesses of some terrible deed, a deed which circumstances demand shall remain a secret between them for ever. In all the wide world, only these two men, and they strangers to each other, know the secret. They separate; continents and oceans, and many eventful years, divide them; but they cannot forget each other, nor the dread mystery which binds them together as with an iron chain. Neither time nor distance can weaken that mighty bond. In that,

---

[1] THOMAS CARLYLE—*Sartor Resartus.*

27

they are *for ever one.*

It is not, then, for any vain or frivolous purpose that Masonry appeals to the principle of secrecy, but, rather, because it creates a family-feeling, insures unity, and throws the charm of mystery and poetry around the Order, making its labors easy and its obligations pleasant.

IN the beginning, God created the heaven and the earth. And the earth was without form, and void; and darkness was upon the face of the deep. And the Spirit of God moved upon the face of the waters. And God said, Let there be light. and there was light.

*   *   *   *   *   *   *

Light is one of the requirements of a candidate at his initiation; and the material light which is afforded him is succeeded by an intellectual illumination, which serves to enlighten his path on the journey from this world to the next.

THE RITE OF ILLUMINATION.

THE RITE OF ILLUMINATION is a very ancient ceremony, and constituted an important feature in all the mysteries of the early ages. In the Egyptian, Cabirian, Sidonian, Eleusinian, Scandinavian, and Druidical Rituals, it held a prominent place, and in them all represented the same ideas. It marked the termination of the mystic pilgrimage through gloom and night, and was emblematical of that moral and intellectual light which pours its divine radiance on the mind after it has conquered prejudice, and passion, and ignorance, with which it has so long been struggling.

The prevailing notion of all those Rites was, that man, society, humanity could arrive at the Perfect only by the ministry of gloom and suffering; that the soul's exaltation and highest enlightenment could be approached only by the dark way of tears and sacrifice. The Rite of Illumination indicates the triumphant conclusion of man's conflicts, sacrifices, and trials; announces that he has found that LIGHT for which he has so persistently sought—that Truth which alone can give dignity to his life, freedom to his spirit, and repose to his soul, and which is the grand recompense for all his journeyings, labors, and combats.

The particular act which now distinguishes this illumination is, comparatively, modern, but is, nevertheless, deeply significant and instructive. It refers to that point of time when "God said, 'Let there be light,' and there was light." The loftiest imagination is utterly powerless to paint a picture of the unspeakable glory of the scene, when the sun, for the first time, poured down his light in a golden deluge on the earth, hitherto a chaotic mass, plunged in eternal night!—when ocean, lake, and river, hill and valley, smiled and sparkled in the new-born splendor! Yet this Rite does not commemorate that event simply as an historical, material fact, but rather because it symbolizes the release of the soul from darkness, and ignorance, and sin—from the chaos and confusion of a sensual and selfish life—and its establishment in the light and glory of virtue and knowledge.

The emblems peculiar to this Rite are the Bible, Square, and Compasses, the Burning Triangle, or the three lighted Tapers illuminating the altar. These all have exclusive reference to the leading idea of the ceremony, viz: *the release, from moral, spiritual, and intellectual darkness*. Hence the first three of these emblems are called the Great Lights of Masonry, and the latter the Lesser Lights.

"Through Night to Light! and though, to mortal eyes,
  Creation's face a pall of horror wear,
Good cheer! good cheer! the gloom of midnight flies,
  And then a sunrise follows, mild and fair."

29

These lines of the great German beautifully and forcibly illustrate the sublime thought which underlies and shines through this Rite. We cannot, of course, enter into any particular descriptions of it, or give any special details thereof, but the above suggestions are all that the intelligent brother will need to assist him to a thorough comprehension of the whole.

—*"isasin oi ntemueménoi."*—*"The initiated know what is meant."*

The three * * * * * * * * * * are the Holy Bible, Square, and Compasses.

The Holy Bible is given us as the rule and guide of our faith and practice; the Square, to square our actions; and the Compasses, to circumscribe our desires, and keep our passions in due bounds with all mankind, especially with the brethren.

The *Holy Writings*, that great light in Masonry, will guide us to all truth; it will direct our paths to the temple of happiness, and point out to us the whole duty of man.

The *Square* teaches us to regulate our actions by rule and line, and to harmonize our conduct by the principles of morality and virtue.

The *Compasses* teach us to limit our desires in every station, that, rising to eminence by merit, we may live respected and die regretted.

The three * * * * * * * * * * * are the Sun, Moon, and Master.

*   *   *   *   *   *   *

The MASTER represents the sun at its rising, that he may open his Lodge, and employ and instruct the brethren in Masonry; to whom it is his duty to communicate light, forcibly impressing upon their minds the dignity and high importance of Freemasonry, and zealously admonishing them never to disgrace it.

The Senior Warden represents the sun at its setting, and his duty is not only to assist the Master, but to look after certain properties of the Lodge, to see that harmony prevails, and that the brethren have their just dues before being dismissed from their labors.

The Junior Warden represents the sun at meridian, which is the most beautiful part of the day, and his duty is to call the brethren from labor to refreshment, and see that the means thereof are not perverted by intemperance or excess, but so regulated that pleasure and profit may be shared by all.

That ancient and spotless ensign of Masonry, the LAMBSKIN, or WHITE APRON[1], is presented in behalf of the Lodge and the Fraternity in general.

It is an emblem of innocence, and the badge of a Mason; more ancient than the Golden Fleece[2] or Roman Eagle[3]; more honorable than the Star and Garter[4], or any other Order that can be conferred upon the candidate at the time of his initiation, or at any future period, by king, prince, potentate, or any other person, except he be a Mason * * * * *. It is hoped you will wear it with pleasure to yourself and honor to the Fraternity.

The investiture of the candidate with the apron, among the primitive Masons, formed an essential part of the ceremony of initiation, and was attended with rites equally significant and impressive. This badge received a characteristic distinction from its peculiar color and material. With the Essenian Masons, it was accomplished by a process bearing a similar tendency, and accompanied by illustrations not less imposing and satisfactory to the newly-initiated neophyte. He was clothed in a long white robe, which reached to the ground, bordered with a fringe of blue ribbon, to incite personal holiness, and fastened tightly round the waist with a girdle, to separate the upper from the lower parts of the body. With feet bare and head uncovered, the candidate was considered a personification of Modesty and Humility, walking in the fear of God.

In the course of this section is exhibited a beautiful and impressive illustration of one of the grand principles of the institution, and concludes with a moral application.

---

[1] An Entered Apprentice's Apron should be a pure white lambskin, from fourteen to sixteen inches wide, and from twelve to fourteen inches deep, with a fall about five inches deep; square at the bottom, with sharp angular corners, and without device or ornament of any kind.
[2] The Order of the Golden Fleece has ever been ranked among the most illustrious and distinguished Orders of Knighthood in Europe. It was instituted on the 10th of January, 1429, at Bruges, by PHILIP III. Duke of Burgundy, the most puissant prince of his age, on the occasion of his marriage with ISABELLA, daughter of King JOHN I. of Portugal.
[3] There is no such Order as the Knights of the Roman Eagle. The expression (which is an unhappy one) probably refers to the fact that the Eagle was the standard of the ancient Roman empire.
[4] The Order of the Garter was instituted by King EDWARD M. In 1344; and though not the most ancient, is one of the most famous of the military orders of Europe. SELDEN says that it "exceeds—in majesty, honor, and fame—all chivalrous orders in the world." The Star and the Garter are the insignia bestowed upon and worn by a Knight.

CHARITY THE CHIEF SOCIAL VALUE

CHARITY is the chief of every social virtue, and the distinguishing characteristic of Masons. This virtue includes a supreme degree of love to the great Creator and Governor of the Universe, and an unlimited affection to the beings of his creation, of all characters, and of every denomination. This last duty is forcibly inculcated by the example of the Deity himself, who liberally dispenses his beneficence to unnumbered worlds.

It is not particularly our province to enter into a disquisition of every branch of this amiable virtue; we shall only briefly state the happy effects of a benevolent disposition towards mankind, and show that charity, exerted on proper objects, is the greatest pleasure man can possibly enjoy.

The bounds of the greatest nation or the most extensive empire cannot circumscribe the generosity of a liberal mind. Men, in whatever situation they are placed, are still in a great measure the same. They are exposed to similar dangers and misfortunes: they have not wisdom to foresee, or power to prevent the evils incident to human nature: they hang, as it were, in a perpetual suspense between hope and fear, sickness and health, plenty and want. A mutual chain of dependence subsists throughout the animal creation. The whole human species are, therefore, proper objects for the exercise of charity.

Beings who partake of one common nature ought to be actuated by the same motives and interests. Hence, to soothe the unhappy, by sympathizing with their misfortunes, and to restore peace and tranquillity to agitated spirits, constitute the general and great ends of the Masonic institution. This humane, this generous disposition, fires the breast with manly feelings, and enlivens that spirit of compassion which is the glory of the human frame, and which not only rivals, but outshines, every other pleasure the mind is capable of enjoying.

All human passions, when directed by the superior principle of reason, promote some useful purpose; but compassion towards proper objects is the most beneficial of all the affections, and excites the most lasting degrees of happiness, as it extends to greater numbers, and tends to alleviate the infirmities and evils which are incident to human existence.

Possessed of this amiable, this god-like disposition, Masons are shocked at misery, under every form and appearance. When we behold an object pining under the miseries of a distressed body or mind, the healing accents which flow from the tongue mitigate the pain of the unhappy sufferer, and make even adversity, in its dismal state, look gay. When our pity is excited, we assuage grief, and cheerfully relieve distress. If a brother be in want, every heart is moved; when he is hungry, we feed him; when he is naked, we clothe him; when he is in trouble, we fly to his relief. Thus we confirm the propriety of the title we bear, and convince the world at large that BROTHER, among Masons, is something more than a name.

The newly-initiated brother is then conducted to his proper station, * * * * * * * * *, where he receives his first lesson in moral architecture, teaching him ever to walk uprightly before God and man.

THE NORTH-EAST CORNER.

IN the important ceremony which refers to the north-east corner of the Lodge, the candidate becomes as one who is to all outward appearance *a perfect and upright man and Mason*, the representative of a spiritual corner-stone on which he is to erect his future moral and Masonic edifice.

This symbolic reference of the corner-stone of a material edifice to a Mason when, at his first initiation, he commences the moral and intellectual task of erecting a spiritual temple in his heart, is beautifully sustained when we look at all the qualities that aye required to constitute a "well-tried, true, and trusty" corner-stone. The squareness of its surface, emblematic of morality—its cubical form, emblematic of firmness and stability of character—and the peculiar finish and fineness of the material, emblematic of virtue and holiness—show that the ceremony of the north-east corner of the Lodge was undoubtedly intended to portray, in the consecrated language of symbolism, the necessity of integrity and stability of conduct, of truthfulness and uprightness of character, and of purity and holiness of life, which just at that time and in that place the candidate is most impressively charged to maintain.

WORKING-TOOLS OF AN ENTERED APPRENTICE.

THE TWENTY-FOUR-INCH GUAGE

Is an instrument used by operative masons to measure and lay out their work; but we, as Free and Accepted Masons, are taught to make use of it for the more noble and glorious purpose of dividing our time. It being divided into twenty-four equal parts, is emblematical of the twenty-four hours of the day, which we are taught to divide into three equal parts; whereby are found eight hours for the service of God and a distressed worthy brother; eight for our usual vocations; and eight for refreshment and sleep.

The Twenty-four-inch Guage is to measure and ascertain the extent of an edifice. Hence we derive a lesson of instruction. It recalls to our mind the division of the day into twenty-four hours, and directs us to apportion them to prayer, labor, refreshment, and repose. It may be further considered as the scale which comprehends the numerical apportionment of the different degrees, according to the several Lodges.

THE COMMON GAVEL

Is an instrument made use of by operative masons to break off the corners of rough stones, the better to fit them for the builder's use; but we, as Free and Accepted Masons, are taught to make use of it for the more noble and glorious purpose of divesting our hearts and consciences of all the vices and superfluities of life; thereby fitting our minds, as living stones, for that spiritual building—that house not made with hands—eternal in the heavens.

The Common Gavel is an important instrument of labor, without which no work of manual skill can be completed; from which we learn that skill without industry will be of no avail, and labor is the lot of man; for the heart may conceive, and the head devise in vain, if the hand be not prompt to execute the design.

Masons are called moral builders. In their rituals they declare, emphatically, that a more noble and glorious purpose than squaring stones and hewing timbers is theirs—fitting immortal nature for that spiritual building not made with hands, eternal in the heavens. It is said that the construction of the pyramids of Egypt employed the labor of one hundred thousand men for many years, but it was only to build monumental piles, beneath whose shadows kings might rest. These pyramids are only temples for the dead; Masons are building one for the living. The pyramids were only mausoleums in which the bones of the mighty dead might repose in imperial magnificence; Masons are erecting a structure in which the God of Israel shall dwell for ever. The pyramid shall crumble away, till not one stone shall be left upon another; but who shall count the years of immortality, the life-time of the soul, which is fitted for its place in the heavens? Who can define its outlines, or fathom its depths, or measure its journey! It is a stream which grows broader and deeper as it flows onward. An angel's eye cannot measure its length, nor an angel's wing travel to its farthest boundary. When earth's proudest monumental piles have crumbled away, and that sand been scattered by the desert winds, and the glory and greatness of earth shall be forgotten, then will the immortal be pluming its wings for loftier flights. It is a fountain whose sources are in the Infinite, and whose placid waters flow on for ever—a spring-time that shall bloom, educating immortal mind for the present, the future, for all ages—is acknowledged to be one of the essential objects of Masonic labors. The builder builds for a century; Masons, for eternity. The painter paints for a generation; they, for everlasting years.

SECTION II.

IN this section is fully explained the symbolic meaning of the ceremonies that take place in the first. Without this explanation, the mind of the novitiate would still be in darkness; all would be mysterious and incomprehensible. When these ceremonies are explained by an intelligent and competent teacher, the mind is favorably impressed with the beautiful system; the mystery is unvailed, and the candidate discovers that his progress is replete with instruction, and that the assertion is confirmed, that every character, figure, and emblem, depicted in a Lodge, has a moral tendency, inculcates the practice of the noblest virtues, and furnishes sufficient proof of the definition, that "Freemasonry is a system of morality, vailed in allegory and illustrated by symbols."

THE PREPARATION.
*   *   *   *   *   *   *

Various passages of Scripture are referred to in this section -as explaining the traditions of Masonry.

"Cut wood out of Lebanon, and bring it on floats by sea to Joppa; and carry it up to Jerusalem."

"And the house was built of stone, made ready before it was brought thither; so that there was neither hammer, nor axe, nor any tool of iron heard in the house, while it was building."

"For to confirm all things, a man plucked off his shoe, and gave it unto his neighbor: and this was testimony in Israel."

"Ask, and it shall be given you; seek, and ye shall find; knock, and it shall be opened unto you."

PRAYER.

Bending the knees, in adoration of JEHOVAH, is one of the most ancient customs among men. We are taught, as Masons, never to commence any great or important undertaking without first invoking the blessing and protection of Deity.

The right hand has in all ages been deemed an emblem of fidelity, and the ancients worshiped Deity under the name of *Fides*, or Fidelity, which was sometimes represented by two right hands joined, and sometimes by two human figures, holding each other by the right hands.

The joining of right hands was esteemed, among the Persians and Parthians, as conveying a most inviolable obligation of fidelity. Hence, when King ARTABANUS desired to hold a conference with his revolted subject ASINEUS, who was in arms against him, he dispatched a messenger to him with the request, who said to ASINEUS, "The king hath sent me to give you his right hand and security,"—that is, a promise of safety in coming and going. And when ASINEUS sent his brother ASILEUS to the proposed conference, the king met him, and gave him his right hand; upon which JOSEPHUS remarks: "This is of the greatest force there with all these barbarians, and affords a firm security to those who hold intercourse with them, for none of them will deceive, when once they have given you their right hands; nor will any one doubt of their fidelity, when that once is given, even though they were before suspected of injustice."

VALERIUS MAXIMUS tells us that the ancients had a moral deity, whom they called FIDES. Her temple was first consecrated by NUMA. . . . FIDES was a goddess of honesty or fidelity; and the writer adds, when they promised any thing of old, they gave the right hand to pledge it, as we do, and, therefore, she is represented as giving her hand and sometimes her two hands conjoined. CHARTARIUS more fully describes this, by observing that the proper residence of faith or fidelity was thought by the ancients to be in the right hand; and, therefore, this deity was sometimes represented by two right hands joined together; sometimes by two little images, shaking each other's right hand: so that the right hand was by them held sacred, and was symbolically made use of in a solemn manner to denote fidelity.

Badge of a Mason.

The LAMB has, in all ages, been deemed an emblem of innocence; the lambskin is, therefore, to remind him of that purity of life and conduct which is so essentially necessary to his gaining admission into the Celestial Lodge above, where the Supreme Architect of the Universe presides.

The Apron, in ancient times, was a universally-received emblem of Truth. Among the Grecian mysteries, the candidate was invested with a white robe and apron. In Persia, the investiture was exceedingly splendid, and succeeded to the commission of Light. It consisted of the girdle, on which the twelve signs of the Zodiac were depicted; the tiara, the white apron, and the purple tunic.

SECTION III.

THIS section fully explains the manner of constituting, and the proper authority for holding a Lodge. Here, also, we learn where Lodges were anciently held; their FORM, SUPPORT, COVERING, FURNITURE, ORNAMENTS, LIGHTS, and JEWELS; how situated, and to whom dedicated, as well in former times as at present.

A Lodge is an assemblage of Masons, duly congregated, having the Holy Bible, Square, and Compasses, and a Charter or Warrant, authorizing them to work.

Where Held.

Lodge meetings, at the present day, are usually held in upper chambers— probably for the better security which such places afford. It may be, however, that the custom had its origin in a practice observed by the ancient Jews, of building their temples, schools, and synagogues on high hills[1], a practice which seems to have met the approbation of the ALMIGHTY, who said unto the Prophet EZEKIEL, "Upon the top of the mountain, the whole limit thereof, round about shall be most holy." Before the erection of temples, the *celestial* bodies were worshiped on HILLS, and the terrestrial ones in VALLEYS[2]. At a later period, the Christians, wherever it was practicable, erected their churches on eminences.

Hills or mountains were always considered the peculiar abode of the Deity; and hence the Masonic tradition, that our ancient brethren held their Lodges most frequently on the highest of hills. The veneration for hills or secret caverns induced the construction of temples for divine worship in such situations. The custom was initiated in the early ages of Christianity; for our ancient churches are usually erected on hills, and, beneath the foundations of those which are cathedral or collegiate, crypts were commonly constructed for private devotion and other secret purposes.

---

[1] The Noachidæ met on the summit of high hills, to practice their simple devotions, which were commemorative of their preservation amidst the destruction of mankind by the Universal Deluge, and of the promise that the world should never again be subjected to a similar judgment.

[2] In imitation of the primitive practice, but with a much more innocent purpose than the worship of idols, before Freemasons possessed the convenience of well-formed Lodges, our ancient brethren used to assemble on the highest of hills or in the lowest of valleys, because such situations afforded the means of security from unlawful intrusion.

Form and Dimensions of the Lodge.

Its form is * * * *. Its dimensions, from east to west, embracing every clime between north and south. In fact, its universal chain of friendship encircles every portion of the human family, and beams wherever civilization extends.

The form of a Lodge should always be an oblong square, in length, between the east and the west; in breadth, between the north and the south; in height, from earth to heaven; and in depth, from the surface to the center. This disposition serves to indicate the prevalence of Freemasonry over the whole face of the globe, guarded by its laws, and ornamented by its beautiful tenets. Every civilized region is illuminated by its presence. Its charity relieves the wretched; its brotherly love unites the Fraternity in a chain of indissoluble affection, and extends its example beyond the limits of the lodge-room, to embrace, in its ample scope, the whole human race, infolding them in its arms of universal love. The square form was esteemed by our ancient operative brethren as one of the Greater Lights, and a component part of the furniture of the Lodge. The double cube is an expressive emblem of the united powers of darkness and light in the creation.

*   *   *   *   *   *   *

The Boundaries of the Lodge.

The Masonic Lodge, bounded only by the extreme points of the compass, the highest heavens, and the lowest depth of the central abyss, is metaphorically supported by three great pillars, which are denominated WISDOM[1], STRENGTH[2], and BEAUTY[3]: because there should be *wisdom* to contrive, *strength* to support, and *beauty* to adorn all great and important undertakings. The universe is the temple of the DEITY whom we serve: Wisdom, Strength, and Beauty are about His throne as pillars of His work; for His wisdom is infinite, His strength is omnipotent, and His beauty shines forth through all His creation in symmetry and order.

---

[1] WISDOM is represented by the Ionic column and the W. M.; because the Ionic column wisely combines the strength without the massiveness of the Doric; with the grace, without the exuberance of ornament, of the Corinthian; and because it is the duty of the W. M. to superintend, instruct, and enlighten the Craft by his superior wisdom. SOLOMON, king of Israel, is also considered as the column of wisdom that supported the temple.

[2] STRENGTH is represented by the Doric column and the S. W.; because the Doric is the strongest and most massive of the Orders, and because it is the duty of the S. W., by an attentive superintendence of the Craft, to aid the W. M. in the performance of his duties, and to strengthen and support his authority. HIRAM, king of Tyre, is also considered as the representative of the column of strength which supported the temple.

[3] BEAUTY is represented by the Corinthian column and the J. W.; because the Corinthian is the most beautiful and highly finished of the Orders, and because the situation of the J. W. in the S. enables him the better to observe that bright luminary which, at its meridian height, is the beauty and glory of the day.—Thus, by the united energies of these three presiding-officers, the system is adorned and established firm as a rock in mid-ocean, braving the malignant shafts of envy and detraction; its summit gilded with the rays of the meridian sun, though stormy winds and waves beat furiously on its base.

As the work of building the temple at Jerusalem was conducted by the wisdom of SOLOMON, the strength of Mutant, king of Tyre, and the beauty, or cunning workmanship of HIRAM ABIFF, so the labors of the Lodge are supported by the wisdom, strength, and beauty of the three presiding-officers, who occupy the prominent stations in the East, West, and South; thus locally forming a triangle, which is a sacred emblem, and unitedly constituting one chief governor, by which the affairs of the Lodge are conducted, and without the presence of all three, or their legally-appointed representatives, no Lodge can be opened for the transaction of business, nor can any candidate be legally initiated therein.

The Covering of the Lodge.

Its covering is no less than the clouded canopy, or starry-decked heaven, where all good Masons hope at last to arrive, by the aid of that theological ladder[1] which JACOB, in his vision, saw extending from earth to heaven; the three principal rounds of which are denominated FAITH, HOPE, and CHARITY; which admonishes us to have *faith* in GOD, *hope* in immortality, and *charity* to all mankind. The greatest of these is CHARITY: for our *faith* may be lost in sight; *hope* ends in fruition; but *charity* extends beyond the grave, through the boundless realms of eternity.

FAITH is the foundation of justice, the bond of amity, and the chief support of society. We live by faith; we walk by faith; by faith we have a continual hope in the acknowledgment of a Supreme Being; by faith we are justified, accepted, and finally saved. Faith is the substance of things hoped for—the evidence of things not seen. If we—with suitable, true devotion—maintain our Masonic profession, our faith will become a beam of light, and bring us to those blessed mansions where we shall be eternally happy with God, the Grand Architect of the Universe.

HOPE is the anchor of the soul, both sure and steadfast, and enters into that within the vail; let a firm reliance in the Almighty's faithfulness animate our endeavors, and teach us to fix our hopes within the limits of His promises, so shall success attend us. If we believe a thing to be impossible, our despondency may render it so; but he who perseveres, will ultimately overcome all difficulties.

---

[1] Standing firmly on the Bible, Square, and Compasses, is a ladder which connects the earth with the heavens, or covering of the Lodge, and is a simile of that which JACOB saw in a vision when journeying to Padanarum, in Mesopotamia. It is composed of staves or rounds innumerable, which point out as many moral virtues; but principally of three, which refer to Faith, Hope, and Charity: Faith in the Great Architect of the Universe; Hope in salvation; and to be in Charity with all mankind, but more particularly with the brethren. It reaches to the heavens, and rests on the volume of the sacred law; because, by the doctrine contained in that Holy Book, we are taught to believe in the wise dispensations of Divine Providence; which belief strengthens our faith, and enables us to ascend the first step. This faith naturally creates in us a hope of becoming partakers of the blessed promises therein recorded; which hope enables us to ascend the second step. But the third and last, being Charity, comprehends the whole; and the Mason who is possessed of that virtue, in its amplest sense, may justly be deemed to have attained the summit of the science.

CHARITY is the brightest gem that can adorn our Masonic profession. Happy is the man who has sowed in his breast. the seeds of benevolence, the produce thereof is love and peace: he envieth not his neighbor; he listeneth not to a tale, when reported by slander; revenge or malice has no place in his breast; he forgives the injuries of men, and endeavors to blot them from his recollection. The objects of true charity among Masons are, merit and virtue in distress; persons who are incapable of extricating themselves from misfortunes in their journey through life; industrious men, who, from inevitable accidents and acts of Providence, have fallen into ruin; widows, who are left survivors of their husbands, by whose labors they subsisted; orphans in tender years, left naked to the world; and the aged, whose spirits are exhausted, whose arms are unbraced by time, and thereby rendered unable to procure for themselves that sustenance they could accomplish in their youthful days. This is Charity, the Keystone to our mystic fabric.

Hail, balm-bestowing CHARITY!
  First of the heaven-born:
Sanctity and Sincerity
  Thy temple still adorn:
Communing with Mortality,
  The humble but thou dost not scorn.
Thou art, in bright reality,
  Friend of the friendless and forlorn.
With joy-induced alacrity,
  Supplying want, assuaging woe.
To every home of misery
  Thy sister-spirits smiling go;
Dispelling all despondency,
  Their blessings they bestow—
Like angels in the ministry
  Of holiness below.

The Furniture of the Lodge

Consists of the Holy Bible, Square, and Compasses. The Bible is dedicated to the service of God, because it is the inestimable gift of God to man, * * * *; the Square to the Master, because it is the proper Masonic emblem of his office; and the Compasses to the Craft, because, by a due attention to their use, they are taught to circumscribe their desires, and keep their passions within due bounds.

The Square is given to the whole Masonic body, because we are all obligated with it, and are consequently bound to act thereon. As it is by the assistance of the Square that all rude matter is brought into due form, so it is by the square conduct of the Master that all animosities are made to subside, should any unfortunately arise in the Lodge, and the business of Masonry is thereby better conducted. The ungovernable passions and uncultivated nature of man stand as much in need of the Square and Compasses to bring them into order, and to adorn us with the beauty of holiness, as those instruments of Masonry are necessary to bring rude matter into form, or to make a block of marble fit for the polished corners of the temple.

The following appropriate illustrations of the three Great Lights of Masonry may be introduced with beautiful effect:

As more immediate guides for a Freemason, the Lodge is furnished with unerring rules, whereby he shall form his conduct.

The Book of the Law is laid before him, that he may not say, through ignorance he erred; whatever the Great Architect of the world hath dictated to mankind, as the mode in which he should be served, and the path in which to tread, is to obtain his approbation; whatever precepts he bath administered, and with whatever laws he hath inspired the sages of old, the same are faithfully comprised in the Book of the Law of Masonry. That book reveals the duties which the Great Master of all exacts from us: open to every eye—comprehensible to every mind. Then who shall say among us, that he knoweth not the acceptable service?

The Rule, the Square, and the Compasses, are emblematical of the conduct we should pursue in society. To observe punctuality in all our engagements, faithfully and religiously to discharge those important obligations which we owe to God and our neighbor; to be upright in all our dealings; to hold the scales of Justice in equal poise; to square our actions by the unerring rule of God's sacred word; to keep within compass and bounds with all mankind, particularly with a brother; to govern our expenses by our incomes; to curb our sensual appetites; to keep within bounds those unruly passions which oftentimes interfere with the enjoyments of society, and degrade both the man and the Freemason; to recall to our minds that, in the great scale of existence, the whole family of mankind are upon a level with each other, and that the only question of preference among Freemasons should be, who is most wise, who is most good? For the time will come, and none of us know how soon, when death, the great leveler of all human greatness, will rob us of our distinctions, and bring us to a level with the dust.

The Ornaments of a Lodge

Are the MOSAIC PAVEMENT, the INDENTED TESSEL, and the BLAZING STAR.

The Mosaic Pavement is a representation of the ground-floor of King Solomon's Temple; the Indented Tessel[1], of that beautiful tessellated border or skirting which surrounded it. The Mosaic Pavement is emblematical of human life, checkered with good and evil; the Indented Tessel, or Tesselated Border, of the manifold blessings and comforts which constantly surround us, and which we hope to enjoy by a firm reliance on Divine Providence, which is hieroglyphically represented by the Blazing Star in the center.

---

[1] The Indented Tessel is a border of stones, of various colors, plead around the pavement, cut or notched into inequalities resembling teeth.

As the steps of man are tried in the various and uncertain incidents of life; as our days are checkered with a strange contrariety of events, and our passage through this existence, though sometimes attended with prosperous circumstances, is often beset by a multitude of evils; hence is the Lodge furnished with Mosaic work, to remind us of the precariousness of our state on earth: to-day, our feet tread in prosperity; to-morrow, we totter on the uneven paths of weakness, temptation, and adversity. While this emblem is before us, we are instructed to boast of nothing; to have compassion, and give aid to those who are in adversity; to walk uprightly, and with humility; for such is this existence, that there is no station in which pride can be stably founded: all men, in birth and in the grave, are on a level. While we tread on this Mosaic work, let our ideas return to the original, which it copies; and let every Freemason act as the dictates of reason prompt him to live in brotherly love.

The Lights of the Lodge.

A Lodge has three symbolic lights:—one in the East, one in the West, and one in the South.

*　　*　　*　　*　　*　　*　　*

The fixed lights of the Lodge were formerly represented by "three windows, supposed to be in every room where a Lodge is held; referring to the cardinal points of the compass, according to the antique rules of Masonry." There was one in the East, another in the West, and another in the South, to light the men *to*, *at*, and *from* labor; but there was none in the North, because the sun darts no rays from thence. These constitute the symbolic situations of the three chief officers. Hence it is affirmed that "a Lodge is, or ought to be, a true representation of King SOLOMON'S temple, which was situated north of the ecliptic; the sun and moon, therefore, darting their rays from the south, no light was to be expected from the north; we, therefore, masonically, term the north a place of darkness." The Master's place is in the East, to call the brethren *to* labor; the Junior Warden is placed in the South, to cheer and encourage them *at* their work; and the Senior Warden in the West, to dismiss them *from* their daily toil.

This description of a Masonic Lodge will be found to embrace a perfect picture of the universe, both in its attributes and its extent. The sun governs the day, the moon the night, and the stars illumine the spangled canopy of heaven; while the earth is spread with a carpet of natural mosaic work, beautiful to the eye, and administering to the necessities of man.

A Lodge has six jewels; three movable and three immovable.

The immovable jewels are the SQUARE, LEVEL, and PLUMB[1].

---

[1] They are called Immovable jewels, because they are always to be found in the East, West, and South parts of the Lodge, being worn by the Master, Senior Warden, and Junior Warden.

The Square inculcates morality; the Level, equality; and the Plumb, rectitude of conduct.

The movable jewels are the ROUGH ASHLAR, the PERFECT ASHLAR, and the TRESTLE-BOARD[1].

The Rough Ashlar is a stone as taken from the quarry in its rude and natural state. The Perfect Ashlar is a stone made ready by the hands of the workmen, to be adjusted by the working-tools of the Fellow Craft. The Trestle-board is for the Master-workman to draw his designs upon.

By the Rough Ashlar we are reminded of our rude and imperfect state by nature; by the Perfect Ashlar, of that state of perfection at which we hope to arrive by a virtuous education, our own endeavors, and the blessing of God; and by the Trestle-board we are also reminded that, as the operative workman erects his temporal building agreeably to the rules and designs laid down by the Master on his Trestle-board, so should we, both operative and speculative, endeavor to erect our spiritual building in accordance with the designs laid down by the Supreme Architect of the Universe, in the Great Book of Nature and Revelation, which is our spiritual, moral, and Masonic Trestle-board.

The Trestle-board is for the Master to draw his plans and designs upon, that the building may be constructed with order and regularity. It refers to the Sacred Volume, which is denominated the Trestle-board of the Grand Architect of the Universe, because in that Holy Book he has laid down such magnificent plans and holy designs, that, were we conversant therein and adherent thereto, it would prepare us for that building not made with hands, eternal in the heavens.

---

[1] Such is the generally-acknowledged division of the jewels in the Lodges in this country; but in the English Lodges, the reverse is the case. There, the Rough and Perfect Ashlars and the Trestle-board are the immovable jewels, and the Square, Level, and Plumb are the movable, because they descend from one set of officers to their successors.

Situation of the Lodge

The Lodge is situated due East and West.[1]

*   *   *   *   *   *   *

Dr. OLIVER assigns the following reasons why the Tabernacle is considered as the type of a Freemason's Lodge: "It was an oblong square, and, with its courts and appendages, it represented the whole habitable globe. Such is also the extent of our Lodges. The former was supported by pillars, and the latter is also sustained by those of Wisdom, Strength, and Beauty. They were equally situated due east and west. The sacred roll of GOD'S revealed will and law was deposited in the Ark of the Covenant; the same Holy Record is placed in a conspicuous part of our Lodges. The altar of incense was a double cube, and so is our pedestal and stone of foundation. The covering of the Tabernacle was composed of three colors, as a representation of the celestial hemisphere; such, also, is the covering of a Freemason's Lodge. The floor of the Tabernacle was so holy, that the priest's were forbidden to tread upon it without taking off their shoes; the floor of the Lodge is holy ground."

CALCOTT says that MOSES, "foreseeing the difficulties which he would have to encounter before he should arrive in the promised land, and having already experienced the instability of the Israelites, caused the Tabernacle to be erected east and west, to excite in them a firm reliance on the omnipotence of that GOD who had then lately wrought so great a miracle in their favor, by causing a wind to blow first east, and then west, whereby they safely escaped from the Egyptians upon dry land, even through the midst of a sea, which, nevertheless, overwhelmed and totally destroyed their pursuers. And as they were liable to meet with many distresses in their sojournment in the wilderness, so, as oft as they should behold the situation of the Tabernacle, their faith might be strengthened, and, by a firm reliance on ALMIGHTY GOD, they might be enabled to proceed with resolution and cheerfulness. And as the Tabernacle was at that time to be a constant exhortation to them, from that great instance of omnipotence, to confide in GOD under all their embarrassments, so the Temple, afterwards built by SOLOMON, in the same form and situation, was to be a lasting monument to their posterity of the mighty works the LORD had performed in conducting their forefathers out of their captivity into the promised land. And this, also, may be deemed a very sufficient reason why places for Christian worship, after the pattern of the said Tabernacle and Temple, have ever been, and still are, generally erected in the same manner;

---

[1] Our Lodges are situated due East and West, because all places of Divine worship, as well as all well-formed and regularly-constituted Lodges, are, or ought to be, so situated; for which we assign three Masonic reasons:—1. The sun, the glory of the LORD, rises in the East and sets in the West; 2. Learning originated in the East, and from thence extended its benign influence to the West; 3. The last and grand reason, refers to the situation of the Tabernacle in the wilderness. The nature of the Lodge—its form, dimensions, and supports—its ground, situation, and covering—its ornaments, furniture, and jewels—all unite their aid to form a perfect code of moral and theological philosophy; which, while it fascinates the understanding, improves the mind, until it becomes polished like the Perfect Ashlar, and can only be tried by the Square of GOD'S word and the unerring Compass of conscience.

for, as human creatures, we, as well as our forefathers, stand in need to be continually reminded of our weakness, and a necessary constant dependence on an Omnipotent and All-gracious Being."

Dedication of Lodges.

Lodges were anciently dedicated to King SOLOMON, as he was our first Most Excellent Grand Master; but Masons professing Christianity, dedicate theirs to St. JOHN the Baptist and St. JOHN the Evangelist, who were two eminent patrons of Masonry; and since their time, there is represented in every regular and well-governed Lodge a certain *Point within a Circle*—the point representing an individual brother; the circle, the boundary-line of his conduct to GOD and man, beyond which he is never to suffer his passions, prejudices, or interests to betray him, on any occasion. This circle is embordered by two perpendicular parallel lines, representing those Saints, who were perfect parallels in Christianity, as well as in Masonry; and upon the vertex rests the Holy Scriptures, which point out the whole duty of man. In going around this circle, we necessarily touch upon these two lines, as well as upon the Holy Scriptures; and while a Mason keeps himself thus circumscribed, it is impossible that he should materially err.

> "But though past all diffused, without a shore
> His essence; local is his Throne, as meet
> To gather the dispersed, as Standards call
> The listed from afar; to fix a point,
> A central point, collective of his sons,
> Since finite every nature but his own,
>   *   *   *   *   *   *   *
> If earth's whole orb by some dire distant eye
> Were seen at once, her towering Alps would sink,
> And level'd Atlas leave an even sphere.
> Thus earth, and all that earthly minds admire,
> Is swallow'd In Eternity's vast round,"—YOUNG.

"Whether we regard this symbol in the purity of its legitimate interpretation, or consider the unlimited corruption which it sustained in its progress through the mysteries of idolatry, the general principle will be found equally significant. It was originally the conservator of a genuine moral precept, founded on a fundamental religious truth; but innovation followed innovation, until this degraded symbol became the dreadful depository of obscenity and lust.

47

"The use of this emblem is coeval with the first created man. A primary idea which would suggest itself to the mind of ADAM, when engaged in reflections on his own situation, the form of the universe, and the nature of all the objects presented to his view, would be, that *the creation was a circle and himself the center*. This figure, implanted without an effort, would be ever present in all his contemplations, and would influence his judgment to a certain extent, while attempting to decide on the mysterious phenomena which were continually before him. To persons unacquainted with the intricate philosophy of Nature, as we may fairly presume ADAM was, this is the plain idea conveyed to the senses by a superficial view of Nature's works. Ask an unlettered hind of the present day, and he will tell you that the earth is a circular plane; and perhaps he will have some indistinct notion that the expanse above his head is spherical, but he will assuredly look upon *himself* as the common center of all. This is consistent with the general appearance of things; for, if he look around, be finds the horizon, unless intercepted by the intervention of sensible objects, equally distant from the point of vision in all its parts. And the experiment uniformly producing the same results, whether made by night or day, he relies on the evidence of his senses, and pronounces his own judgment correct and irrefutable. So the first created man. Himself the center of the system, he would regard Paradise as the limit of the habitable earth, and the expanse as the eternal residence of the omnipresent Deity. A little reflection, however, would soon bring him nearer to the truth. The garden of Eden was of a circular form, and the Tree of Life was placed in the center. Now, as the fruit of this tree was reputed to convey the privilege of immortality, the center would hence be esteemed the most honorable situation, and be ultimately assigned to the Deity, who alone enjoys the attributes of immortality and eternity; for ADAM, in his progress to different parts of this happy abode, would soon conclude that, however he might be deceived by appearances, he himself could not be a permanent center, because he was constantly changing his position.

"To this august Circle the two forbidden trees were the accompanying perpendicular parallel lines, pointing out GOD'S equal *justice* and *mercy*. When ADAM had violated the divine command, and eaten of the tree of knowledge, *justice* demanded that the threatened penalty should be paid. But here *mercy* interposed, and he was expelled from the abode of purity and peace, now violated by transgression, 'lest he should put forth his hand, and take also of the tree of life, and live for ever' in a state of wickedness and sin. Hence arose the Masonic emblem of a Point within a Circle."

* * * * * * *

"When mankind had transferred their adoration from the Creator to his works, they advanced specious reasons to justify a devotion to spheres and circles. Every thing great and sublime, which was continually presented to their inspection, partook of this form. The sun, the unequivocal source of light and heat, was a primary object of attention, and became their chief deity. The earth, the planets, and fixed stars, proceeding in all their majestic regularity, excited admiration, and implanted devout feelings in their hearts. These were all spherical, as was also the arch of heaven, illuminated with their unfading luster. The next progressive observations of mankind would be extended to the unassisted efforts of Nature in the production of plants and trees; and these were found to exhibit, for the most part, the same uniform appearances. From the simple stalk of corn, to the bole of the gigantic lord of the forest, the cylinder and cone, and consequently the circle, were the most common forms assumed by the vegetable creation. Every fruit he plucked—every root he dug from the earth for food—was either globular, cylindrical, or conical, each partaking of the nature of a circle. If a tree were divided horizontally, the section uniformly exhibited the appearance of a Point within a succession of concentric circles. The same will be true of many varieties of vegetables; and similar results would be produced from an inspection of animal bodies. The trunk is a cylinder; and the intestines, so often critically examined for the purposes of augury, presented to the curious inquirer little variation from the general principle. Hence statues bearing these forms were subsequently dedicated to the Olympic gods; a Cylinder, to the earth; and a Cone to the sun.

"In this figure, Nature, in her most sportive mood, appeared exclusively to delight. If a bubble were excited on the water, it was spherical; and if any solid body were cast upon the surface, the ripple formed itself into innumerable concentric circles, rapidly succeeding each other, of which the body, or moving cause, was the common center. If water were cast into the air, they found that the drops invariably arranged themselves into a globular form. This uniformity was soon observed, and thought to be a preternatural indication of divinity; for if Nature assumed one unvarying character in all her works, that character must be an unquestionable symbol of the GOD of Nature. Hence the Circle, with its center distinctly marked, became a most sacred emblem with every nation of idolaters; adopted perhaps from the same symbol used by their forefathers on the plain of Shinar; referring primarily to the immeasurable expanse occupied by infinite space; a proper type of eternity, but now justified by a reference to the works of Nature. This was the general belief, though the expression varied in different ages and among the inhabitants of different nations.

"The tribes contiguous to Judea placed a *Jod* (') in the center of a circle, as a symbol of the Deity surrounded by Eternity, of which He was said to be the inscrutable author, the ornament, and the support. The Samothracians had a great veneration for the Circle, which they considered as consecrated by the universal presence of the Deity; and hence *rings* were distributed to the initiated, as amulets possessed of the power of averting danger. The Chinese used a symbol which bore a great resemblance to that which is the subject of this annotation. The Circle was bounded north and south by two serpents, (equivalent to the two perpendicular parallel lines of the Masonic symbol,) and was emblematical of the *Universe*, protected and supported equally by the *Power* and *Wisdom* of the Creator. The Hindoos believed that the Supreme Being was correctly represented by a perfect sphere, without beginning and without end. The first settlers in Egypt transmitted to their posterity an exact copy of our Point within a Circle, expressed in emblematical language. The widely-extended universe was represented as a circle of boundless light, in the center of which the Deity was said to dwell; or, in other words, the circle was symbolical of His *eternity*; and the perpendicular parallel lines by which it is bounded, were the two great luminaries of heaven, the sun and moon; the former denoting His *virtue*—the latter His *wisdom*. And this idea was generally expressed by a hawk's head in the center of a circle, or an endless serpent inclosing an eye.

"But the most expressive symbol to this effect used by any people who had renounced the true religion, was the famous emblem of PYTHAGORAS, who contrived not merely to express the only one GOD, residing in the midst of eternity, but united with it an idea of the divine Triad, and blended emblems of regeneration, morality, and science. For this purpose he added to the central Jod nine other Jods, disposed about the center in the form of an equilateral triangle, each side consisting of the number FOUR. The disciples of PYTHAGORAS denominated this symbol *Trigonon-mysticum*, because it was the conservator of many awful and important truths.

"1. The *Monad*, or active principle.

"2. The *Duad*, or passive principle.

"3. The *Triad*, or world proceeding from their union.

"4. The sacred *Quarternary*, involving the liberal Sciences, Physics, Morality, etc., etc.

"Of this remarkable emblem, a full explanation may be equally interesting and instructive.

"The symbol of all things, according to PYTHAGORAS, was *one* and *two*. One added to two make *three*; and once the square of two make FOUR, which is the perfect *Tetractys*; and 1+2+3+4=10, the consummation of all things; and therefore the amount of the points contained within the Pythagorean Circle is exactly TEN. Hence, because the first *four* digits added into each other made up the number ten, this philosopher called the number *four* πάντα ἀριθμὸν, *all number*, or the *whole number*, and used it as the symbol of universality[1]. To ascertain, however, the entire meaning of this symbol, it will be necessary to take the numbers included within the Circle in their natural order, and hear what hidden mystery the philosophy of PYTHAGORAS attached to each.

"The number ONE was the Point within the Circle, and denoted the central fire, or GOD; because it is the beginning and ending—the first and the last. It signified, also, love, concord, piety, and friendship; because it is so connected that it cannot be divided into parts. Two meant darkness, fortitude, harmony, and justice; because of its equal parts; and the moon, because she is forked. THREE referred to harmony, friendship, peace, concord, and temperance. All these, and many other virtues, depended on this number and proceeded from it. FOUR referred to the Deity: for it was considered the number of numbers. It is the first solid figure; a point being 1, a line 2, a superficies 3, and a solid 4. It was also the Tetractys; a WORD sacred among the Pythagoreans, and used as a most solemn oath; because they considered it the root and principle, the cause and maker, of all things." *   *   *   *

"The Point within the Circle afterwards became a universal emblem to denote the temple of the Deity, and was referred to the Planetary Circle, in the center of which was fixed the sun, as the universal god and father of nature; for the whole circle of heaven was called GOD." *   *   *   *   *   *

"SERVIUS tells us it was believed that the center of a temple was the peculiar residence of the Deity; the exterior decorations being merely ornamental. Hence the astronomical character used to denote or represent the sun, is a Point within a Circle; because that figure is the symbol of perfection. The most perfect metal, gold, is also designated in chemistry by the same character.

"With this reference the Point within a Circle was an emblem of great importance among the British Druids. Their temples were circular, many of them with a single stone erected in the center; their solemn processions were all arranged in the same form; their weapons of war—the circular shield with a central boss, the spear with a hollow globe at its end, etc.—all partaking of this general principle; and without a circle it was thought impossible to obtain the favor of the gods."

---

[1] The sum of all the principles of PYTHAGORAS is this:—"The Monad is the principle of all things. From the Monad came the Indeterminate Duad, as matter subjected to the cause of Monad; from the Monad and the indeterminate Duad, numbers; *from numbers, points; from points, lines; from lines, superficies; from superficies, solids*; from these solid bodies, whose elements are four—Fire, Water, Air, and Earth—of all which transmuted, and totally changed, the WORLD consists."

The three great tenets of a Freemason's profession inculcate the practice of those truly commendable virtues, BROTHERLY LOVE, RELIEF, and TRUTH.

BROTHERLY LOVE.

By the exercise of Brotherly Love, we are taught to regard the whole human species as one family—the high, the low, the rich, the poor—who, as created by one Almighty Parent, and inhabitants of the same planet, are to aid, support, and protect each other. On this principle, Masonry unites men of every country, sect, and opinion, and conciliates true friendship among those who might otherwise have remained at a perpetual distance.

Brotherly Love or Friendship is regarded by Freemasons as the strong cement of the Order; without this high moral virtue, the Fraternity would soon cease to exist. By Brotherly Love, we are to understand that generous principle of the soul which regards the human species as one family, created by an All-wise Being, and placed on this globe for the mutual assistance of each other. The man who is actuated by the pure principle of Brotherly Love, will not desert his friend when dangers threaten or misfortunes assail him. When he is calumniated, he will openly and boldly espouse his cause, and endeavor to remove the aspersion. When sickness or infirmity occasion him to be deserted by others, he will seize the opportunity, and redouble all the affectionate attentions which love suggests. No society can exist for any length of time, unless Brotherly Love prevail among its members. To "dwell together in unity," is the life and support of the great Masonic institution.

RELIEF.

To relieve the distressed, is a duty incumbent on all men, but particularly on Masons, who are linked together by an indissoluble chain of sincere affection. To soothe the unhappy; to sympathize with their misfortunes; to compassionate their miseries, and to restore peace to their troubled minds, is the great aim we have in view. On this basis, we form our friendships and establish our connections.

Relief flows from brotherly love, as free, pure, and refreshing as the mountain air. It dries up the gushing fountains of grief, banishes want from the abode of a distressed brother, and pours the oil of joy into the wounded hearts of the widow and the orphan.

TRUTH

Is a divine attribute, and the foundation of every virtue. To be good and true, is the first lesson we are taught in Masonry. On this theme we contemplate, and by its dictates endeavor to regulate our conduct. Hence, while influenced by this principle, hypocrisy and deceit are unknown among us; sincerity and plain dealing distinguish us; and the heart and the tongue join in promoting each other's welfare, and rejoicing in each other's prosperity[1].

Truth is the foundation of all Masonic virtues; it is one of our grand principles; for to be good men and true, is a part of the first lesson we are taught; and at the commencement of our freedom we are exhorted to be fervent and zealous in the pursuit of truth and goodness. It is not sufficient that we walk in the light, unless we do so in the truth also. All hypocrisy and deceit must be banished from among us. Sincerity and plain dealing complete the harmony of a Lodge, and render us acceptable in the sight of Him unto whom all hearts are open, all desires known, and from whom no secrets are hid. There is a charm in truth, which draws and attracts the mind continually towards it. The more we discover, the more we desire; and the great reward is wisdom, virtue, and happiness. This is an edifice founded on a rock, which malice cannot shake or time destroy.

The * * * * are explained, in connection with the four cardinal virtues, FORTITUDE, PRUDENCE, TEMPERANCE, and JUSTICE.

FORTITUDE

Is that noble and steady purpose of the mind, whereby we are enabled to undergo any pain, peril, or danger, when prudentially deemed expedient. This virtue is equally distant from rashness or cowardice; and should be deeply impressed upon the mind of every Mason, as a safeguard or security against any illegal attack that may be made, by force or otherwise, to extort from him any of those valuable secrets with which he has been so solemnly intrusted, and which were emblematically represented upon his first admission into the Lodge, and * * * *

In the absence of this virtue, no person can perform his duty, either to GOD, his neighbor, or himself, in an acceptable manner. He will be too much overwhelmed with the cares and troubles of the world to find leisure or resolution to protect himself from the enticing machinations with which he will be continually beset during his progress through life; and may be led unintentionally to rend asunder the sacred ties of brotherhood which unite men of all parties, religions, or politics, by forfeiting the confidence trustingly reposed in him, and thereby becoming the victim of his own weakness.

---

[1] In the ancient mythology of Rome, TRUTH was called the mother of VIRTUE, and was depicted with white and flowing garments. Her looks were cheerful and pleasant, though modest and serene. She was the protectress of honor and honesty, and the light and joy of human society.

PRUDENCE

Teaches us to regulate our lives and actions agreeably to the dictates of reason, and is that habit by which we wisely judge and prudentially determine on all things relative to cur present as well as to our future happiness. This virtue should be the peculiar characteristic of every Mason, not only for the government of his conduct while in the Lodge, but also when abroad in the world. It should be particularly attended to, in all strange and mixed companies, never to let fall the least sign, token, or word, whereby the secrets of Masonry might be unlawfully obtained, and * * * * *

Prudence is among the most exalted objects that demand every Mason's special attention, for it is the rule which governs all other virtues. She directs us to the path which leads to every degree of propriety, inciting us to the performance of worthy actions, and, as a guiding-star, lighting our steps through the dreary and dark-some ways of this life.

TEMPERANCE

Is that due restraint upon our affections and passions, which renders the body tame and governable, and frees the mind from the allurements of vice. This virtue should be the constant practice of every Mason; as he is thereby taught to avoid excess, or contracting any licentious or vicious habits, the indulgence of which might lead him to disclose some of those valuable secrets which he has promised to conceal, and never reveal, and which would consequently subject him to the contempt and detestation of all good Masons.

This virtue should be the constant practice of every Freemason, while its opposite should be carefully guarded against. At the shrine of Intemperance, how many victims are daily offered!—Blooming youth and hoary age have alike bowed before it. They continue offering libations on the unhallowed altar, until their fortunes are wasted, their credit lost, their constitutions impaired, their children beggared, and that life which might have been usefully and honorably employed, becomes a burden to the possessor.

JUSTICE

Is that standard, or boundary of right, which enables us to render to every man his just due, without distinction. This virtue is not only consistent with divine and human laws, but is the very cement and support of civil society; and as justice, in a great measure, constitutes the really good man, so should it be the invariable practice of every Mason never to deviate from the minutest principle thereof. * * *

The exercise of this principle incites us to act toward others, in all the transactions of life, as we wish they would act toward us; and as, in a great measure, it constitutes real goodness, it is therefore represented as the perpetual study of an accomplished Freemason. Without the influence of justice, universal confusion would ensue; lawless force would overcome the principles of equity, and social intercourse would no longer exist.

Here may be given some general instructions peculiar to Freemasons, relative to the manner in which Entered Apprentices serve their * * *, and how represented * * *; together with a few observations regarding the comparison between it and clay, etc., and concluding thus:

Our Mother EARTH alone, of all the elements, has never proved unfriendly to man; the bodies of water deluge him with rain, oppress him with hail, and drown him with inundations. The air rushes in storms, prepares the tempest, and lights up the volcano; but the earth, ever kind and indulgent, is found subservient to his wishes. Though constantly harassed, more to furnish the luxuries than the necessaries of life, she never refuses her accustomed yield; spreading his path with flowers and his table with plenty; though she produces poison, still she supplies the antidote, and returns with interest every good committed to her care; and when at last he is called upon to pass through the "dark valley of the shadow of Death," she once more receives him, and piously covers his remains within her bosom: this admonishes us that from it we came, and to it we must shortly return.

Such is the arrangement of the different sections in the first lecture, which, with the forms adopted at the Opening and Closing of a Lodge, comprehends the whole of the first degree of Masonry. This plan has the advantage of regularity to recommend it, the support of precedent and authority, and the sanction and respect which flow from antiquity.

CHARGE TO THE CANDIDATE.

BROTHER: As you are now introduced into the first principles of Masonry, I congratulate you on being accepted into this ancient and honorable Order:—ancient, as having subsisted from time immemorial; and honorable, as tending, in every particular, so to render all men who will be conformable to its precepts. No institution was ever raised on a better principle or more solid foundation; nor were ever more excellent rules and useful maxims laid down, than are inculcated in the several Masonic lectures. The greatest and best of men, in all ages, have been encouragers and promoters of the art; and have never deemed it derogatory to their dignity to level themselves with the Fraternity, extend their privileges, and patronize their assemblies. There are three great duties which, as a Mason, you are charged to inculcate:—to GOD, your neighbor, and yourself. To GOD, in never mentioning His name but with that reverential awe which is due from a creature to his Creator; to implore His aid in all your laudable undertakings, and to esteem Him as the chief good; to your neighbor, in acting upon the square, and doing unto him as you wish he should do unto you; and to yourself, in avoiding all irregularity and intemperance, which may impair your faculties, or debase the dignity of your profession. A zealous attachment to these duties will insure public and private esteem.

In the state, you are to be a quiet and peaceful citizen, true to your government, and just to your country; you are not to countenance disloyalty or rebellion, but patiently submit to legal authority, and conform with cheerfulness to the government of the country in which you live. In your outward demeanor, be particularly careful to avoid censure and reproach.

Although your frequent appearance at our regular meetings is earnestly solicited, yet it is not meant that Masonry should interfere with your necessary vocations; for these are on no account to be neglected; neither are you to suffer your zeal for the institution to lead you into argument with those who, through ignorance, may ridicule it.

At your leisure hours, that you may improve in Masonic knowledge, you are to converse with well-informed brethren, who will be always as ready to give, as you will be to receive, instruction.

Finally, keep sacred and inviolable the mysteries of the Order; as these are to distinguish you from the rest of the community, and mark your consequence among Masons. If, in the circle of your acquaintance, you find a person desirous of being initiated into Masonry, be particularly careful not to recommend him, unless you are convinced he will conform to our rules; that the honor, glory, and reputation of the institution may be firmly established, and the world at large convinced of its good effects.

CHARGE,
AT THE INITIATION OF A SOLDIER.

BROTHER: Our institution breathes a spirit of general philanthropy. Its benefits, in a social point of view, are extensive. In the most endearing ties, it unites all mankind. In every nation, wherever civilization extends—and not unfrequently among the wild savages of the forest—it opens an asylum to a brother in distress, and grants hospitality to the necessitous and unfortunate. The sublime principles of universal goodness and love to all mankind, which are essential to it, cannot be lost in national distinctions, prejudices, and animosities. The rage of contest and the sanguinary conflict have, by its recognized principles, been abated, and the milder emotions of humanity substituted. It has often performed the part of the Angel of Goodness, in ministering to the wants of the sick, the wounded, and the unfortunate prisoner of war. It has even taught the pride of victory to give way to the dictates of an honorable connection.

Pure patriotism will always animate you to every call of your country to repel an invading foreign foe, or in subduing the rebellious intentions of those within the limits of our own land who become faithless to the high duty of a citizen. But should you, while engaged in the service of your country, be made captive, you may find affectionate brethren where others would only find enemies.

The institution also demands that you shall be a quiet and peaceable citizen, true to your government, and just to your country; yielding obedience to the laws which afford you protection.

In whatever country you travel, when you meet a Mason, you will find a brother and a friend, who will do all in his power to serve you; and who will relieve you, should you be poor or in distress, to the utmost of his ability, and with a ready cheerfulness.

SECOND DEGREE.
FELLOW-CRAFT.

"The Second, or Fellow-Craft's Degree is rendered interesting by those scientific instructions and philosophical lectures which characterize latter parts of the mysteries; though both of these Degrees were made to tend to the glory of that God who had given such wonderful faculties to them, and to the welfare of their fellow creatures."—ARCHDEACON MANT.

FELLOW CRAFT.

SECTION I.

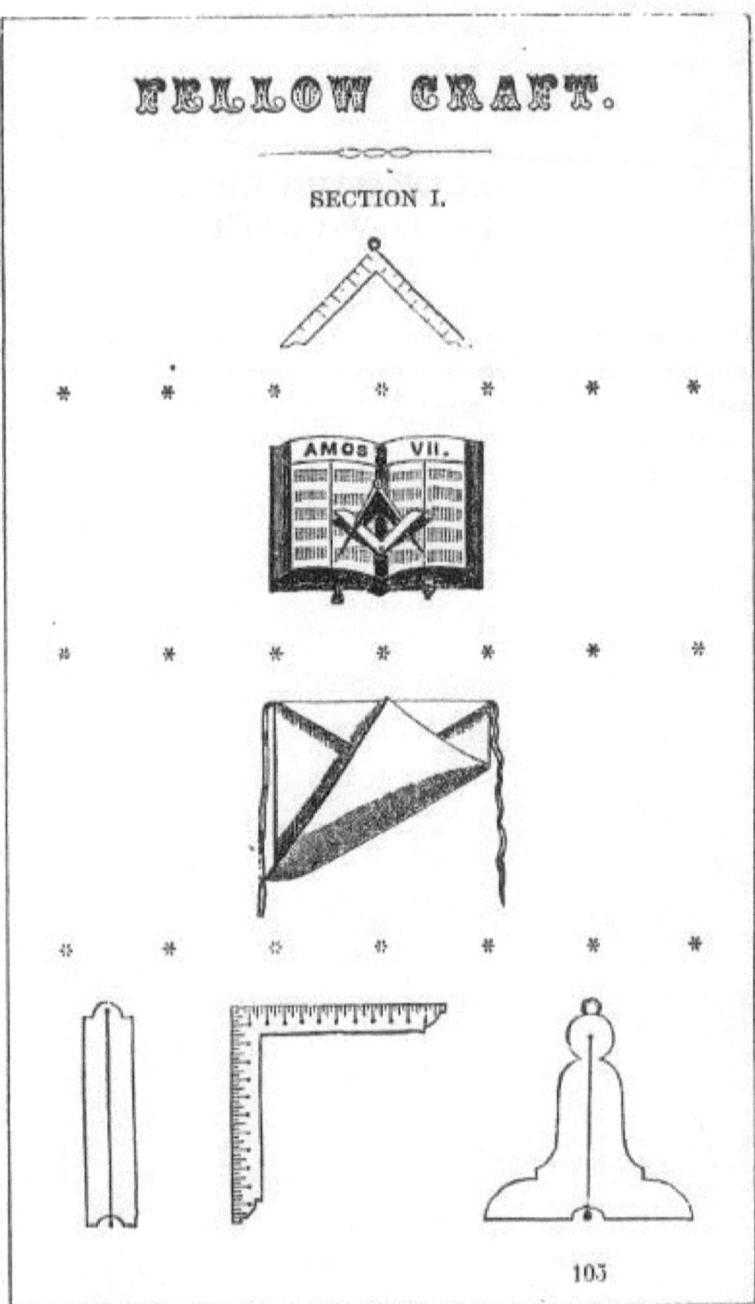

103

107

61

109

111

113

Symbolism of the Degree

IF the object of the first degree be to symbolize the struggles of a candidate groping in darkness for intellectual light, that of the second degree represents the same candidate laboring amid all the difficulties that encumber the young beginner in the attainment of learning and science. The Entered Apprentice is to emerge from darkness to light—the Fellow-Craft is to come out of ignorance into knowledge. This degree, therefore, by fitting emblems, is intended to typify these struggles of the ardent mind for the attainment of truth—moral and intellectual truth—and, above all, that Divine truth, the comprehension of which surpasseth human understanding, and to which, standing in the Middle Chamber, after his laborious ascent of the Winding Stairs, he can only approximate by the reception of an imperfect and yet glorious reward, in the revelation of that "hieroglyphic light which none but Craftsmen ever saw."

SECOND LECTURE.

MASONRY is a progressive science, and is divided into different classes, or degrees, for the more regular advancement in the knowledge of its mysteries. According to the progress we make, we limit or extend our inquiries: and, in proportion to our capacity, we attain to a less or greater degree of perfection.

Freemasonry includes within its circle almost every branch of polite learning. Under the vail of its mysteries is comprehended a regular system of science. Many of its illustrations, to the confined genius, may appear unimportant; but the man of more enlarged faculties will perceive them to be, in the highest degree, useful and interesting. To please the accomplished scholar and ingenious artist, Freemasonry is wisely planned; and, in the investigation of its latent doctrines, the philosopher and mathematician may experience equal delight and satisfaction.

To exhaust the varied subjects of which it treats, would transcend the powers of the brightest genius; still, however, nearer approaches to perfection may be made; and the man of wisdom will not check the progress of his abilities, though the task he attempts may at first seem insurmountable. Perseverance and application remove each difficulty as it occurs; every step he advances, new pleasures open to his view, and instruction of the noblest kind attends his researches. In the diligent pursuit of knowledge, the intellectual faculties are employed in promoting the glory of GOD and the good of man.

The first degree is well calculated to enforce the duties of morality, and imprint on the memory the noblest principles which can adorn the human mind. It is, therefore, the best introduction to the second degree, which not only extends the same plan, but comprehends a more diffusive system of knowledge. Here, practice and theory join in qualifying the industrious Mason to share the pleasures which an advancement in the art must necessarily afford. Listening with attention to the wise opinions of experienced Craftsmen, on important subjects, he gradually familiarizes his mind to useful instruction, and is soon enabled to investigate truths of the utmost concern in the general transactions of life.

From this system proceeds a rational amusement; while the mental, powers are fully employed, the judgment is properly exercised; a spirit of emulation prevails; and all are induced to contend who shall most excel in promoting the valuable rules of the institution.

SECTION I.

THE first section of the second degree accurately elucidates the mode of introduction into that particular class, and instructs the diligent Craftsman how to proceed in the proper arrangement of the ceremonies used on the occasion. It qualifies him to judge of their importance, and convinces him of the necessity of strictly adhering to every established usage of the Order. Here he is intrusted with particular tests, to enable him to prove his title to the privileges of this degree, while satisfactory reasons are given for their origin. Many duties, which cement in the firmest union well-informed brethren, are illustrated in this section; and an opportunity is given to make such advances in Masonry as will always distinguish the abilities of those who have arrived at preferment.

The Square is an important emblem in this degree. The Fellow-Craft is instructed, on his entrance, that this symbol should be the rule and guide of his conduct with all mankind, but especially with a brother Mason.

The following passage of Scripture is rehearsed in this degree:

"Thus he showed me: and behold the LORD stood upon a wall made by a plumb-line, with a plumb-line in his hand. And the LORD said unto me, Amos, what seest thou? and I said, A plumb-line.

Then said the LORD, Behold, I will set a plumb-line in the midst of my people Israel; I will not again pass by them any more."—Amos vii. 7, 8.

Or the following ODE may be sung:

AIR.—*What Fairy-like Music.*

Come, Craftsmen, assembled, our pleasure to share,
Who work by the Plumb, and remember the Square;
While trav'ling, in love, on the Level of time,
Sweet hope shall light on to a far better clime.

We'll seek, in our labors, the Spirit Divine,
Our Temple to bless, and our hearts to refine;
And thus to our altar a tribute we'll bring,
While, joined in true friendship, our anthem we sing.

See Order and Beauty rise gently to view,
Each Brother a column, so perfect and true!
When Order shall cease, and when temples decay,
May each fairer columns immortal survey.

*   *   *   *   *   *   *

*   *   *   *   *   *   *

67

The three ♪ ♪ ♪ allude to the three * * *, which are the Attentive Ear, the Instructive Tongue, and the Faithful Breast.

THE SYMBOLICAL JEWELS.

THE three VIRTUES—symbolically designated "the three Precious Jewels of a Fellow-Craft"—are, if considered from the true point of view, of no mean importance, and are well worthy to be styled "Jewels."

Silence, Secrecy, and Fidelity—rightly understood—are supreme virtues. In silence, the Divine Thought moves through the Eternities, creating and adorning; filling the material world with forms of beauty and glory, and communicating to the moral and spiritual the elements of ever-expanding perfection.

In silence and secrecy, Nature also performs her mysterious labors, and creates that inspiring grandeur and blooming loveliness which ever attracts the attention and charms the vision of man-The human mind, too, withdrawn into silence and secrecy, by attention and meditation, elaborates those grand thoughts—clothed with creative energies—by which man, through Philosophy, Science, and Art, becomes the sovereign of the material world, and demonstrates his close relationship to the unseen and immortal Powers.

Let, then, the Fellow-Craft wear these precious jewels proudly; for they are worthy of his love. Let the attentive ear gather up all those lessons of wisdom which Nature, History, and the World are perpetually proclaiming; and, retiring into the Divine Silence, let the adept study them with solemn earnestness. Let Fidelity—loyalty to Truth and Virtue—having its root in the deep recesses of the faithful heart, bind him eternally to the Good, the Beautiful, and the True, which will crown him with joy on earth, and make him illustrious when he shall be admitted to the "Inner Chamber" of the Temple on high.

Working Tools of a Fellow-Craft

The Working-Tools of a Fellow-Craft are the PLUMB, the SQUARE, and the LEVEL.

The Plumb is an instrument made use of by Operative Masons, to try perpendiculars; the Square, to square their work; and the Level, to prove horizontals: but we, as Free and Accepted Masons, are taught to make use of them for more noble and glorious purposes:—the Plumb admonishes us to walk uprightly in our several stations before GOD and man, squaring our actions by the Square of Virtue, and ever remembering that we are traveling upon the Level of Time, to " that undiscovered country, from whose bourne no traveler returns." * * *

The symbols of those instruments used by architects are unknown to common observers, who merely see in them the simple Square, the Level, and the Plumb; but Free and Accepted Masons recognize them as emblems of certain moral principles and religious duties, which, if followed out as they should be, would render all men valuable members of society. The Square, as an emblem of morality, teaches us to square our lives and actions by the unerring laws of GOD'S Word, and to regulate our conduct according to the doctrine laid down by our divine Creator; to preserve a lively faith in his Holy Gospel, which, in the most impressive manner, teaches us to live in brotherly love with all mankind. The Level is an emblem of equality; and reminds us that, in the sight of GOD, all men are equal; that He causes the sun to shine on the poor man's cottage, as well as on the king's palace; with Him there is no distinction, unless we so far forget our duty as to neglect and disobey the divine commands. The Plumb, signifying uprightness, reminds us to observe justice and equity in all our dealings on earth; so that, through the great mercy of GOD, we may hope to obtain an entrance into the Grand Lodge above, held in that temple not made with hands, eternal in the heavens.

SECTION II.

THE second section of this degree has reference to the origin of the Institution, and views MASONRY under two denominations—OPERATIVE and SPECULATIVE. These are separately considered, and the principles on which both are founded, particularly explained. Their affinity is pointed out by allegorical figures and typical representations. The period stipulated for rewarding merit is fixed, and the inimitable moral to which that circumstance alludes is explained; the creation of the world is described, and many other particulars recited, all of which have been carefully preserved among Masons, and transmitted from one age to another by oral tradition.

Circumstances of great importance to the Fraternity are here particularized, and many traditional tenets and customs confirmed by sacred and profane record. The celestial and terrestrial globes are considered with a minute accuracy; and here the accomplished Craftsman may display his talents to advantage in the elucidation of the ORDERS OF ARCHITECTURE, the SENSES of human nature, and the liberal ARTS AND SCIENCES, which are severally classed in a regular arrangement. In short, this section contains a store of valuable knowledge, founded on reason and sacred record, both entertaining and instructive.

OPERATIVE MASONRY.

We work in Speculative Masonry, but our ancient brethren wrought in both Operative and Speculative.[1] They worked at the building of King SOLOMON'S temple, and many other sacred and Masonic edifices.

By Operative Masonry, we allude to a proper application of the useful rules of architecture, whence a structure will derive figure, strength, and beauty, and whence will result a due proportion and a just correspondence in all its parts. It furnishes us with dwellings and convenient shelters from the vicissitudes and inclemencies of seasons; and while it displays the effects of human wisdom, as well in the choke as in the arrangement of the sundry materials of which an edifice is composed, it demonstrates that a fund of science and industry is implanted in man, for the best, most salutary, and beneficent purposes.

SPECULATIVE MASONRY.

By Speculative Masonry, we learn to subdue the passions, act upon the square, keep a tongue of good report, maintain secrecy, and practice charity. It is so far interwoven with religion, as to lay us under obligations to pay that rational homage to the Deity, which at once constitutes our duty and our happiness. It leads the contemplative to view, with reverence and admiration, the glorious works of creation, and inspires him with the most exalted ideas of the perfection of his Divine Creator.

MASONRY, OPERATIVE AND SPECULATIVE.

FOR a considerable time previous to the building of SOLOMON'S Temple, the Societies of Sidonian Architects and Builders had become celebrated throughout the ancient world. A company of these masons and architects, under the superintendence of HIRAM, the Widow's Son, was sent by the King of Tyre to SOLOMON, to assist in the erection of that stately edifice. At this period commences the history of Masonry among the Jews. Thus introduced into Judea, it flourished greatly under the protection of SOLOMON and some of his successors; but it was also, in the course of years, subject to bitter persecutions, gross misrepresentations, and fierce denunciations. The exclusive and stern Hebrews were slow to appreciate fully its catholic and benign spirit, and its great value as an industrial agent.

---

[1] Freemasonry is to be considered as divided into two parts—the *Operative* and *Speculative*; and these are again subdivided—that is, Craft Masonry—into three distinct branches: the Manual, the Instrumental, and the Scientific. The Manual consists of such parts of business as are performed by hand-labor alone, or by the help of some simple instruments, the uses whereof are not to be learned by any problems or rules of art, but by labor and practice only; and this is more particularly applicable to the brethren of the first degree, called *Entered Apprentices*.

Even at this period, we have reason to believe, the Sidonian Order was not entirely an operative society, but rather was a mixed body, consisting of both operative and speculative Masons. In the formation of its rituals, it had drawn largely on the Rites of the Orphic, Cabirian, and Isianic Mysteries. The speculative character finally triumphed over the operative, and the ancient Order of Hiram was transformed into the Order of the Essen, or Breast-plate, or the Essenian Brotherhood.

At an early period the Sidonian Masons had planted their societies in Rome, and in the reign of NUMA POMPUAUS were highly favored by that monarch. These societies were there known under the name of Colleges of Builders and Artificers. After Christianity had subdued the pagan world, these "Colleges of Builders," or societies of Operative Masons, were engaged in erecting cathedrals, churches, and other public edifices, and continued, in unbroken succession, down to A. D. 1717. In 1459 they held a general convention of the Crafts at Ratisbon, and decided to institute a Grand Lodge at Strasburg, and that the architect of that cathedral, for the time being, should be, ex officio, Grand Master.

These Lodges also preserved the ancient rituals, which gave them a speculative or philosophical character; and thus we find that the history of the Order of Operative Masons in Europe reproduces that of Sidonian Masonry in ancient Judea. As that Order culminated in the Essenian Brotherhood, so the Order of Operative was in 1717 transformed into that of Speculative Masonry.

That Speculative Masonry is the offspring of the ancient corporations of Builders and Masons, there cannot be a doubt. It possesses all the venerable forms of those old societies, their rituals, and their language of signs and symbols. The instruments of the builder's art—the Gavel, Twenty-four-inch Gauge, Trowel, Level, Plumb, Square, Compasses, Spade, Setting-Maul, etc.—it retains, and applies them to moral uses. They have become the most significant and instructive of emblems. All Freemasons are familiar with their symbolical interpretations, and appreciate their beauty and the force of their teaching. The Free or Speculative Mason is also a builder, but not of material edifices. He is, or should be, the constructer of a Temple, more glorious than that of SOLOMON—a Temple of Virtue, of Honor, of Charity, Purity, and Knowledge; and these implements of the Operative Mason's art, in their emblematic use, indicate the labors he is to execute, the dangers he is to encounter, and the preparations he is to make in the great work of uprearing that spiritual fabric wherein his soul may find peace for evermore.

* * * * * * *

This section also refers to the origin of the Jewish Sabbath, as well as to the manner in which it was kept by our ancient brethren.

In six days GOD created the heaven and the earth, and rested upon the seventh day; the seventh, therefore, our ancient brethren consecrated as a day of rest from their labors, thereby enjoying frequent opportunities to contemplate the glorious works of creation, and to adore their great Creator.

THE six days of creation are technically known among Freemasons as the "Grand Architect's Six Periods." These important periods in the world's history may be more particularly illustrated as follows:

Before the Almighty was pleased to command this vast world into existence, the elements and materials of creation lay blended together without distinction or form. Darkness was on the face of the great deep, and the spirit of GOD moved on the surface of the waters. The Almighty, as an example to man, that all things of moment should be done with due deliberation, was pleased to be *six days* in commanding it from chaos to perfection. The *first* instance of his supreme power was made manifest by commanding light; and being pleased with this new operation, he distinguished it by name, calling the light DAY, and the darkness he called NIGHT. And, in order to keep this same framed matter within just limits.

The *second day* was employed in laying the foundations for the heavens, which be called firmament, designed to keep the waters that were within the clouds, and those beneath them, asunder. On the *third day*, he commanded those waters within due limits, and dry land appeared, which he called EARTH; and the mighty congregated waters he called SEA. The earth being yet irregular and barren, GOD spoke the word, and it was immediately covered with a beautiful carpet of grass, designed as pasture for the brute creation. Trees, shrubs, and flowers of all sorts, succeeded in full growth, maturity, and perfection. On the *fourth day*, the two grand luminaries, the SUN and moots, were created; the sum to rule the day, and the MOON to govern the night. And the sacred historian informs us that they were ordained for signs, seasons, days, and years, The Almighty was also pleased to bespangle the ethereal concave of heaven with a multitude of stars, that man, whom he intended to make, might contemplate thereon, and justly admire his majesty and glory. On the *fifth day*, he caused the waters to bring forth a variety of fish for our use; and, in order to imprint on the mind of man a reverential awe of his divine omnipotence, he created the other inhabitants of the mighty deep, which multiplied exceedingly after their kind. On the same day, the Almighty caused the birds to fly in the air, that man might delight his eyes and ears—with some for their beautiful plumage, and others for their melodious notes.

On the *sixth day*, he created the beasts of the field and the reptiles which crawl on the earth. And here we may plainly perceive the wisdom, power, and goodness of the Grand Geometrician of the Universe, made manifest throughout the whole of his proceedings. He produced what effects he pleased without the aid of their natural causes—such as giving light to the world before he created the sun and moon, and making the earth fruitful without the influence of the heavenly bodies. He did not create the beasts of the field until he had provided sufficient herbage for their support; neither did he create man until be had furnished him with a dwelling, and every thing requisite for life and pleasure. Then, to dignify the work of his hands still more, ho made man, who came into the world with greater pomp than any creature which preceded him. They came but with a single command. GOD spake the word, and it was done. But at the formation of man, we are told, there was a consultation, in which GOD said, Let us make man. He was immediately formed out of the dust of the earth. The breath of life was blown into his nostrils, and man became a living soul. In this one creature, there is a combination of every thing throughout the whole creation—such as the quality and substance of an animate being, the life of plants, the senses of beasts; but, above all, the understanding of angels; formed after the immediate image of GOD, thereby intimating to him that integrity and uprightness should ever influence him to adore his Creator, who has so liberally bestowed on him the faculty of speech, and further endued him with that noble instinct called REASON. The Almighty, as his last and best gift to man, created WOMAN. Under his forming hand, the creature grew— man-like, but of different sex—so lovely fair, that what seemed fair in all the world, seemed now mean: all in her summed up—in her contained. On she came, led by her Heavenly Maker, though unseen, yet guided by his voice, adorned with all that heaven could bestow to make her amiable.

"Grace was in all her steps, heaven in her eye,
In every gesture dignity and love."

The Almighty, having finished the sixth day's work, rested on the *seventh*. He blessed, hallowed, and sanctified it. He thereby taught man to work industriously six days, but strictly commanded him to rest on the seventh, the better to contemplate on the beautiful works of creation—to adore him as their Creator—to go into his sanctuaries, and offer up praises for life and every blessing he so amply enjoys at his bountiful hands.

The Pillars of the Porch.

For he cast two pillars of brass, of eighteen cubits high apiece; and a line of twelve cubits (lid compass either of them about.—I. KINGS Vii. 15.

Also he made before the house two pillars of thirty and five cubits high, and the chapter that was on the top of each of them was five cubits.—II. CHRON. iii. 15.

And he made two chapiters of molten brass, to set upon the tops of the pillars; the height of the one chapter was five cubits, and the height of the other chapter was five cubits.—I. KINGS vii. 16.

73

The height of the one pillar was eighteen cubits, and the chapiter upon it was brass: and the height of the chapiter three cubits; and the wreathen work, and pomegranates upon the chapiter round about all of brass: and like unto these had the second pillar with wreathen work.—II. Kiwis xxv. 17.[1]

THE TWO BRAZEN PILLARS

 WHICH ornamented the porch of King SOLOMON'S Temple, were fluted, with sixteen flutes each, a hand's breadth (about four inches) in depth. Their shafts were eighteen cubits high (I. KINGS vii. 15; JEREMIAH lii. 21), about thirty feet seven inches; the circumference of the shaft at the base was fourteen cubits, twenty-three feet eleven inches (LXX. version I. KINGS vii. 15), giving a diameter of about seven feet seven inches. At the top, the circumference was twelve cubits, giving a diameter of six feet eight inches (JEREMIAH lii. 21; I. KINGS vii. 15). They were surmounted by chapiters; the chapiters were composed of seven wreaths of twisted brass, set perpendicularly on an abacus of seven sides, crowning the shaft of each pillar. These wreaths were three cubits high (II. KINGS xxv. 17); upon four of these wreaths, in a *trapezoidal* form was suspended a latticed Net-work of brass and copper, colored yellow and red; around the curved bottom of which was a brass fringe, ornamented with two rows of brazen Pomegranates, fifty in a row (I. KINGS vii. 18; II. CHRON. iv. 12; JEREMIAH lii. 23). The pomegranates being arranged ninety-six on a side (JEREMIAH lii. 23), two of the pomegranates hung on each point of suspension; and eight to the cubit for twelve cubits (LXX. version JEREMIAH lii. 22), which was the entire length of the *cycloidal arc* of the net-work from one point of suspension to the other. Within the net-work was set a hollow Lily of silver, with six pointed leaves; the height of the points of the lily above the abacus was four cubits (I. KINGS vii. 19). This lily circumscribed a SPHERE of *brass* (II. CHRON. iv. 12), whose diameter was exactly equal to the diameter of the top of the column (LXX. version L KINGS vii. 20), whose superior convex surface reached an elevation of five cubits above the abacus, making the whole height of the chapiter

---

[1] The discrepancy as to the height of the pillars, as given in the book of Kings and in Chronicles, is to be reconciled by supposing that in the book of Kings the pillars are spoken of separately, and that in Chronicles their aggregate height is calculated: and the reason that, in this latter book, their united height is placed at thirty-five cubits, instead of thirty-six, which would be the double of eighteen, is because they are there measured as they appear with the chapiters upon them. Now, half a cubit of each pillar was concealed in what Dr. LIGHTFOOT calls "the hole of the chapiter;"—that is, half a cubit's depth of the lower edge of the chapiter covered the top of the pillar, making each pillar apparently only seventeen and a half cubits high, or the two, thirty-five cubits, as laid down in the book of Chronicles.— In a similar way we reconcile the difference as to the height of the chapiters. In I. Kings and II. Chronicles the chapiters are said to be five cubits high, while in II. Kings their height is described as being only three cubits. But it will be noticed that it immediately follows in the same place, that "there was a wreathen work and pomegranates upon the chapiter round about." Now, this expression is conclusive that the height of the chapiters was estimated exclusive and independent of the wreathen work round about them, which was two cubits more, and this, added to the three cubits of the chapiter proper, will make the five cubits spoken of In all other parts of Scripture.—MACKEY'S *Manual of the Lodge*.

five cubits (I. KINGS vii. 15; IL CHRON. iii. 15; JEREMIAH lii. 21).—*Symbols of Freemasonry, esoterically considered, by W. S. ROCKWELL, P. G. M. of Georgia.*

THE SYMBOLS OF
Peace, Unity and Plenty

Are introduced, and their moral application explained.

OF THE GLOBES.

The Globes are two artificial spherical bodies, on the convex surface of which are represented the countries, seas, and various parts of the earth, the face of the heavens, the planetary revolutions, and other important particulars.

THE USE OF THE GLOBES.

Their principal use, besides serving as maps to distinguish the outward parts of the earth, and the situation of the fixed stars, is to illustrate and explain the phenomena arising from the annual revolution and the diurnal rotation of the earth around its own axis. They are invaluable instruments for improving the mind, and giving it the most distinct idea of any problem or proposition, as well as enabling it to solve the same. Contemplating these bodies, we are inspired with a due reverence for the Deity and his works, and are induced to encourage the studies of Astronomy, Geography, Navigation, and the Arts dependent on them, by which society has been so much benefited.

The Winding Stairs.

The door for the middle chamber was in the right side of the house; and they went up with winding stairs into the middle chamber.—I. KINGS vi. 8.[1]

THE SYMBOLICAL STAIRWAY, which leads front the ground-floor to the Middle Chamber of our mystic house, consists of fifteen steps and three divisions. The divisions, we perceive, differ in the number of their steps, each having an odd number—"three, five, and seven." While there is no positive evidence that these divisions have any particular reference to Ancient Craft Masonry, yet the lessons taught us, as we ascend, should impress upon the mind of every Freemason the importance of discipline, as well as a knowledge of natural, mathematical, and metaphysical science It also opens to him an extensive range of moral and speculative inquiry, which may prove a source of peculiar gratification.

Reference is here made to the Masonic organization into three degrees—the Entered Apprentice, the Fellow-Craft, and the Master Mason; and to its system of government by three officers—the Worshipful Master, the Senior Warden, and the Junior Warden.

---

[1] Vide Lecture on the Legend of the Winding Stairs, pp. 159-170.

The ORDERS OF ARCHITECTURE are next considered and explained.

OF ORDER IN ARCHITECTURE.

By order in architecture is meant a system of all the members, proportions, and ornaments of columns and pilasters; or, it is a regular arrangement of the projecting parts of a building, which, united with those of a column, form a beautiful, perfect, and complete whole.

OF ITS ANTIQUITY.

From the first formation of society, order in architecture may be traced. When the rigor of seasons obliged men to contrive shelter from the inclemency of the weather, we learn that they first planted trees on end, and then laid others across, to support a covering. The bands which connected those trees at top and bottom are said to have given rise to the idea of the base and capital of pillars; and from this simple hint originally proceeded the more improved art of architecture.

The first habitations of men were such as Nature afforded, with but little labor on the part of the occupant, and sufficient only to satisfy his simple wants. Each tribe or people constructed, from the materials that presented themselves, such habitations as were best suited to this purpose, and at the same time most convenient.

We thus find, in countries remote from other nations, und where foreign influences did not exist, an architecture at once singular, and as indigenous as the vegetation itself. The *hypogea* of the borders of the Indus, the Nile, and the Ganges—the temporary tents of the nomadic tribes of eastern Asia—the oaks of the Grecian forests, fashioned by the ingenuity of man into the humble cabin (the prototype of the principal Grecian order)—are indubitably the primitive styles of the Egyptian, the Grecian, and the Oriental structures. Anterior to the discovery of printing, the monument was the tablet upon which the various races chronicled for posterity the annals of their history. In the simple, unhewn altar, we recognize the genius of religion: we trace in it the germ of the development of human intelligence; it bespeaks faith, ingenuity, ambition. The ancient Babel, and the altars of Scripture—the monuments of Gilgal and Gilead of the Hebrews—the Celtic Dolmens, the Cromlechs, the Peulvens or Menheirs, the Lichavens, (the Trelithous of the Greeks,) the Nurhags, the Talayots, and the Tumuli, (the Latin Mercuriales,)—are all symbols of pristine faith. With the pagan devotee, the art was made to conform to the moral attributes of the character of the deity in whose honor the monument was erected. With the Greeks, various styles of structure were thus instigated, from the early polygonal formations of the Phoenicians, at Astrea and Tyranthus, to the perfections of design, the imposing Doric, the graceful Ionic, and the magnificent Corinthian orders. Each nation, at every age, possessed its symbolic monuments, revealing its conception of the attributes of the Infinite, with the exception of the Persians, who, as we learn from the Zend Avesta, worshiped in the open air, and who, according to HEEODOTUS, possessed no temples, but revered the whole circuit of the heavens; and the Assyrians, whose Magi interpreted the silent stars, and worshiped the sun. Among such monuments, we must reckon, as the chief, the Temple of SOLOMON, that sublime conception of the spirit of immateriality, true type, in its massive splendor, of a higher and purer belief; at Elora, the temple of Indra, sacred to Swargas, the god of ether, which, according to the Puranas, was designed by Wiswakama, the *stapathi*, or architect of the heavens. In China, the ancient Tings, Taas, and Mikosi, were temples of the gods, and the mias, in Japan and Siam, were sacred structures. The Pyramids were symbolic emblems of the metempsychosian creed of Egypt. The Djebel Pharouni, the pyramids of Rhamses, the temples of Isis end Osiris, and the Memnon, bespeak (in their colossal size) a vast and boundless faith. Athens possessed her Parthenon, over whose magnificence presided Minerva Archegetea, and Rome her Pantheon, "shrine of all saints and altar of all gods." Ancient Cordova had her mosque, on which the Moors spent the riches of their oriental taste. Modern Rome possesses her basilica of St. Peters, on whose sublime structure, amid the visible decadence of classic art, MICHAEL ANGELO lavished his genius.—Of the early achievements and of the progressive steps of the science of architecture, there remain but fragments, though sufficient, with the assistance of history, to teach us their antiquity. The epochs of advancement can be traced progressively from the early elements of structure to the more perfected styles; and throughout the whole globe remains of edifices will be found which proclaim an early possession of certain degrees of architectural knowledge.—The most ancient nation known to us who made any considerable progress in the arts of design is the Babylonian. Their most celebrated monuments were the Temple of Belus, the Kasr, and the hanging gardens which Nebuchadnezzar built for his Lydian bride, the wonderful canal of the Naher Malca, and the Lake of Palacópos. An idea of the colossal size of the structures they once composed can be formed from the dimensions of their ruins. The material employed in cementing the burned or sun-dried bricks—upon which hieroglyphics are to be traced—was the mortar produced by Nature from the fountains of naphtha and bitumen at the river Is, near Babylon. No entire architectural monument has come down to us from the Assyrians, whose capital was embellished with the superb Kalla, Ninoah, and the Khorzabad; nor from the Phoenicians, whose cities—Tyre, Sidon, Arados, and Sarepta—were adorned with equal magnificence; nor from the Israelites, whose temples were wonderful structures; nor from the Syrians, the Philistines, and many other nations. Our want of thorough knowledge concerning the architecture of these Oriental nations is attributable partly to the innumerable devastations which have taken place on this great battle-field of the world; but to the perishability of the materials that were employed—such as gypsum, alabaster, wood, terra cotta, and brick, with which their ruins abound—we must likewise attribute, in part, this ignorance.

The massive temples of the Hindoos at Elora, Salsitte, and the Island of Elephanta, seem in their awful grandeur like the habitations of giants, on whose land some divine malediction has fallen. The Hindoos, in these colossal structures with their endless sculptured panels, their huge figures, and their astounding and intricate excavations, evince a perseverance and industry equaled only by the Egyptians. Their pagodas, towering in the air, are likewise wonderful architectural achievements, quite as admirable as their hypogea. The Indian structures are remarkable for their severe and grotesque appearance. Their temples—whether of BRAHMA, the creator of all; VISHNU, the preserver of all; or of SERB or SHEVA, the destroyer of all—exhibit a striking embodiment of the attributes of the deities in whose honor they were erected.

A remarkable resemblance to the Hindoo constructions has been found in the religious monuments or *teocallis* of Mexico and Yucatan. But the architectural types of these antique structures sink into insignificance when compared with those of Egypt. The obelisks, pyramids, temples, palaces, tombs, and other structures with which that country abounds, are on a colossal scale, and such as can have been executed only by a people far advanced in architectural art, and profoundly versed in the science of mechanics. These works, like the Hindoo structures, were remarkable for their gigantic proportions and massiveness. Intricate and highly painted relievo sculptures or hieroglyphics covered the entire extent of their walls. The prevailing monotony of the hieroglyphic designs which form the chief feature of Egyptian architectural decoration, was superinduced by the circumscribed and limiting laws of their religion. In Egyptian architecture we trace the elements of the early Indian school, blended with more harmonious combinations, as likewise the introduction of architectural orders. Beside skilled organization of parts, and a just appreciation of pleasing effect, their works in their colossal features evince a thorough knowledge of the geometrical branch of the science of construction. The architectural genius of Egypt lavished its power on mausoleums, and on gorgeous temples to the deities, which, in their sublimity, inspire awe. They were constructed of granite, breccia, sandstone, and brick, which different materials are adjusted with much precision. The huge blocks employed in their various monuments exhibit a perfect acquaintance with the laws of mechanics. We cannot but wonder at their monolithic obelisks, especially when we reflect upon the immense distances they had to be transported. The pyramidal shape pervades most of their works, the walls of their temples inclining inward. The jambs to their entrance-gates also were generally inclined. The Egyptians never used columns peripterally, even under the dominion of the Greeks and Romans.

When the column was used externally, the space intervening was walled up to a certain height. To these circumstances, together with the fact that their monuments were terraced, eau be ascribed their massive and solid appearance. With them, columns were employed to form porticos in their interior courts, and also to support the ceilings. The shafts, of different forms, being conical, or cylindrical, or bulging out at the base, sometimes presented a smooth surface; they were rarely fluted, being generally covered with hieroglyphics. Occasionally, they were monoliths, but were generally constructed in layers, and covered with hieroglyphics; a circular plinth formed the base. The capitals resemble the lotus, at times, spreading out at the top; again, the flower appears bound together, assuming the bulbous shape; above is a square tablet forming the abacus. Others, of a later date, present projecting convex lobes; while other capitals are composed of a rectangular block, with a head carved on either side, surmounted by a die, also carved. Caryatic figures were also employed by the Egyptians, and were generally placed against walls or pillars, thus appearing to support the entablature, composed of a simple architrave and a coved cornice, with a large torus intervening, which descends the angles of the walls. The Pelasgians appear to have been the first people settled in Greece, numerous remains of whose structures are still extant. Subsequently, from the knowledge possessed by the indigenous tribes, together with that acquired from the Egyptians and the Asiatic nations, the Greeks extracted and developed a style peculiarly their own; and architectural art passed from the gigantic to the elegant and classic forms. During the reign of PERICLES it flourished with meridian splendor, and some of the most superb edifices the world has ever seen were erected during this period. The Grecian monument belonged to the nation, and upon the public works of the country the government lavished fabulous sums. HEEREN informs us that the Greeks placed the necessary appropriation of funds for the public works at the head of the government expenditures. The thoughts of the whole Grecian nation, it would seem, were turned toward the adornment of the country. They forbade by law any architectural display on private residences, and in fact, until after Greece became subject to Macedonia, architects were permitted to work only for the governments.

The beauty and grace which pervade all their works, whether monumental, mechanical, or industrial, lead us to suppose that, although imperfect as regards comfort, they must yet have exhibited a certain degree of elegance. A just idea of the moldings and ornaments, unequaled for their purity and grace, can be obtained only from personal observation. It is also impossible, from any verbal description, to be able fully to appreciate the beauty and harmony of their different styles. It may not be amiss, however, here to lay down some general principles:—These styles may be classed in systems or orders—the Doric, Ionic, and Corinthian. They also employed, though rarely, caryatides. Innumerable conjectures exist concerning the origin of these different orders. In all probability we are indebted to the Dorians for the invention of the Doric; although CHAMPOLLION sees in an Egyptian order, which he styles the proto-Doric, the type of the Grecian order of that name. The oldest example extant is at Corinth.—To the Ionians, likewise, is attributed the honor of having first employed the Ionic order, no example of which is to be found in Greece, prior to the Macedonian conquest. As for the origin of the Corinthian, without wishing to discredit the interesting narrative of VITRUVIUS, wherein he accords to CALLIMACHUS the invention of the Corinthian capital, it might be well to state, that foliated capitals, of much greater antiquity than any discovered in Greece, are to be found in Egypt and in Asia Minor. The most perfect Grecian example of this order is employed in the choragic monument of LYSICRATES; and there can be little doubt that the Greeks also derived the idea of their caryatic order from the Egyptians, who frequently employed human figures instead of columns in their structures.—The Doric holds the foremost rank among the Grecian orders, not only on account of its being the most ancient, the most generally employed, and, consequently, the most perfected, but more especially on account of its containing, as it were, the principle of all their architecture, as well as an exact imitation of all the parts employed in their primitive constructions, which were undoubtedly of wood. This style, typical of majesty and imposing grandeur, was almost universally employed by the Greeks in the construction of their temples; and certainly monumental art does not furnish us with the equal of a Greek peripteral temple.

To the Etruscans the invention of the arch, constructed on its true principles, has been generally attributed, as likewise the composition of an order styled Tuscan, a species of simple Doric, no entire example of which, however, has been handed down to us by the ancients.

The history of Roman architecture, under its kings and at the beginning of the republic, is somewhat obscure, as but few of the monuments of that period remain. The Roman kings fortified the city, and erected various palaces, temples, and tombs. It became adorned with colossal works of art, whose stupendous features— forming such a contrast with the comparative insignificance of its power and condition—would seem to indicate that the future of imperial Rome had been foreshadowed to its people. The early Romans employed Etruscans in their works. When Greece at length fell under the yoke of the Roman empire, Rome became enriched with the spoils of Athens. The Greek artists sought protection and patronage among their conquerors, and adorned the imperial capital with structures which called forth unbounded praise. The Grecian style was blended with the Etruscan during the more early period of the Roman school. But as the arch, which was the characteristic feature of Roman architecture, revealed its treasures, the Grecian elements were employed but as a system of ornamentation. During the middle ages, the spirit of classic art seems to have waned with the glory of the Roman empire. The science of building became perverted, and the fame which the Romans had attained in architecture became a memory only. At this period it is supposed that the construction of houses in stories became general. The habitations of the mass of the people were poor, and irregularly planted about the town-hall in cities, or clustered about those massive structures (feudal castles) erected as fortresses, into which the arrogant possessor might retire, and whence he might sally at pleasure to harass the country. Many of the castle fortresses were on a plan of great magnitude, consisting of two or more large towers and divers inner buildings, including chapels During the gloom and the disastrous influences of the bloody wars of the middle ages, we find the venerable institution of Freemasonry nourishing, under the ashes of its ancient mysteries, the social fire of architectural art. While the whole of Europe was convulsed with the international and social strife and invasions of barbarians, which resulted in its complete reorganization, the study of the arts, sciences, and literature, took refuge in the monasteries. In Italy, during the tenth century, we find the corporation of Magistri Comacini exercising great influence, and giving to Grecian artists shelter from the political troubles of the East, and from the persecutions of the Iconoclasts. These artists promulgated among the Lombards the Byzantine elements of structure. whose influence, es we have seen, was more or less diffused throughout the architectural schools of Europe. Under ERWIN VON STEINBACH, of Germany, during the thirteenth century, the Mitten, or Lodges, were organized, one object of which was the study of architecture, over which they exercised a powerful influence. In Strasbourg existed the Lodge of the Haupt-Hütte. Under GODOYNE, or JOSSE DOTTZINGER, of Worms, (who in 1444 succeeded the architect J. HULT,) the various sects of the German Freemasons were incorporated into one body, and, in virtue of an act passed at Ratisbon, the same year, the architect of the cathedral of Strasbourg was elected the sole Grand Master of the Fraternity. These *magistri lapidum* were likewise sole directors or supervisors of all the religious structures. Protected by the Church, sole depository of the arcana of the early Masters, architecture passed from the old Gothic through various phases of the pointed or ogean styles. The influence, the enterprise, and daring achievements of its promoters seemed to strike the contemporary ages as well as posterity with a religious awe; and the intellectual power and energy of the people appear to have been concentrated and expended upon architecture. The revival of the spirit of emulation, engendered by the impetus thus given to art, would seem to have possessed a regenerating power, and to have resuscitated Europe from the condition of moral syncope into which it had fallen. The spirit of an age is embodied in its architecture.

The five orders are thus classed:—the TUSCAN, DORIC, IONIC, CORINTHIAN, and COMPOSITE.

THE TUSCAN

Is the most simple and solid of the five orders. It was invented in Tuscany, whence it derives its name. Its column is seven diameters high; and its capital, base, and entablature have but few moldings. The simplicity of the construction of this column renders it eligible where ornament would be superfluous.

THE DORIC,

Which is plain and natural, is the most ancient, and was invented by the Greeks. Its column is eight diameters high, and has seldom any ornaments on base or capital, except moldings—though the frieze is distinguished by triglyphs and metopes, and triglyphs compose the ornaments of the frieze. The solid composition of this order gives it a preference, in structures where strength and a noble simplicity are chiefly required. The Doric is the best proportioned of all the orders. The several parts of which it is composed are founded on the natural position of solid bodies. In its first invention, it was more simple than in its present state. In after-times, when it began to be adorned, it gained the name of Doric: for when it was constructed in its primitive and simple form, the name of Tuscan was conferred on it. Hence the Tuscan precedes the Doric in rank, on account of its resemblance to that pillar in its original state.

THE IONIC

Bears a kind of mean proportion between the more solid and delicate orders. Its column is nine diameters high; its capital is adorned with volutes, and its cornice has dentils. There is both delicacy and ingenuity displayed in this pillar, the invention of which is attributed to the Ionians, as the famous "*Temple of Diana,*" at Ephesus, was of this order. It is said to have been formed after the model of an agreeable young woman, of an elegant shape, dressed in her hair; as a contrast to the Doric order, which was formed after that of a strong, robust man.

THE CORINTHIAN,

The richest of the five orders, is deemed *a masterpiece of art*. Its column is ten diameters high, and its capital is adorned with two rows of leaves, and eight volutes, which sustain the abacus. The frieze is ornamented with curious devices; the cornice with dentils and modillions. This order is used in stately and superb structures. It was invented at Corinth by CALLIMACHUS, who is said to have taken the hint of the capital of this pillar from the following remarkable circumstance:—Accidentally passing by the tomb of a young lady, be perceived a basket of toys, covered with a tile, placed over an acanthus-root, having been left there by her nurse.

As the branches grew up, they encompassed the basket until, arriving at the tile, they met with an obstruction, and bent downwards. CALLIMACHUS, struck with the object, set about imitating the figure; the vase of the capital he made to represent the basket; the abacus, the tile; and the volutes, the bending leaves.

THE COMPOSITE

Is compounded of the other orders, and was contrived by the Romans. Its capital has the two rows of leaves of the Corinthian, and the volutes of the Ionic. Its column has quarter-rounds, as the Tuscan and Doric orders; is ten diameters high, and its cornice has dentils, or simple modillions. This pillar is generally found in buildings where strength, elegance and beauty are displayed.

THE INVENTION OF ORDER IN ARCHITECTURE.

The ancient and original orders of architecture, revered by Masons, are no more than three: the *Doric*, *Ionic*, and *Corinthian*, which were invented by the Greeks. To these, the Romans have added two—the Tuscan, which they made plainer than the Doric, and the Composite, which was more ornamental, if not more beautiful, than the Corinthian. The first three orders alone, however, show invention and particular character, and essentially differ from each other; the two others have nothing but what is borrowed, and differ only accidentally: the Tuscan is the Doric in its earliest state; and the Composite is the Corinthian enriched with the Ionic. To the Greeks, therefore, and not to the Romans, we are indebted for what is great, judicious, and distinct in architecture.

Of these five orders, the IONIC, DORIC, and CORINTHIAN, as the most ancient, are most esteemed by Masons.

*   *   *   *   *   *   *

The five Senses of Human Nature.

An analysis of the human faculties is next given in this section, in which the FIVE EXTERNAL SENSES particularly claim attention.

The senses we are to consider as the gifts of Nature, and though not the acquisition of our reasoning faculty, yet, in the use of them, are still subject to reason. REASON, properly employed, confirms the regulations of Nature, which are always true and wholesome: she distinguishes the good from the bad; rejects the last with modesty—adheres to the first with reverence. The objects of human knowledge are innumerable; the channels by which this knowledge is conveyed are few. Among these, the perception of external things by the senses, and the information we receive from human testimony, are not the least considerable: the analogy between them is obvious. In the testimony of Nature, given by the senses, as well as in human testimony, given by information, things are signified by signs. In one as well as the other, the mind, either by original principles or by custom, passes from the sign to the conception and belief of the thing signified. The signs in the natural language, as well as the signs in our original perceptions, have the same signification in all climates and nations, and the skill of interpreting them is not acquired, but innate.

Having made these observations, we shall proceed to give a brief description of the five senses:

HEARING

Is that sense by which we distinguish sounds, and are capable of enjoying all the agreeable charms of music. By it we are enabled to enjoy the pleasures of society, and reciprocally to communicate to each other our thoughts and intentions—our purposes and desires; and thus our reason is rendered capable of exerting its utmost power and energy. The wise and beneficent Author of Nature intended, by the formation of this sense, that we should be social creatures, and receive the greatest and most important part of our knowledge from social intercourse with each other. For these purposes we are endowed with hearing, that, by a proper exertion of our rational powers, our happiness may be complete.

SEEING

Is that sense by which we distinguish objects, and in an instant of time, without change of place or situation, view armies in battle array, figures of the most stately structures, and all the agreeable variety displayed in the landscape of Nature. By this sense, we find our way on the pathless ocean, traverse the globe of earth, determine its figure and dimensions, and delineate any region or quarter of it. By it we measure the planetary orbs, and make new discoveries in the sphere of the fixed stars. Nay, more, by it we perceive the tempers and dispositions, the passions and affections of our fellow-creatures, when they wish most to conceal them; so that, though the tongue may be taught to lie and dissemble, the countenance will display the hypocrisy to the discerning eye. In fine, the rays of LIGHT which administer to this sense, are the most astonishing parts of the animated creation, and render the eye a peculiar object of admiration.

Of all the faculties, SIGHT is the noblest. The structure of the eye, and its appurtenances, evince the admirable contrivance of Nature for performing all its various external and internal motions; while the variety displayed in the eyes of different animals, suited to their several ways of life, clearly demonstrate this organ to be .the master-piece of Nature's works.

FEELING

Is that sense by which we distinguish the different qualities of bodies:—such as *heat* and *cold*, *hardness* and *softness*, *roughness* and *smoothness*, *figure*, *solidity*, *motion*, and *extension*.

These three senses, *Hearing*, *Seeing* and *Feeling*, are deemed peculiarly essential among Masons.

*   *   *   *   *   *   *

SMELLING

Is that sense by which we distinguish odors, the various kinds of which convey different impressions to the mind. Animal and vegetable bodies, and indeed most other bodies, while exposed to the air, continually send forth effluvia of vast subtility, as well in a state of life and growth, as in the state of fermentation and putrefaction. These effluvia, being drawn into the nostrils along with the air, are the means by which all bodies are distinguished. Hence it is evident, that there is a manifest appearance of design in the great Creator's having planted the organ of smell in the inside of that canal through which the air continually passes in respiration.

TASTING

Enables us to make a proper distinction in the choice of our food. The organ of this sense guards the entrance of the alimentary canal, as that of smelling guards the entrance of the canal for respiration. From the situation of both these organs, it is plain that they were intended by Nature to distinguish wholesome food from that which is nauseous. Every thing that enters into the stomach must undergo the scrutiny of tasting; and by it we are capable of discerning the changes which the same body undergoes in the different compositions of art, cookery, chemistry, pharmacy, etc.

Smelling and tasting are inseparably connected; and it is by the unnatural kind of life men commonly lead in society, that these senses are rendered less fit to perform their natural offices.

The proper use of these five senses enables us to form just and accurate notions of the operations of Nature; and when we reflect on the objects with which our senses are gratified, we become conscious of them, and are enabled to attend to them till they become familiar objects of thought.

On the mind all our knowledge must depend. What, therefore, can be a more proper subject for the investigation of Masons?

To sum up the whole of this transcendent measure of GOD'S bounty to man, we shall add, that Memory, Imagination, Taste, Reasoning, Moral Perception, and all the active powers of the soul, present a vast and boundless field for philosophical disquisition, which far exceeds human inquiry, and are peculiar mysteries, known only to Nature and to Nature's GOD, to whom all are indebted for creation, preservation, and every blessing we enjoy.

The Seven Liberal Arts And Sciences,

Which are Grammar, Rhetoric, Logic, Arithmetic, Geometry, Music, and Astronomy, are here illustrated. Grammar is the science which teaches us to express our ideas in appropriate words, which we may afterward beautify and adorn by means of Rhetoric; while Logic instructs us how to think and reason with propriety, and to make language subordinate to thought. Arithmetic, which is the science of computing by numbers, is absolutely essential, not only to a thorough knowledge of all mathematical science, but also to a proper pursuit of our daily avocations. Geometry, or the application of Arithmetic to sensible quantities, is of all sciences the most important, since by it we are enabled to measure and survey the globe that we inhabit. Its principles extend to other spheres; and, occupied in the contemplation and measurement of the sun, moon, and heavenly bodies, constitute the science of Astronomy; and, lastly, when our minds are filled, and our thoughts enlarged, by the contemplation of all the wonders which these sciences open to our view, Music comes forward, to soften our hearts and cultivate our affections by its soothing influences.

GRAMMAR

Is the key by which alone the door can be opened to the understanding of speech. It is Grammar which reveals the admirable art of language, and unfolds its various constituent parts—its names, definitions, and respective offices; it unravels, as it were, the thread of which the web of speech is composed. These reflections seldom occur to any one before their acquaintance with the art; yet it is most certain that, without a knowledge of Grammar, it is very difficult to speak with propriety, precision, and purity.

RHETORIC.

It is by Rhetoric that the art of speaking eloquently is acquired. To be an eloquent speaker, in the proper sense of the word, is far from being either a common or an easy attainment: it is the art of being persuasive and commanding; the art, not only of pleasing the fancy, but of speaking both to the understanding and to the heart.

LOGIC

Is that science which directs us how to form clear and distinct ideas of things, and thereby prevents us from being misled by their similitude or resemblance. Of all the human sciences, that concerning man is certainly most worthy of the human mind, and the proper manner of conducting its several powers in the attainment of truth and knowledge. This science ought to be cultivated as the foundation or ground-work of our inquiries; particularly in the pursuit of those sublime principles which claim our attention as Masons.

ARITHMETIC

Is the art of numbering, or that part of the mathematics which considers the properties of numbers in general. We have but a very imperfect idea of things without quantity, and as imperfect of quantity itself, without the help of Arithmetic. All the works of the Almighty are made in number, weight, and measure; therefore, to understand them rightly, we ought to understand arithmetical calculations; and the greater advancement we make in the mathematical sciences, the more capable we shall be of considering such things as are the ordinary objects of our conceptions, and be thereby led to a more comprehensive knowledge of our great Creator and the works of the creation.

GEOMETRY

Treats of the powers and properties of magnitudes in general, where length, breadth, and thickness are considered—from a *point* to a *line*, from a line to a *superfices*, and from a superfices to a *solid*.

A *point* is the beginning of all geometrical matter.

A *line* is a continuation of the same.

A *superfices* is length and breadth, without a given thickness.

A *solid* is length and breadth, with a given thickness, which forms a cube, and comprehends the whole.

THE ADVANTAGES OF GEOMETRY.

By this science, the architect is enabled to construct his plans and execute his designs; the general, to arrange his soldiers; the engineer, to mark out grounds for encampments; the geographer, to give us the dimensions of the world, and all things therein contained; to delineate the extent of seas, and specify the divisions of empires, kingdoms, and provinces. By it, also, the astronomer is enabled to make his observations, and to fix the duration of times and seasons, years and cycles. In fine, Geometry is the foundation of architecture, and the root of the mathematics.

The contemplation of this science, in a moral and comprehensive view, fills the mind with rapture. To the true geometrician, the regions of matter with which he is surrounded afford ample scope for his admiration, while they open a sublime field for his inquiry and disquisition.

Every particle of matter on which he treads, every blade of grass which covers the field, every flower which blows, and every infect which wings its way in this expanded space, proves the existence of a First Cause, and yields pleasure to the intelligent mind.

The symmetry, beauty, and order displayed in the various parts of the animate and inanimate creation, is a pleasing and delightful theme, and naturally leads to the source whence the whole is derived. When we bring within the focus of the eye the variegated carpet of the terrestrial theater, and survey the progress of the vegetative system, our admiration is justly excited. Every plant which grows, every flowering shrub which breathes its sweets, affords instruction and delight. When we extend our views to the animal creation, and contemplate the varied clothing of every species, we are equally struck with astonishment. And when we trace the lines of geometry drawn by the Divine pencil in the beautiful plumage of the feathered tribe, how exalted is our conception of the heavenly work! The admirable structure of plants and animals, and the infinite number of fibers and vessels which run through the whole, with the apt disposition of one part to another, is a perpetual subject of study to the geometrician, who, while he adverts to the changes which all undergo in their progress to maturity, is lost in rapture and veneration of the Great Cause which governs the system.

When he descends into the bowels of the earth, and explores the kingdom of ores, minerals, and fossils, he finds the same instances of Divine Wisdom and Goodness displayed in their formation and structure: every gem and pebble proclaims the handiwork of an Almighty Creator.

When he surveys the watery elements, and directs his attention to the wonders of the deep, with all the inhabitants of the mighty ocean, he perceives emblems of the same supreme intelligence. The scales of the largest fish, as well as the penciled shell of the minutest bivalve, equally yield a theme for his contemplation, on which he fondly dwells, while the symmetry of their formation, and the delicacy of their tints, evince the wisdom of the Divine Artist.

When he exalts his view to the more noble and elevated parts of Nature, and surveys the celestial orbs, how much greater is his astonishment! If, on the principles of geometry and true philosophy, he contemplate the sun, the moon, the stars, and the whole concave of heaven, his pride will be humbled, while he is lost in awful admiration of the Maker. The immense magnitude of those bodies, the regularity and velocity of their motions, and the inconceivable extent of space through which they move, are equally wonderful and incomprehensible, so as to baffle his most daring conceptions, while he labors in considering the immensity of the theme!

MUSIC

Is that elevated science which affects the passions by sound. There are few who have not felt its charms, and acknowledged its expression to be intelligible to the heart. It is a language of delightful sensations, far more eloquent than words; it breathes to the ear the clearest intimations; it touches and gently agitates the agreeable and sublime passions; it wraps us in melancholy, and elevates us in joy; it dissolves and inflames; it melts us in tenderness, and excites us to war. This science is truly congenial to the nature of man; for by its powerful charms the most discordant passions may be harmonized, and brought into perfect unison; but it never sounds with such seraphic harmony as when employed in singing hymns of gratitude to the Creator of the universe.

ASTRONOMY

Is that sublime science which inspires the contemplative mind to soar aloft, and read the wisdom, strength, and beauty of the great Creator in the heavens. How nobly eloquent of the Deity is the celestial hemisphere!—spangled with the most magnificent heralds of his infinite glory! They spear-to the whole universe; for there is no speech so barbarous, but their language is understood; nor nation so distant, but their voices are heard among them.

> The heavens proclaim the glory of GOD;
> The firmament declareth the works of his hands.

Assisted by Astronomy, we ascertain the laws which govern the heavenly bodies, and by which their motions are directed; investigate the power by which they circulate in their orbs, discover their size, determine their distance, explain their various phenomena, and correct the fallacy of the senses by the light of truth.[1]

---

[1] Astronomy stands confessedly the most exalted and sublime science that has ever been cultivated by man. By this divine science, the Grand Architect of the Universe leas enabled the mind of man, not only to view his wonderful omnipotency in a much stronger light than he could otherwise effect, but also to demonstrate, even to the skeptic, if any such exist, that nothing less than the Almighty power could establish such innumerable systems of the heavenly bodies, and place them at their relative distances, and finally keep the whole in universal order. To view the starry firmament without this science, mankind are impressed with a reverential awe of heavenly wisdom; but when we explore the science with its demonstrative truths, we are lost in astonishment at the boundless fields of ether, where those vast systems are placed. In short, it is by the help of this sublime science that mankind are enabled to plough the trackless ocean—to traverse the sandy waste of the immense desert; by commerce to civilize rude and savage nations—to unite men of all countries, sects, and opinions—and conciliate true friendship among persons who would otherwise have remained at an immense distance asunder.

An Emblem of PLENTY is introduced and explained.[1]

*   *   *   *   *   *   *

CORN.   WINE.   OIL.

*   *   *   *   *   *   *

THE MORAL ADVANTAGES OF GEOMETRY.

Geometry, the first and noblest of sciences, is the basis on which the superstructure of Freemasonry is erected. By Geometry, we may curiously trace Nature through her various windings, to her most concealed recesses. By it, we discover the power, wisdom, and goodness of the GRAND ARTIFICER of the universe, and view with delight the proportions which connect this vast machine. By it, we discover how the planets move in their respective orbits, and demonstrate their various revolutions. By it, we account for the return of the seasons, and the variety of scenes which each season displays to the discerning eye. Numberless worlds are around us, all framed by the same Divine Artist, which roll through the vast expanse, and are all conducted by the same unerring law of Nature.

A survey of Nature, and the observation of her beautiful proportions, first determined man to imitate the divine plan, and study symmetry and order. This gave rise to societies, and birth to every useful art. The architect began to design; and the plans which he laid down, being improved by time and experience, have produced works which are the admiration of every age.

The lapse of time, the ruthless hand of ignorance, and the devastations of war, have laid waste and destroyed many valuable monuments of antiquity, on which the utmost exertions of human genius have been employed. Even the *Temple of Solomon*, so spacious and magnificent, and constructed by so many celebrated artists, escaped not the unsparing ravages of barbarous force. Freemasonry, notwithstanding, has still survived. The *Attentive Ear* receives the sound from the *Instructive Tongue*, and the mysteries of Masonry are safely lodged in the repository of *Faithful Breasts*. Tools and implements of architecture and symbolic emblems, most expressive are selected by the Fraternity, to imprint on the mind wise and serious truths; and thus, through a succession of ages, are transmitted unimpaired the most excellent tenets of our institution.

---

[1] The passages of Scripture which are referred to in this part of the section will be found in JUDGES xii. 1-6. The Vulgate version gives a paraphrastic translation of a part of the sixth verse, as follows: "Say, therefore, Shibboleth, which, being interpreted, is an *ear of corn*." The same word also in Hebrew signifies a rapid stream of water, from the root *SHaBaL*, to flow copiously. The too common error of speaking, in this part of the ritual, of a "*water-ford*," instead of a "*water-fall*," which is the correct word, must be carefully avoided. A *water-fall* is an emblem of plenty, because it indicates an abundance of water. A *water-ford*, for the converse reason, is, if any symbol at all, a symbol of scarcity.—MACKEY's *Manual of the Lodge*.

90

The lecture closes by paying profound homage to the sacred name of the Grand Geometrician of the Universe, before whom all Masons, from the youngest E. A., who stands in the north-east corner of the Lodge, to the W. M., who presides in the East, humbly, reverently, and devoutly bow.

CHARGE TO THE CANDIDATE.

BROTHER: Being advanced to the second degree of Freemasonry, we congratulate you on your preferment. The internal, and not the external qualifications of a man are what Masonry regards. As you increase in knowledge, you will improve in social intercourse.

It is unnecessary to recapitulate the duties which, as a Fellow-Craft, you are bound to discharge, or to enlarge on the necessity of a strict adherence to them, as your own experience must have established their value. Our laws and regulations you are strenuously to support; and be always ready to assist in seeing them duly executed. You are not to palliate or aggravate the offences of your brethren; but in the decision of every trespass against our rules, you are to judge with candor, admonish with friendship, and reprehend with justice.

The study of the Liberal Arts, that valuable branch of education, which tends so effectually to polish and adorn the mind, is earnestly recommended to your consideration; especially the science of Geometry, which is established as the basis of our art. Geometry, or Masonry, originally synonymous terms, being of a divine and moral nature, is enriched with the most useful knowledge; while it proves the wonderful properties of Nature, it demonstrates the more important truths of morality.

Your past behavior and regular deportment have merited the honor which we have now conferred; and in your new character, it is expected that you will conform to the principles of the Order, by steadily persevering in the practice of every commendable virtue. Such is the nature of your engagements as a Fellow-Craft, and to these duties you are bound by the most sacred ties.

LECTURE
ON THE
LEGEND OF THE WINDING STAIRS.
BY ALBERT G. MACKEY, M. D.

ALTHOUGH the legend of the Winding Stairs forms an important tradition of Ancient Craft Masonry, the only allusion to it in scripture is to be found in a single verse in the 6th chapter of the 1st Book of Kings, and is in these words: "The door for the middle chamber was in the right side of the house; and they went up with winding stairs into the middle chamber, and out of the middle into the third." Out of this slender material has been constructed an allegory, which, if properly considered in its symbolical relations, will be found to be of surpassing beauty. But it is only as a symbol that we can regard this whole tradition; for the historical facts and the architectural details alike forbid us for a moment to suppose that the legend, as it is rehearsed in the second degree of Masonry, is anything more than a magnificent philosophical myth.

Let us inquire into the true design of this legend, and learn the lesson of symbolism which it is intended to teach.

In the investigation of the true meaning of every Masonic symbol and allegory, we must be governed by the single principle that the whole design of Freemasonry as a speculative science is the investigation of Drawn TRUTH. To this great object everything is subsidiary. The Mason is, from the moment of his initiation as an Entered Apprentice to the time at which he receives the full fruition of Masonic light, an investigator—a laborer in the quarry and the Temple—whose reward is to be TRUTH. All the ceremonies and traditions of the Order tend to this ultimate design. Is there light to be asked for? It is the intellectual light of wisdom and truth. Is there a word to be sought? That word is the symbol of truth. Is there a loss of something that had been promised? That loss is typical of the failure of man, in the infirmity of his nature, to discover Divine truth. Is there a substitute to be appointed for that loss? It is an allegory which teaches us that in this world man can approximate only to the full conception of truth.

Hence there is in Speculative Masonry always a progress, symbolized by its peculiar ceremonies of initiation. There is an advancement from a lower to a higher state—from darkness to light—from death to life—from error to truth. The candidate is always ascending; he is never stationary; never goes back, but each step he takes brings him to some new mental illumination—to the knowledge of some more elevated doctrine. The teaching of the Divine Master is, in respect to this continual progress, the teaching of Masonry—"No man having put his hand to the plough, and looking back, is fit for the kingdom of heaven." And similar to this is the precept of Pythagoras: "When traveling, turn not back, for if you do, the furies will accompany you."

92

Now, this principle of Masonic symbolism is apparent in many places in each of the degrees. In that of the Entered Apprentice we find it developed in the theological ladder, which resting on earth, leans its top upon heaven, thus inculcating the idea of an ascent from a lower to a higher sphere, as the objects of Masonic labor. In the Master's degree we find it exhibited in its most religious form, in the restoration from death, to life—in the change from the obscurity of the grave to the holy of holies of the Divine Presence. In all the degrees we find it presented in the ceremony of circumambulation, in which there is a gradual examination by, and a passage from, an inferior to a superior officer. And lastly, the same symbolic idea is conveyed in the Fellow Craft's degree in the legend of the Winding Stairs. In an investigation of the symbolism of the Winding Stairs we will be directed to the true explanation by a reference to their origin, their number, the objects which they recall, and their termination, but above all by a consideration of the great object which an ascent upon them was intended to accomplish.

The steps of this Winding Staircase commenced, we are informed, at the porch of the Temple, that is to say, at its very entrance. But nothing is more undoubted in the science of Masonic symbolism than that the Temple was the representative of the world purified by the Shekinah, or the Divine Presence. The world of the profane is without the Temple; the world of the initiated is within its sacred walls. Hence to enter the Temple, to pass within the porch, to be made a Mason, and to be born into the world of Masonic light, are all synonymous and convertible terms. Here, then, the symbolism of the Winding Stairs begins.

The Apprentice, having entered within the porch of the Temple, has begun his Masonic life. But the first degree in Masonry, like the lesser mysteries of the ancient systems of initiation, is only a preparation and purification for something higher. The Entered Apprentice is the child in Masonry. Thy lessons which he receives are simply intended to cleanse the heart and prepare the recipient for that mental illumination which is to be given in the succeeding degrees.

As a Fellow Craft, he has advanced another step, and as the degree is emblematic of youth, so it is here that the intellectual education of the candidate begins. And therefore, here, at the very spot which separates the Porch from the Sanctuary, where childhood ends and manhood begins, he finds stretching out before him a winding stair which invites him, as it were, to ascend, and which, as the symbol of discipline and instruction, teaches him that here must commence his Masonic labor—here he must enter upon those glorious though difficult researches, the end of which is to be the possession of Divine truth. The Winding Stairs begin after the candidate has passed within the Porch, and between the Pillars of Strength and Establishment, as a significant symbol to teach him that as soon as he had passed beyond the years of irrational childhood, and commenced his entrance upon manly life, the laborious task of self-improvement is the first duty that is placed before him. He cannot stand still, if he would be worthy of his vocation; his destiny as an immortal being requires him to ascend, step by step, until he has reached the summit, where the treasures of knowledge await him.

The number of these steps in all the systems have been odd. VITRUVIUS remarks, and the coincidence is at least curious, that the ancient temples were always ascended by an odd number of steps, and he assigns as the reason, that commencing with the right foot at the bottom, the worshiper would find the same foot foremost when he entered the Temple, which was considered as a fortunate omen. But the fact is that the symbol of numbers was borrowed by the Masons from PYTHAGORAS, in whose system of philosophy it plays an important part, and in which odd numbers were considered as more perfect than even ones. Hence. throughout the Masonic system we find a predominance of odd numbers; and, while three, five, seven, nine, fifteen, and twenty-seven, are all important symbols, we seldom find a reference to two, four, six, eight, or ten. The odd number of the stairs was therefore intended to symbolize the idea of perfection, to which it was the object of the aspirant to attain.

As to the particular number of the stairs, this has varied at different periods. Tracing-boards of the last century have been found, in which only *five* steps are delineated, and others in which they amount to *seven*. The Prestonian lectures used in England, in the beginning of this century, gave the whole number as thirty-eight, dividing them into series of one, three, five, seven, nine, and eleven. The error of making an even number, which was a violation of the Pythagorean principle of odd numbers as the symbol of perfection, was corrected in the HEMMING lectures, adopted at the union of the two Grand Lodges of England, by striking out the eleven, which was also objectionable as receiving a sectarian explanation. In this country the number was still further reduced to *fifteen*, divided into three series of *three*, *five*, and *seven*. We shall adopt this American division as the basis of our explanations, although, after all, the particular number of the steps, or the peculiar method of their division into series, will not in any way affect the general symbolism of the whole legend.

The candidate, then, in the second degree of Masonry, represents a man starting forth on the journey of life, with the great task before him of self-improvement. For the faithful performance of this task, a reward is promised, which reward consists in the development of all his intellectual faculties, the moral and spiritual elevation of his character, and the acquisition of truth and knowledge. Now, the attainment of this moral and intellectual condition supposes an elevation of character, an ascent from a lower to a higher life, and a passage of toil and difficulty, through rudimentary instruction, to the full fruition of wisdom. This is, therefore, beautifully symbolized by the Winding Stairs; at whose foot the aspirant stands ready to climb the toilsome steep, while at its top is placed "that hieroglyphic bright which none but Craftsmen ever saw," as the emblem of Divine truth. And, hence, a distinguished writer has said that "these steps, like all the Masonic symbols, are illustrative of discipline and doctrine, as well as of natural, mathematical, and metaphysical science, and open to us an extensive range of moral and speculative inquiry."

The candidate, incited by the love of virtue and the desire of knowledge, and withal, eager for the reward of truth which is set before him, begins at once the toilsome ascent. At each division, he pauses to gather instruction from the symbolism which these divisions present to his attention.

At the first pause which he makes he is instructed in the peculiar organization of the Order of which he has become a disciple. But the information here given, if taken in its naked, literal sense, is barren and unworthy of his labor. The rank of the officers who govern, and the names of the degrees which constitute the institution, can give him no knowledge which he has not before possessed. We must look, therefore, to the symbolic meaning of these allusions for any value which may be attached to this part of the ceremony.

The reference to the organization of the Masonic institution is intended to remind the aspirant of the union of men in society, and the development of the social state out of the state of nature. He is thus reminded, in the very outset of his journey, of the blessings which arise from civilization, and of the fruits of virtue and knowledge which are derived from that condition. Masonry itself is the result of civilization; while in grateful return it has been one of the most important means of extending that condition of mankind.

All the monuments of antiquity, that the ravages of time have left, combine to prove that man had no sooner emerged from the savage into the social state than he commenced the organization of religious mysteries, and the separation, by a sort of divine instinct, of the sacred from the profane. Then came the invention of architecture as a means of providing convenient dwellings and necessary shelter from the inclemencies and vicissitudes of the seasons, with all the mechanical arts connected with it, and lastly, geometry, as a necessary science to enable the cultivators of land to measure and designate the limits of their possessions. All these are claimed as peculiar characteristics of speculative Masonry, which may be considered as the type of civilization, the former bearing the same relation to the profane world as the latter does to the savage state. Hence, we at once see the fitness of the symbolism which commences the aspirant's upward progress in the cultivation of knowledge and the search after truth, by recalling to his mind the condition of civilization and the social union of mankind as necessary preparations for the attainment of these objects. In the allusions to the officers of a Lodge, and the degrees of Masonry as explanatory of the organization of our own society, we clothe in our symbolic language the history of the organization of society.

Advancing in his progress, the candidate is invited to contemplate another series of instructions. The human senses, as the appropriate channels through which we receive all our ideas of perception, and which, therefore, constitute the most important sources of our knowledge, are here referred to as a symbol of intellectual cultivation. Architecture, as the most important of the arts which conduce to the comfort of mankind, is also alluded to here, not simply because it is so closely connected with the operative institution of Masonry, but also, as the type of all the other useful arts. In his second pause, in the ascent of the Winding Stairs, the aspirant is, therefore, reminded of the necessity of cultivating practical knowledge.

So far, then, the instructions he has received relate to his own condition in society as a member of the great social compact and to his means of becoming, by a knowledge of the arts of practical life, a necessary and useful member of that society.

But his motto will be "EXCELSIOR." Still must he go onward and forward. The stair is still before him; its summit is not yet reached, and still further treasures of wisdom are to be sought for, or the reward will not be gained, nor the *middle chamber*, the abiding place of truth, be reached.

In his third pause, he, therefore, arrives at that point in which the whole circle of human science is to be explained. Symbols, we know, are in themselves arbitrary and of conventional signification, and the complete circle of human science might have been as well symbolized by any other sign or series of doctrines as by the seven liberal arts and sciences. But Masonry is an institution of the olden time; and this selection of the liberal arts and sciences as a symbol of the completion of human learning is one of the most pregnant evidences that we have of its antiquity.

In the seventh century, and for a long time afterward, the circle of instruction to which all the learning of the most eminent schools and most distinguished philosophers was confined, was limited to what was then called the liberal arts and sciences, and consisted of two branches, the *trivium* and the *quadrivium*.[1] The *trivium* includes grammar, rhetoric, and logic; the *quadrivium* comprehended arithmetic, geometry, music, and astronomy.

These seven heads were supposed to include universal knowledge. He who was master of these was thought to have no need of a preceptor to explain any books or to solve any questions which lay within the compass of human reason; the knowledge of the *trivium* having furnished him with the key to all language, and that of the *quadrivium* having opened to him the secret laws of nature.

---

[1] The words themselves are purely classical, but the meanings here given to them are of a mediæval or corrupt Latinity. Among the old Romans, a *trivium* meant a place where three ways met, and a *quadrivium*, where four, or what we now call a cross-road. When we speak of the *paths of learning*, we readily discover the origin of the signification given by the scholastic philosophers to these terms.

At a period when few were instructed in the *trivium*, and very few studied the *quadrivium*, to be master of both was sufficient to complete the character of a philosopher. The propriety, therefore, of adopting the seven liberal arts and sciences as a symbol of the completion of human learning is apparent. The candidate having reached this point is now supposed to have accomplished the task upon which he had entered—he has reached the last step, and is now ready to receive the full fruition of human learning.

So far, then, we are able to comprehend the true symbolism of the Winding Stairs. They represent the progress of an inquiring mind with the toils and labors of intellectual cultivation and study, and the preparatory acquisition of all human science, as a preliminary step to the attainment of divine truth, which it must be remembered is always symbolized in Masonry by the WORD.

Here we may again allude to the symbolism of numbers, which is for the first time presented to the consideration of the Masonic student in the legend of the Winding Stairs. The theory of numbers as the symbols of certain qualities was originally borrowed by the Masons from the school of PYTHAGORAS. We do not expect, however, to develop this doctrine, in its entire extent, on the present occasion, for the numeral symbolism of Masonry would itself constitute materials for an ample essay. It will be sufficient to advert to the fact that the total number of the steps, amounting in all to fifteen, in the American system, is a significant symbol. For fifteen was a sacred number among the Orientals, because the letters of the holy name JAH, הי, were, in their numerical value, equivalent to fifteen; and hence a figure, in which the nine digits were so disposed as to make fifteen either way when added together perpendicularly, horizontally, or diagonally, constituted one of their most sacred talismans. The fifteen steps in the Winding Stairs are therefore symbolic of the name of GOD.

But we are not yet done. It will be remembered that a reward was promised for all this toilsome ascent of the Winding Stairs. Now what are the wages of a Speculative Mason? Not money, nor coin, nor wine, nor oil. All these are but symbols. His wages are TRUTH, or that approximation to it which will be most appropriate to the degree into which he has been initiated. It is one of the most beautiful, but at the same time most abstruse, doctrines of the science of Masonic symbolism, that the Mason is ever to be in search of truth, but is never to find it. This divine truth, the object of all his labors, is symbolized by the WORD, for which we all know he can only obtain a *substitute*; and this is intended to teach the humiliating but necessary lesson that the knowledge of the nature of GOD and of man's relation to him, which knowledge constitutes divine truth, can never be acquired in this life. It is only when the portals of the grave open to us, and give us an entrance into a more perfect life, that this knowledge is to be attained. "Happy is the man," says the father of lyric poetry, "who descends beneath the hollow earth, having beheld these mysteries; he knows the end, he knows the origin of life."

The Middle. Chamber is therefore symbolic of this life, where only the symbol of the word can be given, where only the truth is to be reached by approximation, and yet where we are to learn that that truth will consist in a perfect knowledge of the G. A. O. T. U. This is the reward of the inquiring Mason; in this consists the wages of a Fellow Craft; he is directed to the truth, but must travel further and ascend still higher to attain it.

It is then, as a symbol, and a symbol only, that we must study this beautiful legend of the Winding Stairs. If we attempt to adopt it as an historical fact, the absurdity of its details stares us in the face, and wise men will wonder at our credulity. Its inventors had no desire thus to impose upon our folly; but offering it to us as a great philosophical myth, they did not for a moment suppose that we would pass over its sublime moral teachings to accept the allegory as an historical narrative, without meaning, and wholly irreconcilable with records of scripture, and opposed by all the principles of probability. To suppose that eighty thousand craftsmen were weekly paid in the narrow precincts of the Temple chambers, is simply to suppose an absurdity. But to believe that all this pictorial representation of an ascent by a Winding Stairs to the place where the wages of labor were to be received, was an allegory to teach us the ascent of the mind from ignorance, through all the toils of study and the difficulties of obtaining knowledge, receiving here a little and there a little, adding something to the stock of our ideas at each step, until, in the middle chamber of life—in the full fruition of manhood—the reward is attained, and the purified and elevated intellect is invested with the reward, in the direction how to seek GOD and GOD'S truth—to believe this is to believe and to know the true design of Speculative Masonry, the only design which makes it worthy of a good or a wise man's study.

Its historical details are barren, but its symbols and allegories are fertile with instruction.

And so we close with this theory: *The Fellow Craft represents a man laboring in the pursuit of truth; and the Winding Stairs are the devious pathways of that pursuit.*

THIRD DEGREE.
MASTER MASON.

"In the ceremonial of the Third Degree the last grand mystery is attempted to be illustrated in a forcible and peculiar manner, showing, by striking analogy, that the Master Mason cannot be deemed perfect in the glorious science until by the cultivation of his intellectual powers he has gained such moral government of his passions, such serenity of mind, that in synonymous apposition with mastership in operative art his thoughts, like his actions, have become as useful as human intelligence will permit; and that, having passed through the trials of life with fortitude and faith, he is fitted for that grand, solemn, and mysterious consummation by which alone he can become acquainted with the great security of Eternity. Unlike the Entered Apprentice and Fellow-Craft, who each anticipate improvement as they advance, the Master Mason can learn nothing beyond the Third Degree; his hopes, therefore, with his thoughts and wishes, should be directed to the Grand Lodge above, where the world's great Architect lives and reigns forever. The ceremonial and the lecture beautifully illustrate this all. engrossing subject, and the conclusion we arrive at is that youth properly directed leads us to honorable and virtuous maturity, and that the life of man regulated by morality, faith and justice, will be rewarded at its closing hour by the prospect of Eternal Bliss."—DR. CRUCEFIX.

MASTER MASON.

SECTION I.

173

* * * * * * * *

175

177

8*

179

SECTION III.

1,453 COLUMNS.	3,300 OVERSEERS.
2,906 PILASTERS.	80,000 FELLOW CRAFTS.
3 GRAND MASTERS.	70,000 ENTERED APPRENTICES.

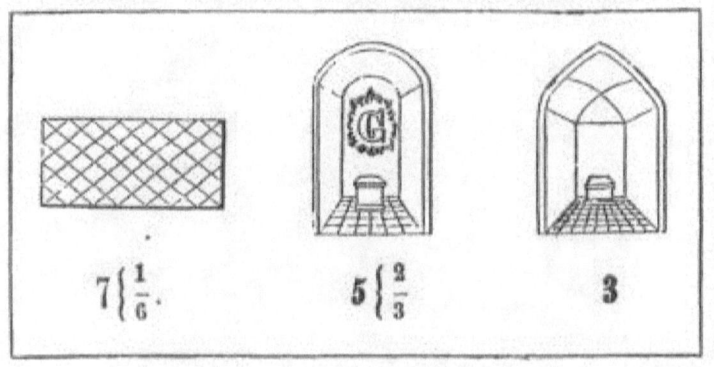

$$7\left\{\frac{1}{6}.\right. \qquad 5\left\{\frac{2}{3}\right. \qquad 3$$

181

104

183

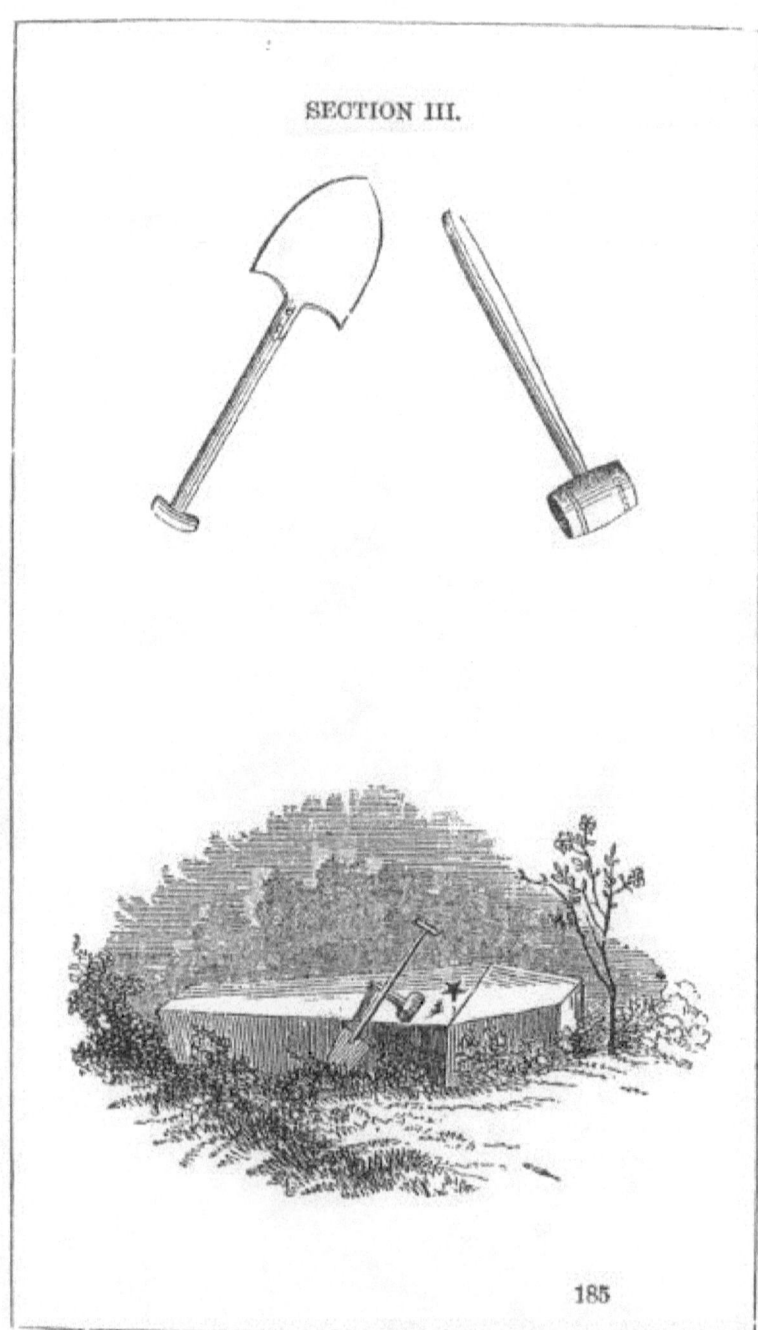

185

DEGREE OF MASTER MASON.
Symbolism of the Degree

WE have seen the type of man complete in moral worth and intellectual culture—not left to acquire knowledge, but first prepared to use that knowledge well, when it shall have been obtained. What more is left? Communion with our Maker. The mere knowledge of the Deity, as given us heretofore, is that of an august Creator, whom we are to reverence, and in whom alone we are to place our trust. But we have not yet seen him walking upon the earth, and holding open communion with the sons of men. Man has not yet been ennobled by personal contact with the All-Holy.

Let us imagine a conception perfectly in accordance with the ideas and opinions of our early brethren. "Who has at any time seen GOD, and lived?" "ADAM, our first progenitor." "But only in the days of his innocence. Since the day when all mankind was corrupted by his fall, no living man has looked upon the face of the Almighty."

Now, what would be the natural opinion of our ancient brethren as to the means of securing GOD'S actual presence? We know that, for a thousand years, men labored to find the true name of JEHOVAH, which they believed would be a talisman, giving them power over all the secrets of the Universe. Union, of the most unselfish nature, formed the grand characteristic of our Fraternity. Ambition, desire for fame—every passion which appeals to the self-love of man—was merged in the perfect union engendered by an adherence to the tenets of the Order to such a degree, that the names even of our great architects have not come down to us, though their works still stand, to attest their excellence. All was the work of brethren, and each was allowed his share of the glory.

Now, with this perfect union, and with the knowledge that the belief .existed that it was through the weakness of man only that he could not endure the presence of his Creator, what so natural as to suppose that if three brethren be found as types respectively of moral, intellectual, and physical perfection, and they be joined together in holy fellowship which should make their very souls as one, they might, in mystic union, call upon the great and sacred name of the Deity, and receive an answer to their prayer? That this idea did prevail, we have sufficient proof; and it is to this, rather than to any more utilitarian views, that we are to look for the rule which, in a purely speculative institution, so sternly demands physical, as well as moral and intellectual integrity.

We know that the wise and good of the days of SOLOMON regarded his idolatry as an evidence that the countenance of the All-Holy had been darkened to him; that he no longer held the interviews with the ONLY-WISE GOD, through which they deemed that his superhuman wisdom came. And indeed it would seem to them a thing monstrous and wholly unnatural, that the being whose intellect had been illumined from above, and to whom JEHOVAH had promised wisdom beyond that of men, should grovel in adoration before false gods, did they not also believe that it was only through direct and constant communion with the Almighty that this wisdom could continue; and now that he no longer sought that presence, he was given over to the blind guidance of his passions

This degree is a type of the communion of man with GOD. Long before the incarnation of that great Being, was the hope entertained of seeing him with mortal eyes, and no exertions were deemed too great to insure that consummation. With us, these ideas are but a type; for we have that realization so longed for by the brethren of old. And yet, as a type, how interesting it is to look back upon their struggles to look forward into what is now bright and clear!

The practical lessons to be found in the full exposition of the ceremonies of this degree, require us to be complete in our duty to our neighbor, before we can venture to direct him. Step by step, mounting from the lowest to the highest, we must prove to ourselves that we would serve him—pray for him—sympathize with his inmost feelings, and sustain him from falling, before we can venture to counsel him, even to his good—far less, dictate to him.

We now find man complete in morality and intelligence, with the stay of RELIGION added, to insure him of the protection of the Deity, and guard him against ever going astray. These three degrees thus form a perfect and harmonious whole; nor can we conceive that any thing can be suggested more, which the soul of man requires.

THIRD LECTURE.

FREEMASONRY, in every degree, as before remarked, is progressive. A knowledge of it can only be attained by time, patience, and application. In the first degree, we are taught the duties we owe to GOD, our neighbor, and ourselves. In the second, we are more thoroughly inducted into the mysteries of moral science, and learn to trace the goodness and majesty of the Creator, by minutely analyzing his works. But the third degree is the cement of the whole. It is calculated to bind men together by mystic points of fellowship, as in a bond of fraternal affection and brotherly love. It is among brethren of this degree that the ancient Landmarks of the Order are preserved, and it is from them that we derive that fund of information which none but ingenious and expert Masons can supply.

It is also from brethren of this degree that the rulers of the Craft are selected; because it is only from those who are capable of giving instruction that we can reasonably expect to receive it.

SECTION I.

THE first section in this, as in the two preceding degrees, is initiatory; and a knowledge of it is indispensable to every brother who would make himself useful in the ceremonial transactions of a Lodge.

The Compasses are peculiarly consecrated to this degree, because within their extreme points, when properly extended, are emblematically said to be inclosed the principal tenets of our profession; and hence the moral application of the Compasses, in the third degree, is to those precious jewels of a Master Mason—Friendship, Morality, and Brotherly Love.

The following passage of Scripture is introduced during the ceremonies:

Remember now thy Creator in the days of thy youth, while the evil days come not, nor the years draw nigh, when thou shalt say, I have no pleasure in them; while the sun, or the light, or the moon, or the stars, be not darkened, nor the clouds return after the rain; in the day when the keepers of the house shall tremble, and the strong men shall bow themselves, and the grinders cease, because they are few, and those that look out of the windows be darkened, and the doors shall be shut in the streets when the sound of the grinding is low, and he shall rise up at the voice of the bird, and all the daughters of Music shall be brought low; also, when they shall be afraid of that which is high, and fears shall be in the way, and the almond-tree shall flourish, and the grasshopper shall be a burden, and desire shall fail; because man goeth to his long home, and the mourners go about the streets: or ever the silver cord be loosed, or the golden bowl be broken, or the pitcher be broken at the fountain, or the wheel broken at the cistern. Then shall the dust return to the earth as it was; and the spirit shall return unto GOD who gave it.—ECCL. xii. 1-7.

The passage of Scripture here selected is a beautiful and affecting description of the body of man suffering under the infirmities of old age, and metaphorically compared to a worn-out house about to fall into decay. How appropriate is such an introduction to the sublime and awful ceremonies of that degree, in which death, the resurrection, and life eternal are the lessons to be taught by all its symbols and allegories!—MACKEY's Manual of the Lodge.

Or the following ODE may be sung:

AIR—*Bonny Doon.*

Let us remember in our youth,
  Before the evil days draw nigh,
Our great Creator, and his Truth!
  Ere mem'ry fail and pleasures fly;
Or sun, or moon, or planets' light
  Grow dark, or clouds return in gloom;
Ere vital spark no more incite;
  When strength shall bow and years consume.

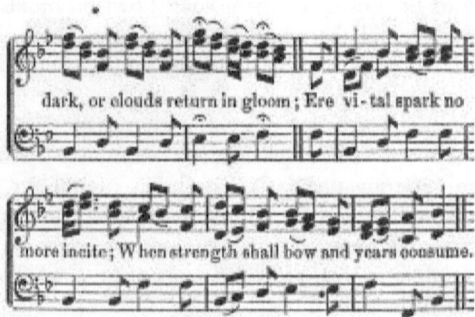

Let us in youth remember HIM!
  Who formed our frame, and spirits gave,
Ere windows of the mind grow dim
  Or door of speech obstructed wave;
When voice of bird fresh terrors wake,
  And Music's daughters charm no more,
Or fear to rise, with trembling shake
  Along the path we travel o'er.

In youth, to GOD let memory cling,
  Before desire shall fail or wane,
Or ere be loosed life's silver string,
  Or bowl at fountain rent in twain;
For man to his long home doth go,
  And mourners group around his urn;
Our dust, to dust again must flow,
  And spirits unto GOD return.

Working Tools of the Master Mason

All the implements in Masonry, indiscriminately, properly belong to this degree, and may be illustrated in this section. The TROWEL, however, is more particularly referred to.

THE TROWEL

Is an instrument made use of by operative Masons to spread the cement which unites the building into one common mass; but we, as Free and Accepted Masons, are taught to make use of it for the more noble and glorious purpose of spreading the cement of brotherly love and affection; that cement which unites us into one sacred band, or society of friends and brothers, among whom no contention should ever exist, but that noble contention, or rather emulation, of who best can work and best agree.

The three precious jewels of a Master Mason—FRIENDSHIP, MORALITY, and BROTHERLY LOVE.

SECTION II.

Trim section recites the historical traditions of the Order, and presents to view a picture of great moral sublimity. It recites the legend of which the symbolic interpretation testifies our faith in the resurrection of the body and the immortality of the soul; while it also exemplifies an instance of integrity and firmness seldom equaled and never excelled, and is in strong contrast with the development of those passions which debase and ruin all who indulge in them.

*   *   *   *   *   *   *

THE ceremonial of the Degree of Master Mason is unquestionably the most important, impressive, and instructive portion of the Ritual of Ancient Freemasonry. It transcends all others in the profoundness of its philosophy, in the wide range of ideas it aims to elucidate, and the dramatic interest with which it is invested. Wrong interpretations, however, assuming what is evidently a philosophical and ethical Mythus, to be the description of a literal fact, have, in a certain degree, weakened the effects which it is capable, otherwise, of producing.

That portion of the Rite which is connected with the legend of the Tyrian Artist, is well worthy the deep and earnest study of thoughtful men. But it should be studied as a myth, and not as a fact; and, if thus accepted, it will be found exceedingly rich in instructive lessons, and lessons, too, which admit of an immense variety of applications; whereas, if it be regarded simply as a ceremony commemorative of historical occurrences, it has no philosophical importance nor significance whatever.

Against the notion that it is the representation of a scene that actually occurred in the Temple, it may well be urged that, outside of Masonic tradition, there is no proof that an event, such as is related in connection with the Temple-Builder, ever transpired; and, besides, the ceremony is *older*, by more than a thousand years, than the age of SOLOMON. There are characters impressed upon it which cannot be mistaken. It is thoroughly Egyptian, and is closely allied to the supreme rite of the Isianic mysteries.

OSIRIS, ISIS, and TYPHON are the three principal figures in the ancient Egyptian mythology. TYPHON—i.e., *Evil*—made war upon OSIRIS—i.e., *Beauty, Goodness*, and *Truth*. A fierce conflict long raged between these spiritual forces, of which all the combats, antagonisms, and disorders of the outward, visible world, were only far-distant. echoes, or feeble reverberations. TYPHON (*Evil*), for a period, appeared to triumph. With his wiles and arts, he overcame OSIRIS (*Truth*), dismembered his body, and concealed the fragments in the several quarters of the earth. Then the whole universe was shrouded in gloom, and resounded with lamentations and mourning over the fall of the Beautiful and Good! ISIS set forth, on her woful pilgrimage, to find the remains of the beloved OSIRIS. After many disappointments and trials, her efforts were crowned with success. The great day of triumph came. TYPHON (*Evil*) was destroyed by HORUS; the tomb of OSIRIS opened, and HE—*Order, Truth, Justice*—came forth, victorious, in the possession of immortal life, and harmony, peace, and joy prevailed through the universe.

The Egyptian rite was a dramatic representation of these events, and its purpose is sufficiently obvious. It pictured, in an impressive and solemn manner, the mighty and unceasing conflict of *Truth* with *Error*, *Light* with *Darkness*, *Beauty* with *Deformity*, *Virtue* with *Vice*, and *Life* with *Death*; and the final certain triumph of the former, and the sure defeat and destruction of the latter.

This myth is the antetype of the Temple-legend. OSIRIS and the Tyrian Architect are one and the same—not a mortal individual, but an idea—an IMMORTAL PRINCIPLE! In Egyptian Freemasonry, OSIRIS was the type of Beauty, Goodness, Order, and Truth. So, in the Temple-myth, the Tyrian is the symbol of Beauty and Order, and of that Creative Art which is ever ready to seize the Ideal, and incarnate it in material forms—that divine art which robes the physical world in immortal splendors—embellishes and beautifies life—idealizes all Nature, transforming dull and prosy reality to a sunny, flowery dream;

"Clothing the palpable and the familiar
With golden exhalations of the dawn."

TYPHON was slain, and the iniquitous triad of the Temple met a deserved doom. The Master's rite, from this point of view, has a wider scope and deeper significance, than if recognized as merely the record of an historical fact. In the one case, it simply tells us that a good man fell in the discharge of his duty, and that his foes were punished. In the other, it embraces all the possible conditions of Humanity, ranges through all worlds, reveals the Law of Eternal Justice, announces the omnipotence of Truth, and proclaims the immortality of man.

In this sense, the myth of the Tyrian is perpetually repeated in the history of human affairs. ORPHEUS was murdered, and his body thrown into the Hebrus; SOCRATES was made to drink the hemlock; and, in all ages, we have seen Evil temporarily triumphant, and Virtue and Truth calumniated, persecuted, crucified, and slain. But Eternal Justice marches surely and swiftly through the world: the TYPHONS, the children of darkness, the plotters of crime, all the infinitely varied forms of evil, are swept into oblivion; and Truth and Virtue—for a time laid low—come forth, clothed with diviner majesty, and crowned with everlasting glory!

"TRUTH, crushed to earth, will rise again;
 The eternal years of GOD are hers:
While ERROR, wounded, writhes in pain,
 And dies amid her worshipers."

THE TWELVE MESSENGERS.

In the old philosophies, the number 12 always concealed a mystical sense, and was considered a symbol of divine ideas. But here the twelve F. C. represent the companions of Isis, who assisted her in her long and wearisome search after the body of the slain OSIRIS.

THE ACACIA-TREE.

The "sprig of acacia" has, in the Masonic system, a solemn importance. It is a handsome tree, noted for its remarkably graceful and flexible leaves, of yellowish green, which droop down, and wave in the breeze, like luxuriant locks of hair. It held a sacred place in the ancient initiations, and, like the weeping-willow, was the symbol of tender sympathy and undying affection. An emblem, too, of immortality, it was most fittingly employed to mark the last resting-place of the distinguished dead.

THE LETTER G.

This letter is deservedly regarded as one of the most sacred of the Masonic emblems. Where it is used, however, as a symbol of Deity, it must be remembered that it is the Saxon representative of the Hebrew *Yod* and the Greek *Tau*—the initial letters of the Eternal in those languages.

This symbol proves that Freemasonry always prosecuted its labors with reference to the grand ideas of Infinity and Eternity. By the letter **G**—which conveyed to the minds of the brethren, at the same time, the idea of GOD and that of Geometry—it bound heaven to earth, the divine to the human, and the infinite to the finite.

Masons are taught to regard the Universe as the grandest of all symbols, revealing to men, in all ages, the ideas which are eternally revolving in the mind of the Divinity, and which it is their duty to reproduce in their own lives and in the world of art and industry. Thus GOD and Geometry, the material worlds and the spiritual spheres, were constantly united in the speculations of the ancient Masons. They, consequently, labored earnestly and unweariedly, not only to construct cities, and embellish them with magnificent edifices, but also to build up a temple of great and divine thoughts and of ever-growing virtues for the soul to dwell in.

The symbolical letter G—

* * * "That Hieroglyphic bright,
Which none but Craftsmen ever saw,"

and before which every true Mason reverently uncovers, and bows his head—is a perpetual condemnation of profanity, impiety, and vice. No brother who has bowed before that emblem, can be profane. He will never speak the name of the Grand Master of the Universe but with reverence, respect, and love. He will learn, by studying the mystic meaning of the letter G, to model his life after the divine plan; and, thus instructed, he will strive to be like GOD in the activity and earnestness of his benevolence, and the broadness and efficiency of his charity.

FUNERAL DIRGE.

Music—*Pleyel's Hymn.*

Solemn strikes the fun'ral chime,
Notes of our departing time;
As we journey here below,
Thro' a pilgrimage of woe.

Mortals, now indulge a tear,
For Mortality is here!
See how wide her trophies wave
O'er the slumbers of the grave!

Here another guest we bring;
Seraphs of celestial wing,
To our fun'ral altar come,
Waft our friend and brother home.

There, enlarged, thy soul shall see
What was wailed in mystery;
Heavenly glories of the place
Show his Maker, face to face.

LORD of all! below—above—
Fill our hearts with truth and love;
When dissolves our earthly tie,
Take us to thy Lodge on high.

Prayer at raising a brother to Master Mason's degree:

THOU, O GOD! knowest our down-sitting and our up-rising, and understandeth our thoughts afar off. Shield and defend us from the evil intentions of our enemies, and support us under the trials and afflictions we are destined to endure, while traveling through this vale of tears. Man that is born of a woman is of few days, and full of trouble. He cometh forth like a flower, and is cut down; he fleeth also as a shadow, and continueth not. Seeing his days are determined, the number of his months are with thee; thou hast appointed his bounds that he cannot pass; turn from him that he may rest, till he shall accomplish his day. For there is hope of a tree, if it be cut down, that it will sprout again, and that the tender branch thereof will not cease. But man dieth, and wasteth away; yea, man giveth up the ghost, and where is he? As the waters fail from the sea, and the flood decayeth and drieth up, so man lieth down, and riseth not up till the heavens shall be no more. Yet, O LORD! have compassion on the children of thy creation; administer them comfort in time of trouble, and save them with an everlasting salvation.—AMEN.

Response.—So mote it be.

RITES OF SEPULTURE.
HEBREW CUSTOMS.

ALL nations of the earth, from time immemorial, however much they have differed in most things, have ever agreed in this, viz: that it is a sacred duty to dispose of the bodies of the departed in a reverential manner. The most prevalent custom has been to bury them in the earth or place them in tombs. Among the Greeks, the duty of burying the dead was considered so important, that they enacted a law, requiring that whoever should meet a corpse in his path, should cover it with earth, turning the eyes to the evening-star. In some of the Oriental nations, the practice of burning the dead, and preserving their ashes in funereal urns, prevailed; but this custom was not tolerated in Judea. The Jews celebrated their funerals with great ceremony. Large crowds generally followed the body to its last resting-place, and—what seems strange to us—hired mourners, with lamentations and tears, proclaimed the grief of the surviving friends.

The prejudices of the people would not allow interments to be made in cities, and, consequently, every town had its cemetery without its walls. This fact would seem to be contradicted by a statement made in this section of the third degree, and Masonic writers have been much perplexed to find a means of reconciling the contradiction. But the subject is really free of all difficulty. The scene referred to is not historically true. Neither the supreme act of this degree—as we have heretofore remarked—nor the final one here described, are to be considered as commemorative of historical facts. The whole together forms a sublime myth, whose significance we have explained in our annotations elsewhere.

The Hebrews had cheerful views of death, and awaited its approach with calmness. With confidence and filial trust they closed their eyes on life, its splendors and enjoyments, and departed joyfully to join the great assembly of the blessed. "Yea, though I walk through the valley of the shadow of death, I will fear no evil!" was the exulting exclamation of one of them. When loved ones were stricken down, and consigned to the grave, they did not speak of them as dead, but said "*they sleep with their fathers!*" Hence, their burial-places were generally selected for their agreeable scenery, and were shaded with the Cypress and Cedar, and adorned with the Tamarisk and "golden-haired" Acacia.

The Jews undoubtedly erected monuments, bearing appropriate emblems and inscriptions, to commemorate the virtues of distinguished men; but the mausoleums which they best loved, were those that Nature supplies. Obelisks of granite and marble will crumble to dust as the ages revolve, but Nature's monuments—the trees and the flowers, symbols of Love, Hope, and Immortality—are perpetually renewed.

Some of the ancient Oriental cemeteries yet exist. A late traveler found one near Babylon, and growing near one of its venerable graves was a Tamarisk, which seemed to belong to the epoch when the Chaldean State was at the summit of its glory. "It appears," he says, "to be of the highest antiquity, and has been a superb tree—perhaps a scion of the monarch of the hanging gardens. Its present height is only twenty-three feet; its trunk has been of great circumference; though now rugged and rifted, it still stands proudly up; and, although nearly worn away, has still sufficient strength to bear the burden of its limbs in the stern grandeur of its decaying greatness. The fluttering and rustling sound produced by the wind sweeping through its delicate branches, has an indescribably melancholy effect, and seems as if entreating the traveler to remain, and unite in mourning over those who slumber below. I scarcely dared ask why, while standing beneath this precious relic of the past and prophet of the future, I had nearly lost the power of forcing myself from the spot.

"I turned from all it brought to those it could not bring."[1]

The emblems of the second class, which are peculiar to this degree—the Spade, Coffin, Sprig of Acacia, etc.—are well known to all thoroughly-qualified Masons. They are all expressive and eloquently instructive; but we have always regarded the acacia as the most beautiful and significant; for it speaks of immortality. So the trees, the shrubs, and flowers with which the old Hebrews were wont to surround the tombs and graves of their "loved and lost," were carefully selected with reference to their symbolic meaning. They were types of sympathy, affection, hope, and of the love which is eternal.

---

[1] Travels in the Holy Land and Chaldea, by Capt. ROBT. MIQUARI. 1829.

This should also be the practice of modern Freemason. The adorning of our graves with those symbols of sympathy and everlasting affection which Nature so richly furnishes, takes away the gloom and terror of the "narrow house." Let the rose, the amaranth, and the myrtle bloom around the places where our loved departed rest from the toils and conflicts of life. Let the acacia, cypress, and cedar be planted there, and embellish the soil which is consecrated to the dead. Thus, on every returning Spring, each swelling bud and opening flower will seem to declare that the night of death is passing;

"And beauty immortal awakes from the tomb."

Thus every wind that softly breathes through the green foliage, and fans the verdant coverings of the dead, will seem to be an echo of the voice of GOD, or the Archangel's trump, commanding the dead to rise. Then will holy and trustful thoughts and bright hopes hover over their tombs, as crowns of stars. The grave will be transfigured, and shine with a light immortal

By following the example of our brethren of the old days, we render a homage, justly due, to the spirits of the honored dead. Each grave thus becomes an altar, consecrated by sighs, and tears, and holy affections; and the flowers that bloom thereon, are the offerings which unforgetting love presents to the cherished being who slumbers beneath.

"Then, like the Hebrew, bear your dead
To fields with pleasant verdure spread,
  And lay him down to rest,
Where th' Acacias, with the Cypress blent,
Weep mutely o'er the tenement
  Which holds a slumbering guest.
Oh, bear along the sable pall
Without the crowded city's wall!"

WHEN the necessities of a Brother call for my aid and support, I will be ever ready to render him such assistance, to save him from sinking, as may not be detrimental to myself or connections, if I find him worthy thereof.

118

Indolence shall not cause my footsteps to halt, nor shall wrath turn them aside; but, forgetting every selfish consideration, I will be ever swift of foot to save, help, and execute benevolence to a fellow-creature in distress, particularly to a brother Mason.

When I offer up my devotions to Almighty God, I will remember a Brother's welfare as my own; for, most assuredly, will the petitions of a fervent heart be acceptable at the Throne of Grace; and our prayers are certainly required for each other.

A Brother's secrets, delivered to me as such, I will keep as I would my own, because, by betraying that trust, I might be doing him the greatest injury he could possibly sustain.

A Brother's character I will support in his absence as I would in his presence; I will not wrongfully revile him myself, nor will I suffer it to be done by others, if in my power to prevent it.

Thus are we linked together in one indissoluble chain of sincere affection, brotherly love, relief, and truth.

It has been the practice in all ages to erect monuments to the memory of departed worth; and the section closes with a tribute to the memory of that distinguished artist who preferred to lose his life rather than betray his trust.

King Solomon's Temple

*   *   *   *   *   *   *

SECTION III.

THIS section illustrates certain hieroglyphical emblems, and inculcates many useful and impressive moral lessons. It also details many particulars relative to the building of the Temple at Jerusalem.

This magnificent structure was founded in the fourth year of the reign of SOLOMON, on the second day of the month Zif, being the second month of the sacred year. It was located on Mount Moriah, near the place where ABRAHAM was about to offer up his son ISAAC, and where DAVID met and appeased the destroying angel. JOSEPHUS informs us that, although more than seven years were occupied in building it, yet, during the whole term, it did not rain in the day-time, that the workmen might not be obstructed in their labor. From sacred history we also learn, that there was not the sound of ax, hammer, or any tool of iron, heard in the house while it was building. It is said to have been supported by fourteen hundred and fifty-three columns, and two thousand nine hundred and six pilasters, all hewn from the finest Parian marble.

It was symbolically supported, also, by three columns—WISDOM, STRENGTH, and BEAUTY.

*   *   *   *   *   *   *

In the British and other mysteries, these three pillars represented the great emblematical *Triad of Deity*, as with us they refer to the three principal officers of the Lodge. It is a fact that, in Britain, the *Adytum* or Lodge was actually supported by three stones or pillars, which were supposed to convey a regenerating purity to the aspirant, after having endured the ceremony of initiation in all its accustomed formalities. The delivery from between them was termed a *new birth*. The corresponding pillars of the Hindoo mythology were also known by the names of Wisdom, Strength, and Beauty, and placed in the East, West, and South, crowned with three human heads. They jointly referred to the Creator, who was said to have planned the Great Work by his infinite *Wisdom*, executed it by his *Strength*, and to have adorned it with all its *Beauty* and usefulness for the benefit of man. These united powers were not overlooked in the mysteries; for we find them represented in the solemn ceremony of initiation by the three presiding Brahmins or Hierophants. The chief Brahmin sat in the East, high exalted on a brilliant throne, clad in a flowing robe of azure, thickly sparkled with golden stars, and bearing in his hand a magical rod; thus symbolizing BRAHMA, the creator of the world. His two compeers, clad in robes of equal magnificence, occupied corresponding situations of distinction. The representative of VISHNU (the setting sun) was placed on an exalted throne in the West; and he who personated SIVA, the meridian sun, occupied a splendid throne in the South.

There were employed in its building three Grand Masters; three thousand and three hundred Masters or Overseers of the work; eighty thousand Fellow-Crafts; and seventy thousand Entered Apprentices, or bearers of burdens. All these were classed and arranged in such manner, by the wisdom of SOLOMON, that neither envy, discord, nor confusion, were suffered to interrupt or disturb the peace and good-fellowship which prevailed among the workmen.

In front of the magnificent porch were placed the two celebrated pillars—one on the left hand and one on the right hand. They are supposed to have been placed there as a memorial to the children of Israel of the happy deliverance of their forefathers from Egyptian bondage, and in commemoration of the miraculous pillars of fire and cloud. The pillar of fire gave light to the Israelites, and facilitated their march; and the cloud proved darkness to PHARAOH and his host, and retarded their pursuit. King SOLOMON, therefore, ordered these pillars to be placed at the entrance of the Temple, as the most conspicuous part, that the children of Israel might have that happy event continually before their eyes, in going to and returning from divine worship.

KING SOLOMON'S TEMPLE.

THE place chosen for the erection of this magnificent structure was Mount Moriah, a lofty hill, situated in the north-easterly part of the city of Jerusalem, having Mount Zion on the south-west, Mount Acra on the west, and Mount Olives on the east. The summit of this mountain was unequal, and its aides irregular; but it was a favorite object of the Jews to level and extend it. The plan and model of the Temple was in the same form as the Tabernacle of Moses, but was of much larger dimensions.

King SOLOMON commenced the erection of the Temple in the year B.C. 1011, about 480 years after the Exodus and the building of the Tabernacle in the wilderness; and it was finished B.C. 1004, having occupied seven years and six months in the building.

The foundations were laid at a profound depth, and consisted of stones of immense size and great durability. They were closely mortised into the rock, so as to form a secure basis for the substantial erection of the sacred edifice.

The building does not appear to have been so remarkable for its magnitude, as for the magnificence of its ornaments and the value of its materials. The porch was 120 cubits, or 210 feet high, and the rest of the building was in height but 30 cubits, or 52½ feet; so that the form of the whole house was thus:—It was situated due east and west, the holy of holies being to the westward, and the porch or entrance toward the east. The whole length, from east to west, was 70 cubits, or 122½ feet. The breadth, exclusive of the side chambers, was 20 cubits, or 35 feet; the height of the holy place and the holy of holies was 30 cubits, or 52½ feet, and the porch stood at the eastern end, like a lofty steeple, 120 cubits, or 210 feet high. In fact, as LIGHTFOOT remarks, the Temple much resembled a modern church, with this difference, that the steeple, which was placed over the porch, was situated at the east end.

Around the north and south sides and the west end were built chambers of three stories, each story being 5 cubits in height, or 15 cubits, 26 feet 9 inches in all—and these were united to the outside wall of the house.

The windows, which were used for ventillation rather than for light, which was derived from the sacred candlesticks, were placed in the wall of the Temple that was above the roof of the side chambers. But that part which included the holy of holies was without any aperture whatever, to which SOLOMON alludes in the passage, "The LORD said that HE would dwell in the thick darkness."

The Temple was divided, internally, into three parts—the porch, the sanctuary, and the holy of holies; the breadth of all these was of course the same, namely, 20 cubits, or 35 feet, but they differed in length. The porch was 17 feet 6 inches in length, the sanctuary 70 feet, and the holy of holies 35, or, in the Hebrew measure, 10, 40, and 20 cubits. The entrance from the porch into the sanctuary was through a wide door of olive posts and leaves of fir; but the door between the sanctuary and the holy of holies was composed entirely of olive-wood. These doors were always open, and the aperture closed by a suspended curtain. The partition between the sanctuary and the holy of holies partly consisted of an open network, so that the incense daily offered in the former place might be diffused through the interstices into the latter.

In the sanctuary were placed the golden candlestick, the table of shew-bread, and the altar of incense. The holy of holies contained nothing but the ark of the covenant, which included the tables of the law.

The frame-work of the Temple consisted of massive stone, but it was wainscoted with cedar, which was covered with gold. The boards within the Temple were ornamented with carved work, skillfully representing cherubim, palm-leaves, and flowers. The ceiling was supported by beams of cedar-wood, which, with that used in the wainscoting, was supplied by the workmen of HIRAM, King of Tyre, from the forest of Lebanon. The floor was throughout made of cedar, but boarded over with planks of fir.

The Temple, thus constructed, was surrounded by various courts and high walls, and thus occupied the entire summit of Mount Moriah. The first of the courts was the Court of the Gentiles, beyond which Gentiles were prohibited from passing. Within this, and separated from it by a low wall, was the Court of the Children of Israel, and inside of that, separated from it by another wall, was the Court of the Priests, in which was placed the altar of burnt offerings. From this court there was an ascent of twelve steps to the porch of the Temple, before which stood the two pillars of JACHIN and BOAZ.

For the erection of this magnificent structure, besides the sums annually appropriated by SOLOMON, his father, DAVID, had left one hundred thousand talents of gold and a million talents of silver, equal to nearly four thousand millions of dollars.

The year after the Temple was finished, it was dedicated with those solemn ceremonies which are alluded to in this degree. The dedicatory ceremonies commenced on Friday, the 30th of October, and lasted for fourteen days, terminating on Thursday, the 12th of November, although the people were not dismissed until the following Saturday. Seven days of this festival were devoted to the dedication exclusively, and the remaining seven to the Feast of Tabernacles, which followed.

Emblems of Master Mason's Degree

In this section are also explained a variety of appropriate emblems, with which the skillful brother will not fail to make himself familiarly acquainted, and they are thus explained:

THE THREE STEPS,

Usually delineated upon the Master's carpet, are emblematical of the three principal stages of human life, viz:—YOUTH, MANHOOD, and AGE. In *Youth*, as Entered Apprentices, we ought industriously to occupy our minds in the attainment of useful knowledge; in *Manhood*, as Fellow-Crafts, we should apply our knowledge to the discharge of our respective duties to GOD, our neighbor, and ourselves; that so, in *Age*, as Master Masons, we may enjoy the happy reflection consequent on a well-spent life, and die in the hope of a glorious immortality.

The morning is the youth of the day; youth is vigorous till noon; then comes the age of man; to which succeeds the evening of old age; sunset follows the evening or death of the day. Frugality is a great revenue, but no where greater than in this case.

THE POT OF INCENSE

Is an emblem of a pure heart, which is always an acceptable sacrifice to the Deity; and as this glows with fervent heat, so should our hearts continually glow with gratitude to the great and beneficent Author of our existence, for the manifold blessings and comforts we enjoy.

THE BEE-HIVE

Is an emblem of industry, and recommends the practice of that virtue to all created beings, from the highest seraph in heaven to the lowest reptile of the dust. It teaches us that, as we carne into the world rational and intelligent beings, so we should ever be industrious ones; never sitting down contented while our fellow-creatures around us are in want, especially when it is in our power to relieve them without inconvenience to ourselves.

When we take a survey of Nature, we view man in his infancy, more helpless and indigent than the brute creation: he lies languishing for days, months, and years, totally incapable of providing sustenance for himself, of guarding against the attack of the wild beasts of the field, or sheltering himself from the inclemencies of the weather.

It might have pleased the great Creator of heaven and earth to have made man independent of all other beings; but as dependence is one of the strongest bonds of society, mankind were made dependent on each other for protection and security, as they thereby enjoy better opportunities of fulfilling the duties of reciprocal love and friendship. Thus was man formed for social and active life—the noblest part of the work of GOD; and he that will so demean himself as not to be endeavoring to add to the common stock of knowledge and understanding, may be deemed a *drone* in the *hive* of Nature, a useless member of society, and unworthy of our protection as Masons.

THE BOOK OF CONSTITUTIONS, GUARDED BY THE TILERS SWORD,

Reminds us that we should be ever watchful and guarded in our thoughts, words, and actions, particularly when before the enemies of Masonry—ever bearing in remembrance those truly Masonic virtues, *silence* and *circumspection.*

THE SWORD, POINTING TO A NAKED HEART,

Demonstrates that justice will sooner or later overtake us; and although our thoughts, words, and actions may be hidden from the eyes of man, yet that

ALL-SEEING EYE,

whom the SUN, MOON, and STARS obey, and under whose watchful care even COMETS perform their stupendous revolutions, pervades the inmost recesses of the human HEART, and will reward us according to our merits.

THE ANCHOR AND ARK

Are emblems of a well-grounded *hope* and a well-spent life. They are emblematical of that divine *Ark* which safely wafts us over this tempestuous sea of troubles, and that *Anchor* which shall safely moor us in a peaceful harbor, where the wicked cease from troubling, and the weary shall find rest.

THE FORTY-SEVENTH PROBLEM OF EUCLID.

This was an invention of our ancient friend and brother, the great PYTHAGORAS, who, in his travels through Asia, Africa, and Europe, was initiated into the several orders of priesthood. and raised to the sublime degree of Master Mason. This wise philosopher enriched his mind abundantly in a general knowledge of things and more especially in Geometry, or Masonry. On this subject he drew out many problems and theorems; and, among the most distinguished, he erected this, which, in the joy of his heart, he called EUREKA, in the Grecian language signifying *I have found it;* and upon the discovery of which he is said to have sacrificed a hecatomb. It teaches Masons to be general lovers of the arts and sciences.

THE HOUR-GLASS

Is an emblem of human life. Behold! how swiftly the sands run, and how rapidly our lives are drawing to a close! We cannot without astonishment behold the little particles which are contained in this machine; how they pass away almost imperceptibly; and yet, to our surprise, in the short space of an hour they are all exhausted! Thus wastes man. To-day, he puts forth the tender leaves of Hope; to-morrow, blossoms, and bears his blushing honors thick upon him; the next day comes a frost, which nips the shoot; and when he thinks his greatness is still, aspiring, he falls like autumn leaves, to enrich our mother-earth.

THE SCYTHE

Is an emblem of Time, which cuts the brittle thread of life, and launches us into eternity. Behold! what havoc the scythe of Time makes among the human race! If by chance we should escape the numerous evils incident to childhood and youth, and with health and vigor arrive to the years of manhood; yet, withal, we must soon be cut down by the all-devouring scythe of Time, and be gathered into the land where our fathers have gone before us.

*　　*　　*　　*　　*　　*　　*

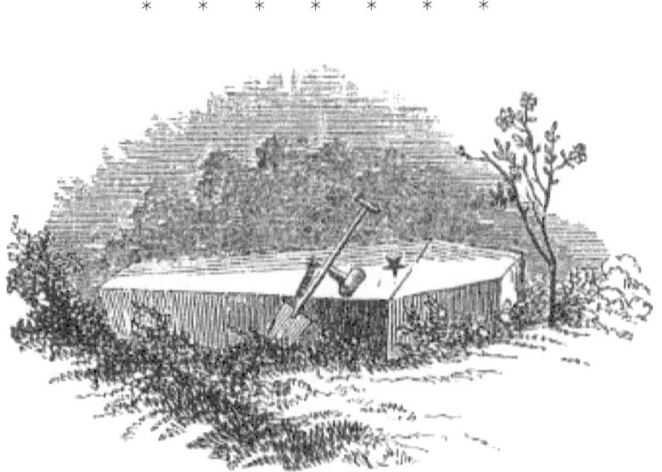

Thus we close the explanation of the emblems upon the solemn thought of death, which, without revelation, is dark and gloomy; but we are suddenly revived by the *ever-green* and ever-living *sprig* of Faith in the merits of the Lion of the tribe of Judah; which strengthens us, with confidence and composure, to look forward to a blessed immortality; and doubt not, but in the glorious morn of the resurrection, our bodies will rise, and become as incorruptible as our souls.

Then let us imitate the good man in his virtuous and amiable conduct; in his unfeigned piety to GOD; in his inflexible fidelity to his trust; that we may welcome the grim tyrant Death, and receive him as a kind messenger sent from our Supreme Grand Master, to translate us from this imperfect to that all-perfect, glorious, and celestial Lodge above, where the Supreme Architect of the Universe presides.

CHARGE TO THE CANDIDATE.

BROTHER: Your zeal for our institution, the progress you have made in our mysteries, and your steady conformity to our useful regulations, have pointed you out as a proper object for this peculiar mark of our favor.

Duty and honor now alike bind you to be faithful to every trust; to support the dignity of your character on all occasions; and strenuously to enforce, by precept and example, a steady obedience to the tenets of Freemasonry. Exemplary conduct, on your part, will convince the world that merit is the just title to our privileges, and that on you our favors have not been undeservedly bestowed.

In this respectable character, you are authorized to correct the irregularities of your less informed brethren; to fortify their minds with resolution against the snares of the insidious, and to guard them against every allurement to vicious practices. To preserve unsullied the reputation of the Fraternity ought to be your constant care; and, therefore, it becomes your province to caution the inexperienced against a breach of fidelity. To your inferiors in rank or office, you are to recommend obedience and submission; to your equals, courtesy and affability; to your superiors, kindness and condescension. Universal obedience you are zealously to inculcate; and by the regularity of your own conduct, endeavor to remove every aspersion against this venerable institution. Our ancient landmarks you are carefully to preserve, and not suffer them on any pretense to be infringed, or countenance a deviation from our established customs.

Your honor and reputation are concerned in supporting with dignity the respectable character you now bear. Let no motive, therefore, make you swerve from your duty, violate your vows, or betray your trust; but be true and faithful, and imitate the example of that celebrated artist whom you have this evening represented. Thus you will render yourself deserving of the honor which we have conferred, and worthy of the confidence we have reposed in you.

Having thus given a general summary of the Lectures restricted to the three Degrees of the Order, and made such remarks on each Degree as might illustrate the subjects treated, little farther can be wanted to encourage the zealous Mason to persevere in his researches. He who has traced the Art in a regular progress, from the commencement of the First to the conclusion of the Third Degree, according to the plan here laid down, must have amassed an ample store of knowledge, and will reflect with pleasure on the good effects of his past diligence and attention. By applying the improvements he has made to the general advantage of society, he will secure to himself the veneration of Masons and the approbation of all good men.

LODGE JEWELS.

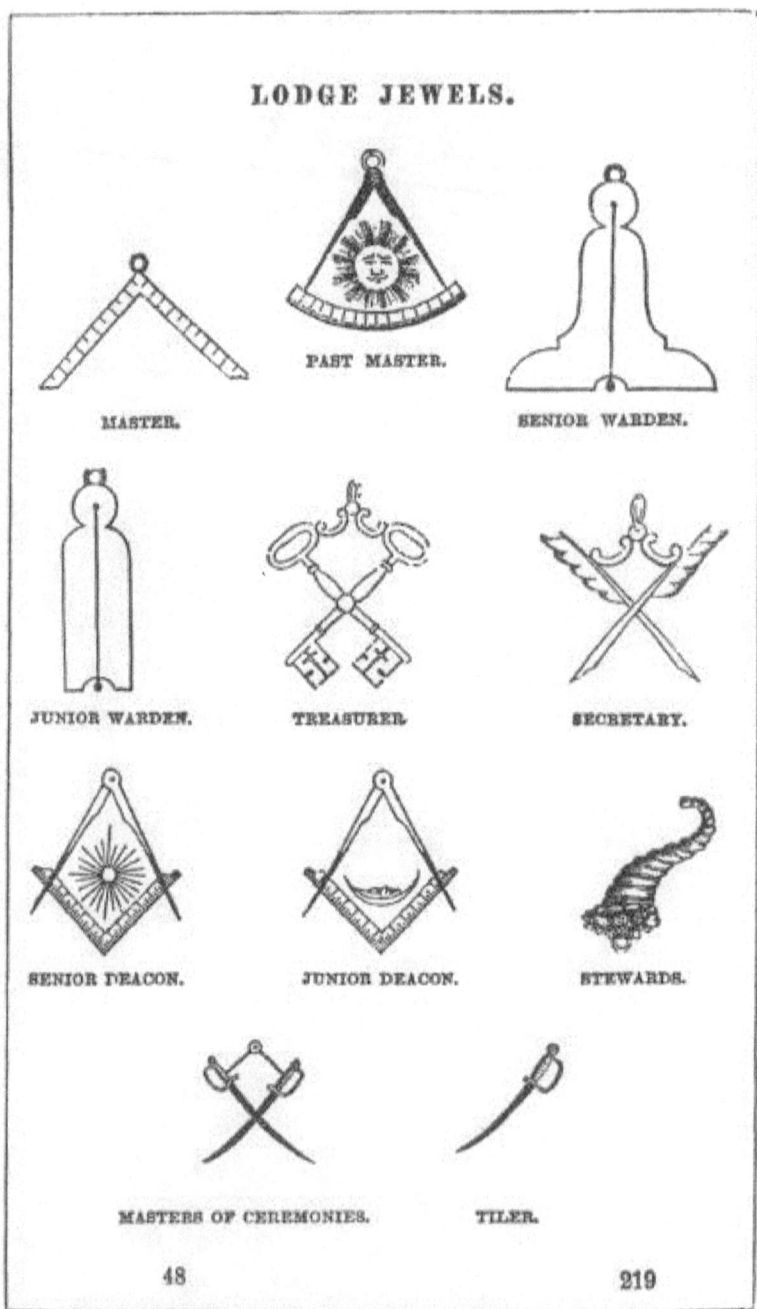

MASTER.

PAST MASTER.

SENIOR WARDEN.

JUNIOR WARDEN.

TREASURER.

SECRETARY.

SENIOR DEACON.

JUNIOR DEACON.

STEWARDS.

MASTERS OF CEREMONIES.

TILER.

48

219

128

OFFICERS' CLOTHING AND JEWELS.

SUBORDINATE LODGE.

The COLLAR must be blue, (of velvet, silk, or merino,) trimmed with material of same color, bordered with silver lace. They may be ornamented with embroidery or stars. The Jewel is to be suspended from the point of the Collar.

The APRON is white lambskin, square at the corners—13x15 in., with flap triangular shape, 5 inches deep at the point, lined and bordered with blue. On the flap is delineated an eye, irradiated; on the area the square and compass and the letter G, irradiated, with flat Masonic tags suspended on either side from under the flap. See illustration p.100.

JEWELS (silver).

Past Master	wears	a compass opened on a quarter circle, sun in the center.[1]
Master	,,	a square.
Senior Warden	,,	a level.
Junior Warden	,,	a plumb.
Treasurer	,,	cross keys.
Secretary	,,	cross pens.
Senior Deacon	,,	square and compass, sun in the center.
Junior Deacon	,,	square and compass, quar. moon in center.
Stewards	,,	a cornucopia.
Chaplain	,,	an open Bible.
Marshal	,,	cross batons.
Organist	,,	a lyre.
M's of Ceremonies	,,	cross swords.
Tiler	,,	a sword, sabre shape.

---

[1] This Jewel may be made of gold, and enclosed to a wreath.

129

GRAND LODGE JEWELS.

GRAND MASTER.

DEP. GR. MASTER.

SEN. GR. WARDEN.

JUN. GR. WARDEN.

GR. TREASURER.

GR. SECRETARY.

GR. CHAPLAIN.

GR. MARSHAL.

GR. STAND. BEARER.

GR. SWORD BEARER.

GR. STEWARDS.

GR. DEACONS.

GR. PURSUIVANT.

GR. LECTURER.

GR. TILER.

GRAND LODGE.

The COLLARS of a Grand Lodge should be made of royal purple silk velvet, enriched with gold embroidery, trimmed with gold lace, and lined with purple silk. The Jewel is to be suspended from the point of the Collar.

The APRON is white lambskin, 13×15 in., square at the corners, trimmed with purple and gold, and flat Masonic tags. The Apron and Collar should be made to correspond in richness to the grade of the officer for whom they were intended.

JEWELS.

The Jewels of a Grand Lodge are made of gold (or yellow metal), and suspended in a circle or wreath.

Grand Master	wears	a compass opened on a quarter circle, sun in the center.
Past Grand Master	,,	the same, with triangle.
Deputy Grand Master	,,	a square.
Senior Grand Warden	,,	a level.
Junior Grand Warden	,,	a plumb.
Grand Treasurer	,,	cross keys.
Grand Secretary	,,	cross pens.
Grand Chaplains	,,	the Holy Bible.
Grand Marshal	,,	a scroll and sword crossed.
G. Standard Bearer	,,	a plate, representing a banner.
Grand Sword Bearer	,,	a straight sword.
Grand Stewards	,,	a cornucopia.
Grand Deacons	,,	a dove, bearing an olive branch.
Grand Pursuivant	,,	a sword and trumpet crossed.
Grand Tiler	,,	cross swords.

ANCIENT CEREMONIES.

THESE CEREMONIES should be carefully studied and well understood by every Master of a Lodge. They include the ceremonies of Opening and Closing Lodges; Form of Petition, and Directions for Organizing Lodges; Consecrating, Dedicating, and Constituting new Lodges; Installing Officers of Grand and Subordinate Lodges; Grand Visitations; Annual Festivals; Laying Foundation Stones; Dedication of Masonic Halls; Sorrow Lodges; Funeral Services; Processions, etc., etc.

SECTION I.

CONSECRATION, DEDICATION, CONSTITUTION, AND INSTALLATION OF OFFICERS OF A NEW LODGE.

ANY number of Master Masons, not less than seven, desirous of forming a new Lodge, must apply, by petition[1], to the Grand Master, Deputy Grand Master, or Grand Lodge of the State in which they reside, as follows;

---

[1] The mode of applying by petition to the Grand Master for a warrant to meet as a regular Lodge, commenced only in the year 1718; previous to that time, Lodges were empowered, by inherent privileges vested in the Fraternity at large, to meet and act occasionally under the direction of some able architect; and the proceedings of those meetings being approved by the majority of the brethren convened at another Lodge assembled in the same district, were deemed constitutional. By such an inherent authority the Lodge of Antiquity in London now acts, having no warrant from any Grand Lodge, but an authority traced from time Immemorial, which has been long and universally admitted and acknowledged by the whole Fraternity throughout the world, and which no warrant or other instrument of any particular Masonic jurisdiction can possibly supersede.

133

FORM OF PETITION FOR A NEW LODGE.

To the M. W. Grand Master of Masons of the State of ....:

THE undersigned petitioners, being Ancient Free and Accepted Master Masons, having the prosperity of the Fraternity at heart, and willing to exert their best endeavors to promote and diffuse the genuine principles of Masonry, respectfully represent—That they are desirous of forming a new Lodge in the .... of ...., to be named , No .... They therefore pray for Letters of Dispensation, to empower them to assemble as a regular Lodge, to discharge the duties of Masonry, in a regular and constitutional manner, according to the original forms of the Order and the regulations of the Grand Lodge. They have nominated and do recommend Brother A. B. to be the first Master; Brother C. D. to be the first Senior Warden; and Brother F. F. to be the first Junior Warden of said Lodge. If the prayer of this petition shall be granted, they promise a strict conformity to the edicts of the Grand Master, and the Constitution, laws, and regulations of the Grand Lodge[1].

---

[1] This petition, being signed by at least seven regular Masons, and recommended by a Lodge or Lodges nearest to the place where the new Lodge is to be holden, is delivered to the Grand Secretary, who lays it before the G. Lodge.

In many jurisdictions, the Grand and Deputy Grand Masters, respectively, are invested with authority to grant dispensations at pleasure during the recess of the Grand Lodge; in some, they are never issued without the special direction of the Grand Lodge.

Lodges working under dispensation are merely the agents of the G. Lodge or Grand officer granting the authority; their presiding officers are not entitled to the rank of Past Masters; their officers are not privileged with a vote or voice in the Grand Lodge; they cannot change their officers without the special approbation and appointment of the Grand Lodge or Grand officer granting the authority; and in case of the cessation of such Lodges, their funds, jewels, and other property accumulated by initiations into the several degrees, become the property of the Grand Lodge, and must be delivered over to the G. Treasurer.

When Lodges that are at first instituted by dispensation have passed a proper term of probation, they make application to the Grand Lodge for a Charter of Constitution. If this be obtained, they are then confirmed in the possession of their property, and possess all the rights and privileges of regularly-constituted Lodges, as long as they conform to the Constitutions of Masonry. After a Charter is granted by the Grand Lodge, the Grand Master appoints a day and hour for consecrating and constituting the new Lodge, and for installing its Master, Wardens, and other officers. If the Grand Master, in person, attends the ceremony, the Lodge Is said to be constituted In AMPLE FORM; if the Deputy Grand Master only, it is said to be constituted in DUE FORM; but if the power of performing the ceremony is vested in any other person, it is said to be constituted in FORM.

When the Charters of Constitution are granted for places where the distance is so great as to render it inconvenient for the Grand Officers to attend, the Grand Master or his Deputy issues a written instrument, under his hand and private seal, to some worthy Present or Past Master, with full power to congregate, dedicate, and constitute the Lodge, and install its officers.

CONSECRATION.

ON the day and hour appointed, the Grand Master and his officers, or their representatives, meet in a convenient room, near to that in which the Lodge is to be consecrated, and open the Grand Lodge.

After the officers of the new Lodge are examined, they send a messenger to the Grand Master with the following message:

MOST WORSHIPFUL: The Officers and Brethren of ...... Lodge, who are now assembled at ....., have instructed me to inform you that the Most Worshipful Grand Lodge (or Grand Master) was pleased to grant them a Letter of Dispensation, bearing date the .... day of ....., in the year ...., authorizing them to form and open a Lodge of Free and Accepted Masons, in the ...... of .....; that since that period they have regularly assembled, and conducted the business of MASONRY according to the best of their abilities; that their proceedings having received the approbation of the Most Worshipful Grand Lodge, they have obtained a Charter of Constitution, and are desirous that their Lodge should be consecrated, and their Officers installed, agree ably to the ancient usages and customs of the Craft; for which purpose they are now met, and await the pleasure of the Most Worshipful Grand Master.

The Grand Lodge then walk in procession to the room of the new Lodge. When the Grand Master enters, the grand honors[1] are given, under direction of the

---

[1] The Grand Honors of Masonry are those peculiar acts and gestures by which the Craft have always been accustomed to express their homage, their joy, or their grief, on memorable occasions. They are of two kinds, the private and public, and carp of them are used on different occasions and for different purposes,

The private Grand Honors of Masonry are performed in a manner known only to Master Masons, since they can only be used in a Master's Lodge. They are practiced by the Craft only on four occasions:— when a Masonic Hall is to be consecrated, a new Lodge to be constituted, a Master slept to be installed, or a Grand Master or his Deputy to be received on an official visitation to a Lodge. They are used at all these ceremonies as tokens of congratulation and homage. And as they can only be given by Master Masons, it is evident that every consecration of a hall, or constitution of a new Lodge, every installation of a Worshipful Master, and every reception of a Grand Master, must be done in the third degree. It is also evident, from what has been said, that the mode and manner of giving the private Grand Honors can only be personally communicated to Master Masons. They are among the *aporreta*—the things forbidden to be divulged.

The public Grand Honors, as their name imports, do not partake pr this secret character. They are given on all public occasions, in the presence of the profane as well as the initiated. They are used at the laying of corner-stones of public buildings, or in other services in which the ministrations of the Fraternity are required, and especially in funerals. They are given in the following manner: Both arms are crossed on the breast, the left uppermost, and the open palms of the bands sharply striking the shoulders; they are then raised above the head, the palms striking each other, and then made to fall smartly upon the thighs. This is repeated three times, and as there are three blows given each time—namely, on the breast, on the palms of the hands, and on the thighs—making nine concussions in all, the Grand Honors are technically said to be given "by three times three." On the occasion of funerals, each one of these honors is accompanied by the words, "*The will of God is accomplished; so mote it be!*" audibly pronounced by the brethren.

Master of the new Lodge. The officers of the new Lodge resign their seats to the Grand Officers, and take their stations on their left.

If the ceremonies are performed in public, the Grand Marshal then forms the procession in the following order:

Tiler, with drawn sword;

Two Stewards, with white rods;

Master Masons, two and two;

Junior Deacons;

Senior Deacons;

These Grand Honors of Masonry have undoubtedly a classical origin, and are but an imitation of the plaudits and acclamations practiced by the ancient Greeks and Romans, in their theaters, their senates, and their public games. There is abundant evidence in the writings of the ancients that, in the days of the empire, the Romans had circumscribed the mode of doing homage to their emperors and great men when they made their appearance in public, and of expressing their approbation of actors at the theatre within as explicit rules and regulations as those that govern the system of giving the Grand Honors in Freemasonry. This was not the case in the earlier ages of Rome; for OVID, speaking of the Rabbles, says that, when they applauded, they did so without any rules of art:

"In medio plausu, plausus tunc arte carebat."

And PROPERTIUS speaks, at a later day, of the ignorance of the country people, who, at the theatres, destroyed the general harmony, by their awkward attempts to join in the modulated applauses of the more skillful citizens.

The ancient Romans had carried their science on this subject to such an extent, as to have divided these honors into three kinds, differing from each other in the mode in which the hands were struck against each other, and in the sound that thence resulted. SUETONIUS, in his Life of NERO, (cap. xx.) gives the names of these various kinds of applause, which he says were called *bombi, imbrices,* and *testæ;* and SENECA, in his *"Naturales Quæstiones,"* gives a description of the manner in which they were executed. The "bombi," or *hums,* wore produced by striking the palms of the hands together, while they were in a hollow or concave position, and doing this at frequent intervals, but with little force, so as to imitate the humming sound of a swarm of bees. The "imbrices," or *tiles,* were made by briskly striking the flattened and extended palms of the hands against each other, so as to resemble the sound of hail pattering upon the tiles of a roof. The "testæ," or *earthen vases,* were executed by striking the palm of the left hand with the fingers of the right collected into one point. By this blow a sound was elicited, which imitated that given out by an earthen vase when struck by a stick.

The Romans and other ancient nations having invested this system of applauding with all the accuracy of a science, used it in its various forms, not only for the purpose of testifying their approbation of actors in the theatre, but also bestowed it, as a mark of respect or a token of adulation, on their emperors and other great men, on the occasion of their making their appearance in public. Huzzas and cheers have, in this latter case, been generally adopted by the moderns, while the manual applause is only appropriated to successful public speakers and declaimers. The Freemasons, however, have altogether preserved the ancient custom of applause, guarding and regulating its use by as strict, though different rules, as did the Romans; and thus showing, as another evidence of the antiquity of their institution, that the "Grand Honors" of Freemasonry are legitimately derived from the "pietism" or applaudings practiced by the ancients on public occasions.—MACKEY'S *Lexicon of Freemasonry.* SEE NOTE, p. 207.

Secretaries;

Treasurers;

Past Wardens;

Junior Wardens;
Senior Wardens;

Past Masters;

Members of the higher degrees;

THE NEW LODGE.

Tiler, with drawn sword;

Stewards, with white rods;

Master Masons;

Junior and Senior Deacons;

Secretary and Treasurer;

Two brethren, carrying the Lodge;

Junior and Senior Wardens;

The Holy Writings, carried by the oldest member not in office.

Worshipful Master;

Music.

THE GRAND LODGE;

Grand Tiler, with drawn sword;

Grand Stewards, with white rods;

Grand Pursuivant, with sword;

Grand Secretary and Grand Treasurer;

A. Past Master, bearing the Holy Writings, Square, and Compasses, supported
by two Stewards, with rods;

Two Burning Tapers, borne by two Past Masters;

Grand Chaplain and Orator;

The Tuscan and Composite Orders;

The Doric, Ionic, and Corinthian Orders;

Past Grand Wardens;

Past Deputy Grand Masters;

Past Grand Masters;

The Celestial and Terrestrial Globes, borne by two brethren;

Junior Grand Warden, carrying a silver vessel with oil;

Senior Grand Warden, carrying a silver vessel with wine;

Deputy Grand Master, carrying a golden vessel with corn;

Master of the oldest Lodge, carrying the Book of

Constitutions;

GRAND MASTER,

Supported by the Grand Deacons, with white rods;

Grand Standard-Bearer;

Grand Sword-Bearer, with drawn sword.

The procession moves on to the church or house where the services are to be performed. When the front of the procession arrives at the door, they halt, open to the right and left, and face inward, while the Grand Master and others, in succession, pass through, and enter the house.

A platform is erected in front of the pulpit, and provided with seats for the accommodation of the Grand Officers.

The Bible, Square, and Compasses, and Book of Constitutions, are placed upon a table in front of the Grand Master; the Lodge[1] is placed in the center, upon a platform covered with white linen, and encompassed by the three tapers and the vessels of corn, wine, and oil.

The following services then take place:

ODE.

AIR—*Shirland.* S. M.

Great Source of Light and Love,
  To thee our songs we raise!
Oh! in thy temple, Lord above,
  Hear and accept our praise!

Shine on this festive day,
  Succeed its hoped design,
And may our Charity display
  A love resembling thine!

May this fraternal band,
  Now Consecrated—blest—
In union all distinguished stand,
  In purity be drest!

---

[1] The *Lodge*, technically speaking, is a piece of furniture, made in imitation of the Ark of the Covenant, which was constructed according to the form of the Temple. The instrument usually used on occasions of Constituting, Consecrating, and. Dedicating Lodges, is a box, of an oblong-square shape, covered with white linen.

The following, or an extemporaneous Prayer, will be offered by the Grand Chaplain:

Great, Adorable, and Supreme Being! We praise thee for all thy mercies, and especially for giving us desires to enjoy, and powers of enjoying, the delights of society. The affections which thou hast implanted in us, and which we cannot destroy without violence to our nature, are among the chief blessings which thy benign wisdom hath bestowed upon us. Help us duly to improve all our powers to the promotion of thy glory in the world, and the good of our fellow-creatures. May we be active under thy divine light, and dwell in thy truth.

Extend thy favor to us who are now entering into a Fraternal compact under peculiar obligations. Enable us to be faithful to thee, faithful in our callings in life, faithful Masons in all the duties of the Craft, and faithful to each other as members of this society. Take us under the shadow of thy protection; and to thy service and glory may we consecrate our hearts. May we always put faith in thee, have hope in salvation, and be in charity with all mankind!—AMEN.

Response by the brethren.—So mote it be.

An ORATION, by some competent brother, when practicable.

ODE.

AIR—*Duke Street.* L. M.

How blest the sacred tie, that binds,
In sweet communion kindred minds!
How swift the heavenly course they run,
Whose hearts, whose faith, whose hopes are one.

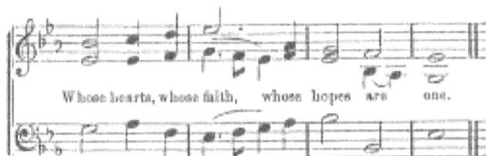

Together oft they seek the place
Where Masons meet with smiling face;
How high, how strong their raptures swell,
There's none but kindred souls can tell.

Nor shall the glowing flame expire,
When dimly burns frail Nature's fire;
Then shall they meet in realms above,
A heaven of joy, a heaven of love.

The Grand Marshal then forms the officers and members of the new Lodge in front of the Grand Master. The Deputy Grand Master addresses the Grand Master as follows:

MOST WORSHIPFUL: A number of brethren, duly instructed in the mysteries of Masonry, having assembled together at stated periods, for some time past, by virtue of a Dispensation granted them for that purpose, do now desire to be *constituted* into a *regular Lodge*, agreeably to the ancient usages and customs of the Fraternity.

The records are then presented to the Grand Master, who examines them, and, if found correct, proclaims

The records appear to be correct, and are approved. Upon due deliberation, the Grand Lodge have granted the brethren of this new Lodge a Warrant, establishing and confirming them in the rights and privileges of a regularly-constituted Lodge; which the Grand Secretary will now read.

After the Warrant is read, the Grand Master then says:

We shall now proceed, according to ancient usage, to constitute these brethren into a regular Lodge.

Whereupon the several officers of the new Lodge deliver up their jewels and badges to their Master, who presents them, with his own, to the Deputy Grand Master, and he to the Grand Master.

The Deputy Grand Master presents the Master elect to the Grand Master; saying,

MOST WORSHIPFUL: I present you Brother ...., whom the members of the Lodge now to be constituted have chosen for their Master.

The Grand Master asks the brethren if they remain satisfied with their choice. [*They bow in token of assent.*]

The Master elect then presents, severally, his Wardens and other officers, naming them and their respective offices. The Grand Master asks the brethren if they remain satisfied with ' ach and all of them. [*They bow, as before.*]

The officers and members of the new Lodge form in front of the Grand Master; and the ceremonies of Consecration commence.

The Grand Master and Grand Officers now form themselves in order around the Lodge—all kneeling.

A piece of solemn music is performed while the Lodge is being uncovered.

After which, the first clause of the *Consecration Prayer* is rehearsed by the Grand Chaplain, as follows:

Great Architect of the Universe! Maker and Ruler of all Worlds! Deign, from thy celestial temple, from realms of light and glory, to bless us in all the purposes of our present assembly! We humbly invoke thee to give us at this, and at all times, *wisdom* in all our doings, *strength* of mind in all our difficulties, and the *beauty* of harmony in all our communications! Permit us, O thou Author of Light and Life, great Source of Love and Happiness, to erect this Lodge, and now solemnly to consecrate it to the honor of thy glory!

Response.—As it was in the beginning, is now, and ever shall be; world without end.—AMEN.

The Deputy Grand Master presents the golden vessel of corn, and the Senior and Junior Grand Wardens the silver vessels of wine and oil, to the Grand Master, who sprinkles the elements of Consecration upon the Lodge.

VESSELS OF CONSECRATION.

The Grand Chaplain then continues:

Grant, O Lord our God, that those who are now about to be invested with the government of this Lodge may be endowed with wisdom to instruct their brethren in all their duties. May *brotherly love*, *relief*, and *truth* always prevail among the members of this Lodge! May this bond of union continue to strengthen the Lodges throughout the world!

Bless all our brethren, wherever dispersed; and grant speedy relief to all who are either oppressed or distressed.

We affectionately commend to thee all the members of thy whole family. May they increase in grace, in the knowledge of thee, and in the love of each other.

Finally: May we finish all our work here below with thy approbation; and then have our transition from this earthly abode. to thy heavenly temple above, there to enjoy light, glory, and bliss, ineffable and eternal!

Response.—As it was in the beginning, is now, and ever shall be. So mote it be.—AMEN.

DEDICATION.

A piece of solemn music is performed.

The Grand Master, then standing with his hands stretched forth over the Lodge, exclaims,

To the memory of the Holy SAINTS JOHN, we dedicate this Lodge. May every brother revere their character and imitate their virtues!

Response.—As it was in the beginning, is now, and ever shall be; world without end.—AMEN.

A piece of music is performed while the brethren of the new Lodge advance in procession to salute the Grand Lodge, with their hands crossed upon their breasts, and bowing as they pass. They then take their places as they were.

CONSTITUTION.

The Grand Master then rises, and Constitutes the new Lodge in the following form, all the brethren standing at the same time:

In the name of the Most Worshipful Grand Lodge, I now constitute and form you, my beloved brethren, into a regular Lodge of Free and Accepted Masons. From henceforth I empower you to meet as a regular Lodge, constituted in conformity to the rites of our Order, and the Charges of our Ancient and Honorable Fraternity; and may the Supreme Architect of the Universe prosper, direct, and counsel you in all your doings!

Response.—So mote it be.—AMEN.

The public grand honors are then given.

The powers and privileges of a Subordinate or Warranted Lodge are such as are defined in its Warrant, by the Constitutions of the Grand Lodge granting the same, and the Ancient Landmarks and General Regulations. They are divided into—

1. EXECUTIVE: in the direction and performance of its work, under the control of its Master, and in all other matters in aid of the Master, who has the primary executive power of a Lodge.

2. LEGISLATIVE: embracing all matters relating to its internal concerns, not in derogation of the Ancient Landmarks, the Constitutions and General Regulations of the Grand Lodge, and its own particular By-Laws; and

3. JUDICIAL: embracing the exercise of discipline, and settlement of controversies between and over all its members (except the Master), and over all Masons and non-affiliated brethren within its jurisdiction, subject to an appeal to the Grand Lodge.

The powers of a Warranted Lodge are, therefore, divided into two classes, INHERENT and CONSTITUTIONAL:

The inherent powers of a Lodge, controlled only by the Ancient Landmarks, are—

1. To decide who shall be admitted members of or initiated therein; that is, of persons properly qualified.

2. To make Masons (not more than five at one meeting), of those it has decided to admit.

3. To place on trial a member against whom charges may have been preferred, to pronounce sentence, and enforce discipline.

144

4. To elect and install its officers.

5. To fix its time of meeting.

6. To require its members to contribute to its funds.

7. To be represented at all communications of the Grand Lodge.

8. To instruct its representatives, for their government, at all such communications of the Grand Lodge.

The constitutional powers of a Lodge, subject to control by the Grand Lodge, are—

1. To make a code of By-Laws for its internal government, not in derogation of its inalienable rights, or of those of its members.

2. To perform all the work pertaining to the three degrees of Ancient Craft Masonry.

3. To transact all business that can be legally transacted by a duly-constituted Lodge of Freemasons.

4. To appeal to the Grand Master or Grand Lodge from the decision of the presiding-officer.

5. To change its place of meeting.

6. To control its funds.

INSTALLATION
OF THE
OFFICERS OF A LODGE.

THE new Lodge having been Consecrated, Dedicated and Constituted, the officers are then to be installed.

At every annual election in a warranted Lodge, it is necessary that the officers should be installed. This ceremony may be performed by any Past Master. At the Annual Installation, the Installing Officer appoints some Present or Past Master, or, if none be present, an old well-informed Master Mason, to act as Marshal, whose duties will be to present the officers elect severally in front of the altar for installation.

The jewels of the several officers are collected, and laid in an orderly manner upon the altar, for convenient use.

The Grand Master or Installing Officer then says:

RIGHT WORSHIPFUL DEPUTY: Have you carefully examined the Master nominated in the warrant (or elect), and do you find him well-skilled in the noble science and the royal art?

The Deputy replies:

MOST WORSHIPFUL GRAND MASTER: I have carefully examined, and so find him[1].

G. M. You will then present him at the altar for installation.

The Deputy, taking the Master elect, presents him at the altar, saying:

MOST WORSHIPFUL GRAND MASTER: I present my worthy Brother, A. B., to be installed Master of this [new] Lodge. I find him to be of good morals and of great skill, true and trusty; and as he is a lover of the Fraternity, I doubt not he will discharge his duties with fidelity and with honor.

The Grand Master then addresses him:

BROTHER: Previous to your investiture, it is necessary that you should signify your assent to those Ancient Charges and Regulations which point out the duty of a Master of a Lodge.

The Grand Master then reads a summary of the Ancient Charges to the Master elect, as follows:

---

[1] A private examination is understood to precede the installation of the Master.

I. You agree to be a good man and true, and strictly to obey the moral law?

Ans. I do.

II. You agree to be a peaceful citizen, and cheerfully to conform to the laws of the country in which you reside?

Ans. I do.

III. You promise not to be concerned in plots and conspiracies against the government, but patiently to submit to the law and the constituted authorities?

Ans. I do.

IV. You agree to pay a proper respect to the civil magistrates, to work diligently, live creditably, and act honorably by all men?

Ans. I do.

V. You agree to hold in veneration the original rulers and patrons of the Order of Masonry, and their regular successors, supreme and subordinate, according to their stations; and to submit to the awards and resolutions of your brethren, in Lodge convened, in every case consistent with the Constitutions of the Order?

Ans. I do.

VI. You agree to avoid private piques and quarrels, and to guard against intemperance and excess?

Ans. I do.

VII. You agree to be cautious in your behavior, courteous to your brethren, and faithful to your Lodge?

Ans. I do.

VIII. You promise to respect genuine brethren, and to discountenance impostors, and all dissenters from the original plan of Masonry?

Ans. I do.

IX. You agree to promote the general good of society, to cultivate the social virtues, and to propagate the knowledge of the mystic art?

Ans. I do.

X. You promise to pay homage to the Grand Master for the time being, and to his officers when duly installed; and strictly to conform to every edict of the Grand Lodge, or General Assembly of Masons, that is not subversive of the principles and ground-work of Masonry?

Ans. I do.

XI. You admit that it is not in the power of any man, or body of men, to make innovations in the body of Masonry?

Ans. I do.

XII. You promise a regular attendance on the committees and communications of the Grand Lodge, on receiving proper notice; and to pay attention to all the duties of Masonry, on convenient occasions?

Ans. I do.

XIII. You admit that no new Lodge shall be formed without permission of the Grand Lodge; and that no countenance be given to any irregular Lodge, or to any person clandestinely initiated therein, being contrary to the Ancient Charges of the Order?

Ans. I do.

XIV. You admit that no person can be regularly made a Mason in, or admitted a member of, any regular Lodge, without previous notice, and due inquiry into his character?

Ans. I do.

XV. You agree that no visitors shall be received into your Lodge without due examination, and producing proper vouchers of their having been initiated into a regular Lodge?

Ans. I do.

These are the Regulations of Free and Accepted Masons.

The Grand Master then addresses the Master elect as follows:

Do you submit to these Charges, and promise to support these Regulations, as Masters have done in all ages before you?

The Master having signified his cordial submission, as before, the Grand Master thus addresses him;

BROTHER A. B.: In consequence of your conformity to the Charges and Regulations of the Order, you are now to be installed Master of this Lodge, in full confidence of your care, skill, and capacity to govern the same.

The Master is then regularly invested with the insignia of his office, and the furniture and implements of his Lodge. The various implements of his profession are emblematical of our conduct in life, and upon this occasion are carefully enumerated.

The *Holy Writings*, that great light in Masonry, will guide you to all truth; it will direct your paths to the temple of happiness, and point out to you the whole duty of man.

The *Square* teaches us to regulate our actions by rule and line, and to harmonize our conduct by the principles of morality and virtue.

The *Compasses* teach us to limit our desires in every station, that, rising to eminence by merit, we may live respected and die regretted.

The *Rule* directs that we should punctually observe our duty; press forward in the path of virtue, and, neither inclining to the right nor to the left, in all our actions have eternity in view.

The *Line* teaches us the criterion of moral rectitude, to avoid dissimulation in conversation and action, and to direct our steps to the path which leads to immortality.

The *Book of Constitutions* you are to search at all times. Cause it to be read in your Lodge, that none may pretend ignorance of the excellent precepts it enjoins.

You now receive in charge the *Charter*, by the authority of which this Lodge is held. You are carefully to preserve, and in no case should it ever be out of your immediate control, and duly transmit it to your successor in office.

You will also receive in charge the *By-Laws* of your Lodge, which you are to see carefully and punctually executed.

You will now be solemnly inducted into the oriental chair of King SOLOMON; during the performance of this ceremony it is requested that all but regularly-installed Masters of Lodges and Past Masters will retire[1].

---

[1] If the installation is performed in a public place, this as well as other private ceremonies are omitted.

All but actual Masters and Past Masters of Warranted Lodges[1] are required to retire (or, if more convenient, are requested to face to the West); the new Master is then invested with the mysteries of the Past Master's degree, and solemnly inducted into the oriental chair of SOLOMON. When the doors are opened, the brethren return (or are requested to face the East); and, forming an avenue on each side, from the West to the East, the new Master being in the chair, the Grand Master says:

Master, behold your brethren!

Brethren, behold your Master!

The grand honors are then given.

When the grand honors are given, a procession is formed, and the brethren pass around the Lodge, signifying their respect and obedience by the usual distinctive marks in the different degrees; during which time the following Installation Ode may be sung:

---

[1] Chapter Past Masters, who have never presided over a Symbolic Lodge are not permitted to be present at this ceremony.

Music—*Italian Hymn.*

Hail, Masonry divine,
Glory of ages, shine;
  Long mayst thou reign!
Where'er thy Lodges stand,
May they have great command,
And always grace the land;
Thou art divine.

Great fabrics still arise,
And grace the azure skies—
  Great are thy schemes;
Thy noble orders are
Matchless beyond compare;
No art with thee can share;
Thou art divine.

HIRAM, the architect,
Did all the Craft direct
  How they should build;
SOLOMON, great Israel's king,
Did mighty blessings bring,
And left us room to sing,
Hail, Royal Art!

After the singing of the ode, the Master calls the Lodge to order, and the other officers are respectively presented in the same manner as the Master, by the Conductor, When the installing officer delivers to each a short Charge, as follows:

THE SENIOR WARDEN.

BROTHER C. D.: You are appointed[1] Senior Warden of this Lodge, and are now invested with the insignia of your office.

The *Level* demonstrates that we are descended from the same stock, partake of the same nature, and share the same hope; and though distinctions among men are necessary to preserve subordination, yet no eminence of station should make us forget that we are brethren; for he who is placed on the lowest spoke of Fortune's wheel may be entitled to our regard; because a time will come, and the wisest knows not how soon, when all distinctions, but that of goodness, shall cease; and Death, the grand leveler of human greatness, reduce us to the same state.

Your regular attendance on our stated meetings is essentially necessary. In the absence of the Master, you are to govern this Lodge; in his presence, you are to assist him in the government of it. I firmly rely on your knowledge of Masonry and attachment to the Lodge for the faithful discharge of the duties of this important trust. *Look well to the West.*

He is conducted to his station in the Lodge.

THE JUNIOR WARDEN.

BROTHER E. F: You are appointed Junior Warden of this Lodge, and are now invested with the badge of your office.

The *Plumb* admonishes us to walk uprightly in our several stations; to hold the scales of Justice in equal poise; to observe the just medium between intemperance and pleasure; and to make our passions and prejudices coincide with the line of our duty. To you is committed the superintendence of the Craft during the hours of refreshment: it is, therefore, indispensably necessary that you should not only be temperate and discreet in the indulgence of your own inclinations, but carefully observe that none of the Craft be suffered to convert the purposes of refreshment into intemperance and excess.—Your regular and punctual attendance is particularly requested, and I have no doubt that you will faithfully execute the duty which you owe to your present appointment.—*Look well to the South.*

He is conducted to his station.

---

[1] When the Installation is not of the officers of a new Lodge, the words "have been elected," should be substituted for the words "are appointed." in all cases where the officer is chosen by ballot.

THE TREASURER.

BROTHER G. H.: You are appointed Treasurer of this Lodge, and are now invested with the badge of your office. It is your duty to receive all moneys from the hands of the Secretary; keep just and regular accounts of the same, and pay them out by order of the Worshipful Master and the consent of the Lodge. I trust your regard for the Fraternity will prompt you to the faithful discharge of the duties of your office.

He is conducted to his station.

THE SECRETARY.

BROTHER I. K.: You are appointed Secretary of this Lodge, and are now invested with the badge of your office. It is your duty to observe all the proceedings of the Lodge; make a fair record of all things proper to be written; receive all moneys due the Lodge, and pay them over to the Treasurer. Your good inclination to Masonry and this Lodge, I hope, will induce you to discharge the duties of your office with fidelity, and, by so doing, you will merit the esteem and applause of your brethren.

He is conducted to his station.

THE CHAPLAIN.

REV. BROTHER L. M.: You are appointed Chaplain of this Lodge, and are now invested with the badge of your office. It is your duty to perform those solemn services which we should constantly render to our infinite Creator; and which, when offered by one whose holy profession is "to point to heaven, and lead the way," may, by refining our souls, strengthening our virtues, and purifying our minds, prepare us for admission into the society of those above, whose happiness will be as endless as it is perfect.

THE SENIOR AND JUNIOR DEACONS.

BROTHERS L. M. AND N. O.: You are appointed Deacons of this Lodge, and are now invested with the badge of your office. It is your province to attend on the Master and Wardens, and to act as their proxies in the active duties of the Lodge; such as in the reception of candidates into the different degrees of Masonry; the introduction and accommodation of visitors, and in the immediate practice of our rites. The Square and Compasses, as badges of your office, I intrust to your care, not doubting your vigilance and attention.

They are conducted to their stations.

THE STEWARDS, OR MASTERS OF CEREMONIES[1].

BROTHERS R. S. AND T. U.: You are appointed Stewards (Masters of Ceremonies) of this Lodge, and are now invested with the badge of your office. You are to assist the Deacons and other officers in performing their respective duties. Your regular and early attendance at our meetings will afford the best proof of your zeal and attachment to the Lodge.

THE TILER.

BROTHER V. W.: You are appointed Tiler of this Lodge, and I invest you with the implement of your office. As the sword is placed in the hands of the Tiler, to enable him effectually to guard against the approach of cowans and eavesdroppers, and suffer none to pass or repass but such as are duly qualified, so it should admonish us to set a guard over our thoughts, a watch at our lips, post a sentinel over our actions; thereby preventing the approach of every unworthy thought or deed, and preserving consciences void of offense toward GOD and toward man. Your early and punctual attendance will afford the best proof of your zeal for the institution.

He is conducted to his station.

CHARGES TO THE OFFICERS.

WORSHIPFUL MASTER: The Grand Lodge having committed to your care the superintendence and government of the brethren who are to compose this Lodge, you cannot be insensible of the obligations which devolve on you as their head, nor of your responsibility for the faithful discharge of the important duties annexed to your appointment. The honor, reputation, and usefulness of your Lodge will materially depend on the skill and assiduity with which you manage its concerns; while the happiness of its members will be generally promoted, in proportion to the zeal and ability with which you propagate the genuine principles of our institution.

For a pattern of imitation, consider the great luminary of Nature, which, rising in the East, regularly diffuses light and luster to all within the circle. In like manner, it is your province to spread and communicate light and instruction to the brethren of your Lodge. Forcibly impress upon them the dignity and high importance of Masonry; and seriously admonish them never to disgrace it. Charge them to practice out of the Lodge those duties which they have been taught in it; and by amiable, discreet, and virtuous conduct, to convince mankind of the goodness of the institution; so that when a person is said to be a member of it, the world may know that he is one to whom the burdened heart may pour out its sorrows; to whom distress may prefer its suit; whose hand is guided by justice, and whose heart is expanded by benevolence. In short, by a diligent observance of the By-laws of

---

[1] Many Lodges have abolished the title of Stewards, and substituted that of Masters of Ceremonies, who perform the duties appertaining to the former.

your Lodge, the Constitutions of Masonry, and, above all, the Holy Scriptures, which are given as a rule and guide to your faith, you will be enabled to acquit yourself with honor and reputation, and lay up a *crown of rejoicing*, which shall continue when time shall be no more.

BROTHER SENIOR AND JUNIOR WARDENS: You are too well acquainted with the principles of Masonry, to warrant any distrust that you will be found wanting in the discharge of your respective duties. Suffice it to say, that what you have seen praiseworthy in others, you should carefully imitate; and what in them may have appeared defective, you should in yourselves amend. You should be examples of good order and regularity; for it is only by a due regard to the laws, in your own conduct, that you can expect obedience to them from others. You are assiduously to assist the Master in the discharge of his trust; diffusing light and imparting knowledge to all whom he shall place under your care. In the absence of the Master, you will succeed to higher duties; your acquirements must, therefore, be such, as that the Craft may never suffer for want of proper instruction. From the spirit which you have hitherto evinced, I entertain no doubt that your future conduct will be such as to merit the applause of your brethren and the testimony of a good conscience.

The members of the Lodge then, all standing, the Grand Master delivers the following

CHARGE TO THE BRETHREN OF THE LODGE.

Such is the nature of our constitution, that as some must of necessity rule and teach, so others must, of course, learn to submit and obey. Humility, in both, is an essential duty. The officers who are appointed to govern your Lodge are sufficiently conversant with the rules of propriety, and the laws of the institution, to avoid exceeding the powers with which they are intrusted; and you are of too generous dispositions to envy their preferment. I, therefore, trust that you will have but one aim, to please each other, and unite in the grand design of being happy and communicating happiness.

Finally, my brethren, as this association has been formed and perfected in so much unanimity and concord, in which we greatly rejoice, so may it long continue. May you long enjoy every satisfaction and delight, which disinterested friendship can afford. May kindness and brotherly affection distinguish your conduct, as men and as Masons. Within your peaceful walls, may your children's children celebrate with joy and gratitude the annual recurrence of this auspicious solemnity. And may the *tenets of our profession* be transmitted through your Lodge, pure and unimpaired, from generation to generation.

The Grand Marshal then proclaims the new Lodge, as follows:

In the name of the Most Worshipful Grand Lodge of the State of ...., I proclaim this new Lodge, by the name of ...... Lodge, No. ...., legally consecrated, dedicated, constituted, and the officers duly installed.

The grand honors are then given.

The following, or some other appropriate ODE may he sung:

Music—*Italian hymn.*

Hail! Brother Masons! hail!
Let friendship long prevail,
 And bind us fast;
May harmony and peace
Our happiness increase,
And friendship never cease,
 While life doth last.

We on the level meet,
And every brother greet,
 Skilled in our art;
And when our labor's past,
Each brother's hand we'll grasp,
Then on the square, at last,
 Friendly we'll part.

156

May Wisdom be our care,
And Virtue form the square
  By which we live;
That we at last may join
The Heavenly Lodge sublime,
Where we shall perfect shine
  With GOD above.

The new Master may return thanks.

The Grand Chaplain then pronounces the following, or some other appropriate

BENEDICTION.

ALMIGHTY and everlasting GOD, from whom cometh every good and perfect gift, send down upon thy servants here assembled the healthful spirit of thy grace, that they may truly please thee in all their doings. Grant, O LORD, power of mind and great understanding unto those whom we have this day clothed with authority to preside over and direct the affairs of this Lodge; and so replenish them with the truth of thy doctrine, and adorn them with humility of life, that, both by word and good example, they may faithfully serve thee, to the glory of thy holy name, and to the advancement, for all good purposes, of our beloved institution.— AMEN.

Response.—So mote it be.

The Grand Lodge returns to its own hall, and closes.

INSTALLATION
OF THE
OFFICERS OF A GRAND LODGE.

AT the hour appointed for the installation of the officers of the Grand Lodge, the Installing Officer (who should be the retiring Grand Master, the actual Grand Master of another jurisdiction, or a Past Grand Master) will assume the chair, call to order, and announce the business before the Grand Lodge. The officers to be installed will then vacate their places respectively, and substitutes will be appointed for the occasion.

The Grand Master and the other Grand Officers elect, to be installed, will be in waiting in an adjoining apartment.

The announcement of the Installing Officer may be in the following form:

BRETHREN: Your Grand Master and other Grand Officers for the ensuing year, having been duly elected, we are now in readiness to perform the ceremony of installation. The R. W. Grand Marshal will announce to them that we are waiting to receive them.

The Grand Marshal then retires, and on his return reports:

MOST WORSHIPFUL: The Grand Master and other Grand Officers elect are without, in readiness to be installed into office, when it is your pleasure to receive them.

Installing Officer. The R. W. Grand Marshal will admit them, and conduct them to the East before the altar.

(Should there be objection to the installation of any or either of them, it must now be made.)

As they enter the room, the Grand Lodge is called up by the Installing Officer in the usual manner, and remain standing.

The Grand Marshal conducts them to the altar in procession, two and two, in order of rank, the Grand Master elect and the Deputy Grand Master being first. Ile then says:

MOST WORSHIPFUL: The Grand Officers elect are before you, and await your pleasure. I have the honor to present to you for installation Brother A. B., who has been duly elected Grand Master of Masons of the State of ...... for the ensuing year.

Ins. Off: (to the Grand Master elect). MY BROTHER: The exalted station to which the free choice of your Brethren has called you, involves great responsibilities, and requires to be inaugurated by solemn sanctions. It elevates you to a position from which the power and prerogative may depart with the expiration of your term of service, but the honor and dignity, except by your own act, never. Have you been instructed in the secret rites and ceremonies appertaining to the high office of Grand Master of Masons preparatory to your installation, and by which you may acquire and forever retain the evidence of your rank among Masons?

G. M. elect. I have not.

Ins. Off. My Brother, it will be necessary for you to retire, and receive those instructions from our M. W. Past Grand Masters here present, who will escort you. And as we are now upon the threshold of a great and important undertaking, Masonic teachings-require that we should bow in solemn prayer with cur R. W. Grand Chaplain.

Grand Chaplain. Brethren, let us pray.

The Grand Chaplain may then make an appropriate extemporaneous prayer, or use the following:

ETERNAL Source of Life and Light! We thine unworthy creatures reverently bow before thee in adoration and praise. As when we first saw the light at our mystic altar, we first implored thy guidance, protection, and aid, so now we seek thee for thy divine blessing and direction. In thy might we are strong, and without thee, in our best and highest estate, we are but frail and feeble beings. We humbly implore thy divine favor upon this occasion, and upon the institution in whose services we are now engaged. Make it yet more helpful and beneficial to our race, and inspire all who are connected with it with an ardent love to thee, to each other, and to every member of the human family. Bless now thy servant before thee, who is about to assume a new and important relation to his brethren. Give him wisdom; give him strength; give him love. Enable him so to bear rule that he may keep in view the best interests of the great brotherhood now about to be committed to his charge. Teach him to feel that he is about to assume great and trying responsibilities, and enable him so to discharge them as to win all hearts. Add thy blessing upon the brethren who are to be associated with him in office. May they feel a just sense of their accountability to thee and to the Fraternity; and may they ever be faithful and zealous, and assist to uphold the hands of their chief in all good deeds. In thee, O GOD! as in the days of our apprenticeship, do we put our trust. Be thou our faithful Friend, Conductor, and Guide, in the unseen vicissitudes of life before us, and bring us all, at last, to see the Great Light, inaccessible and full of glory, in thy presence, where we shall behold thee with unclouded vision for evermore.—AMEN.

Response.—So mote it be!

Ins. Off. The Most Worshipful Brethren, Past Grand Masters present, will now retire with the Grand Master, and give him suitable instructions in the manner known to them only, preliminary to the further ceremonies of installation.

He then calls down, and the Grand Officers elect, other than the Grand Master, are provided with seats near the altar. The Past Grand Masters retire to some suitable apartment, and engage in ceremonies, not proper to be written, with the Grand Master elect.

When this is done, they return, having previously given notice of their approach by the Grand Marshal. Upon their entrance, the Grand Lodge is again called up, and after they have arrived near the East, one of their number says:

Past Grand Master. MOST WORSHIPFUL: Our distinguished Brother having been duly instructed by us, is now prepared to assume his installation vows.

Ins. Off. It is well; and with pleasure do we now proceed in our further services. R. W. Grand Marshal, you will conduct our Brother to the altar, to take upon himself the obligation appertaining to the duties of his office.

The Grand Marshal conducts him to the altar, where he kneels, the acting Grand Deacons holding their rods crossed over his head. The Installing Officer then administers the oath of office, the Grand Master elect. repeating after him, as follows:

I, A. B., in the presence of Almighty GOD, and before the Grand Lodge of the State of ......, do promise and swear, that, to the best of my ability, I will faithfully, honestly, and impartially perform the duties of Grand Master of Masons in this jurisdiction during my term of office; and that I will conform to and maintain the Constitutions, laws, rules, and regulations of the Grand Lodge of the State of ......, and the usages and customs of Free and Accepted Masons, and at all times enforce a strict obedience thereto. So help me GOD.

He then rises, and the Grand Marshal conducts him near the chair of the Installing Officer.

Ins. Off. MOST WORSHIPFUL BROTHER (for from henceforth you are entitled thus to be hailed): In inducting you to your chair of office, as a symbol of the commencement of your government over the Craft, I am performing a most solemn duty. By immemorial usage and the irrevocable landmarks of Masonry, you are invested, as Grand Master of Masons, with powers and prerogatives which are well nigh absolute. The interests of the Craft, for weal or wo, are placed in your hands during your term of office. The good resolutions which I doubt not that you have formed in your own mind that these powers shall not be abused or perverted by you, I would gladly strengthen by a word of admonition, which it will not become me henceforth to utter. The very consciousness of the possession of a great power will ever make a generous mind cautious and gentle in its exercise. To rule has been the lot of many, and requires neither strength of intellect or soundness of judgment; to rule WELL has been the fortune of but few, and may well be the object of an honorable ambition. It is not by the strong arm or the iron will that obedience and order, the chief requisites of good government, are secured, but by holding the key to the hearts of men.

The office of Grand Master is of great antiquity and respect, and is one of the highest dignities to which we may aspire. Its incumbent, to rule well, should possess and practice several important requisites.

As a *man*, he should be of approved integrity and irreproachable morals; freed from the dominion of hasty temper and ill-governed passions; of good repute in the world; and practicing, as an example to the Craft, the cardinal virtues of Fortitude, Prudence, Temperance, and Justice.

As a *citizen*, he should be loyal to his government, obedient to its laws, prompt in the duties he owes to society, and a pattern of fidelity in all social and domestic relations.

As a *Mason*, he should cling to the old landmarks, and be sternly opposed to their infringement; be a proficient in the laws, language, and literature of the Fraternity; be desirous to learn, and apt to teach; though not for the time a workman, yet be master of the work, and qualified to earn his wages; be prompt to aid and relieve, and slow to demand it; be ever mindful that, though elevated for a time above his fellows, that he is elevated by them, and that he is yet a Craftsman, more sacredly bound by a Craftsman's obligation; and that he should cultivate every where and at all times the golden tenets of Brotherly Love, Relief, and Truth.

As an *officer*, he should remember, first of all, that he is an individual Mason, sharing in that respect a common lot with his Brethren, and therefore interested in the welfare of each and all; be devoid of undue ostentation and haughty overbearing; be accessible to all, cultivating the closest friendship and the most unlimited confidence with his associate officers; be eager to take counsel with his Brethren, and ready to give it; be patient in investigation and hearing; be deliberate in judgment; be prompt in execution; be forbearing long and much with evildoers; be ready to reward good; be devoid of favoritism, and wholly impartial; be watchful over the treasury; having an eagle eye upon every portion of his jurisdiction; and breasting over the restless spirit of innovation.

Such are some of the most important qualifications which a Grand Master should possess, and the leading errors which he should avoid. It may be that most, if not all, of your predecessors have failed to reach this standard: but it is attainable; and be it your purpose to reach it, and be a bright and shining example to those who shall come after you!

It now but remains for me to clothe you with the external insignia of your rank and authority.

I now with great pleasure invest you with this jewel of your office, whose symbolic meaning will now have a new and striking significance to you. (*Presents the jewel.*)

I also present you with this gavel, as the potent emblem of Masonic power, which, in your hands, should never be sounded in vain. (*Presents gavel.*)

I now surrender to you this seat of authority. (*Places him in the chair.*)

And render you this, the first act of homage due to you as Grand Master.

The Grand Master having been covered on taking the chair, the Installing Officer uncovers, and bows very low.

Ins. Off. I now hail, salute, and proclaim you Grand Master of Masons of the State of ......! Brethren, behold your Grand Master!

Senior Grand Warden. Brethren, behold our Grand Master!

Junior Grand Warden. Brethren, behold our Grand Master 1

The Brethren, with their arms crossed, * * * * *; and then all, under the direction of the Installing Officer, salute with the public grand honors.

The retiring Grand Master may then address his newly-installed successor and brethren, and the Grand Master may, if he chooses, also address the Grand Lodge. If he does not wish to do so, he may call down, and the brethren continue seated during the remainder of the installation, except as called up during the obligations.

It will be proper for the Grand Master here to announce the names of the appointed officers, that they may be installed with the rest.

In case of the reëlection of a Grand Master, the preceding ceremony will be omitted, except that he be conducted near the chair, the Charge given him, he is invested with the jewel and gave, inducted and saluted as above directed. So in the case of any other officer being reëlected, he will be invested, and given the Charge only.

The Grand Master then proceeds with the installation of the remaining officers, or he may place the Installing Officer again in the chair, delivering to him, without ceremony, the gavel and jewel. In designating the officers hereafter, we will suppose the last to have been done.

Ins. Off. R. W. Grand Marshal, you will now present the Deputy Grand Master elect for installation.

Grand Marshal. MOST WORSHIPFUL: I have the pleasure to present to you, for installation, Brother C. D., who has been duly elected to the office of Deputy Grand Master.

The foregoing address of the Installing Officer, and presentation by the Grand Marshal, may be used for all the remaining officers, simply changing the name and title of the officer. It may also be used for the Grand Master, when reelected. The order of the Installing Officer, next following, will be omitted when the officer to be installed has been reelected.

Ins. Off. R. W. Grand Marshal, you will conduct our Brother to the altar, to take upon himself the obligation appertaining to the duties of his office.

The Grand Marshal conducts him to the altar, when he kneels, and is attended by the Grand Deacons, as in the case of the Grand Master, and takes the same obligation, with the change of name and designation of office.

162

Ins. Off. R. W. BROTHER: You have not been an inattentive observer of the ceremony of installing the M. W. Grand Master; for you are aware that, in case of his incapacity to act in contingencies mentioned in our constitutions, you succeed to his duties and prerogatives, as you do also when acting as his substitute in any matters specially delegated to you. Your office, therefore, is one of great dignity and importance; and it was in view of these considerations that your Brethren selected you to fill it. Treasure up, therefore, the suggestions made to the M. W. Grand Master; for you know not how soon they may have a personal application to you; and remember, also, that usage, as well as our particular regulations, have placed you in most intimate and confidential relations to him, as supporter and counselor.

I now, with pleasure, proceed to invest you with your jewel of office (*gives it*), and proclaim you Deputy Grand Master of Masons of the State of ...... You will now be seated in your place, which is at the right hand of the M. W. Grand Master.

Before he is seated, the Installing Officer calls up the Grand Lodge, and the Deputy Grand Master is saluted with the grand honors.

The others of the first six elective Grand Officers are presented and obligated in like manner as the Deputy Grand Master, but without being saluted with the grand honors.

The Charges to the remaining officers installed (which may be varied at the pleasure of the Installing Officer, when special occasion requires,) are as follows:

TO THE SENIOR GRAND WARDEN.

RIGHT WORSHIPFUL BROTHER: The position which you occupy in the Grand Lodge-and among the Fraternity is one of no little importance. In the Grand Lodge, to control practically the admission of all visitors, to announce specially those who are of rank or eminence, and to aid in the preservation of order, and at all times to render counsel and advice to the Grand Master, are high and responsible duties, requiring circumspection, vigilance, and reflection; but when to these is superadded the more onerous labor, in conjunction with the Junior Grand Warden, of diligently preserving the ancient landmarks throughout the jurisdiction, it then becomes a trust of deep moment to the welfare of the Craft. Your fitness for the discharge of such a trust undoubtedly led to your selection for the office by your Brethren, and it will be your duty and pleasure so to act as to justify their confidence.

In investing you with the jewel of your office, and directing you to the place of your immediate official action, in the West, I am performing a grateful duty.

TO THE JUNIOR GRAND WARDEN.

RIGHT WORSHIPFUL BROTHER: As the duties of your office and the qualifications for it are almost identical with those of the Senior Grand Warden, except as it respects the introduction of visitors, I will only add to the Charge given to that officer, that you be equally vigilant and circumspect, not only at your station in the Grand Lodge, but in the broader field of action without, dividing with him his labors, and taking due care that the great object of your united solicitude shall remain inviolate.

Accept the jewel of your office, and repair to the South, being ever watchful, whether in labor or at refreshment, that the *high twelve* of observation do not find you with your work, and that of the Craft you superintend, unperformed.

TO THE GRAND TREASURER.

RIGHT WORSHIPFUL BROTHER: In intrusting you with the books and funds of the Grand Lodge, as appertaining to your office, I am but their organ in placing them in your possession, as one well qualified to keep and manage them, as your past integrity, accuracy, and prompt business habits testify, an appreciation of which has been evinced by their choice of you as Grand Treasurer.

The keys forming the jewel of your office have a twofold significance: They are instruments to bind as well as to loose; to make fast, as well as to open. They will never, I am confident, be used by you in any other manner than the constitutions, laws, rules, and regulations of the Grand Lodge shall direct.

TO THE GRAND SECRETARY.

RIGHT WORSHIPFUL BROTHER: Usage, as well as positive enactments from time to time, have rendered the duties of the office of Grand Secretary more onerous and varied than that of any other officer. Brought by his official position more immediately into communication with the whole body of the Fraternity, it is requisite that he should possess ability, skill, and industry, to meet the various demands upon him. Placed in a position where ho holds almost constant correspondence with our Masonic brethren of every state and country, upon him devolves, in a large degree, the good name and credit of the Masonic family of this State. The Fraternity should enable him to maintain it; ho should strive that it be maintained. Courtesy and patience are to be elements in his manners and character. Vigilance and fidelity must also be necessary qualities.

Our constitutions, my Brother, point out to you fully the duties of your office, and I will not recapitulate them. Your capability for their prompt and faithful execution has induced your Brethren to confide this trust to you, and I feel assured that it is well placed.

In investing you with your official jewel, the pens, I am persuaded that they will make an endearing record, not only to your praise, but to the welfare of a Craft so largely dependent upon your experience and integrity.

TO THE GRAND CHAPLAIN.

REVEREND AND RIGHT WORSHIPFUL BROTHER: That Holy Book, which is the chart and text-book of your sacred calling, is also the great light of Masonry, and forever sheds its benignant rays upon every lawful assemblage of Free and Accepted Masons. Teach us from its life-giving precepts; intercede for us with that Divine Majesty which it so fully reveals and unfolds to us; and warm us by its lessons of infinite wisdom and truth, and you will have faithfully per formed your sacred functions and fulfilled your important trust.

It is fitting that an emblem of the sacred volume should be the jewel of your office, with which I now invest you.

TO THE GRAND LECTURER

RIGHT WORSHIPFUL BROTHER: The care and preservation of our ancient ritual, and the perpetuation of the time-honored landmarks embraced in it, and which may not be written, devolves upon you. And as that ritual has enshrined within it, in symbol and allegory, certain great and essential moral truths, you should be as perfect in the symbolism as in the mere formula of language which teach us how our rites are to be administered. As Grand Lecturer, also, you should be Master of the ceremonial observances of the Fraternity, and give instructions in the manner of rendering them most striking and effective. You are the preceptor of the Fraternity, and your deportment should be consistent with the nature of your office-work. For upon your teachings depend not only the uniformity and perpetuity, but the character and impressiveness of our rites, and they should be imparted, both by oral communication and example. On no point are the Craft so punctilious and exacting as upon the beauty and accuracy of the work and lectures: hence many eyes will be upon you. A courteous manner, an unwearied patience, and a diligent application are requisites for your place, and no rash or innovating hand will be tolerated in your department of labor.

In installing you into office, and presenting your jewel, I am happy to be enabled to say that your established skill and learning, and your ability to undergo the constitutional tests, have proved you to be a Master Workman.

TO THE GRAND MARSHAL.

RIGHT WORSHIPFUL BROTHER: The duties of your office require energy, activity, and quickness of perception. The good order of the Fraternity, in its general assemblies and processions, depends upon your care, skill, and assiduity. Possessing these qualifications, you have been appointed Grand. Marshal, and I now with pleasure install you into office, and invest you with your appropriate jewel. It denotes command, as the organ of the Grand Master, to whom you will be near at hand to execute his orders.

TO THE GRAND STANDARD-BEARER.

RIGHT WORSHIPFUL BROTHER: Your duty is to carry and uphold the banner of the Grand Lodge on occasions of ceremony and public procession. The emblems upon it are as ancient as the march of the children of Israel from bondage, and the Ark is the symbol of hope and safety. Bear them well aloft, for the world, as well as the Craft, ever honors them. Receive the jewel of your office, and let it remind you that you are never to part with that standard, when under your care, while you have life to defend it.

TO THE GRAND SWORD-BEARER.

RIGHT WORSHIPFUL BROTHER: The sword which you bear is the time-honored symbol of Justice and Authority. It reminds the beholder of the dignity of the body whose emblem it is. It is also the guardian and protector of the standard of the Grand Lodge. Be ever faithful to your trust. Let this jewel of your office remind you of its nature.

TO THE GRAND STEWARDS.

RIGHT WORSHIPFUL BROTHERS: In olden times, your province was to superintend and provide for the festivals of the Craft, and that duty still remains to you, although there is rarely occasion for its exercise. But we are taught that "it is better to go to the house of mourning, than to the house of feasting," and hence on you has been appropriately disposed the dispensation of our beneficent charities. That it is a grateful duty, all hearts testify, and we know that yours most fully responds to it. Receive the jewels of your office, together with the white rods.

TO THE GRAND DEACONS.

RIGHT WORSHIPFUL BROTHERS: As messengers of the Grand Officers, and as useful assistants in our ceremonies, your respective official positions are of very great value and importance to the comfort and good order of the Grand Lodge. Vigilance and zeal are necessary requisites of your offices, and wo know that you possess them.

As Senior and Junior Deacons of this Grand Lodge, you are now invested with the jewels of office, together with these rods, as tokens of your authority.

TO THE GRAND PURSUIVANT.

WORSHIPFUL BROTHER: You are to act as the messenger of the Grand Lodge, and the herald to announce the approach of visitors and strangers. In so doing, possess yourself of the necessary information to announce their rank and position properly, and exercise a sound discretion, so as not to interfere with its labors. Be cautious and vigilant, that no improper person may gain admittance. You, also, have in your keeping the clothing and jewels of the Grand Officers, which you should be careful to keep in a good condition, and neatly and orderly arranged for use at all times. Receive your emblem of office, and repair to your station inside the door.

TO THE GRAND TILER.

WORSHIPFUL BROTHER: The importance of the duties of your place can not be overrated. Care and watchfulness are indispensably requisite, and in all cases, unless thoroughly satisfied with the character and identity of those desiring admittance, let your doubts prevail. Ours is a sanctuary, intrusted to you faithfully and vigilantly to guard, and you have always at hand the means of being fully satisfied. Irreparable injury might result from a negligent or careless discharge of your duty. Your station is ever outside the door, and to which you will now repair with this jewel, and also with this implement of your office. (*Giving a sword.*)

The several officers being now duly installed, the Installing Officer will retire, after surrendering the jewel and gavel to the Grand Master. It may be proper and expedient before doing so, to have an appropriate ode or piece of music.

Grand Master. RT. WORSHIPFUL GRAND MARSHAL.: I now declare the several officers of the Most Worshipful Grand Lodge of the State of .... duly installed into office for the ensuing year, in AMPLE form. You will cause proclamation to be made in the South, West, and East.

The Junior Grand Deacon proclaims in the South, the Senior Grand Deacon in the West, and the Grand Marshal in the East, each as follows, the Grand Lodge being called up:

By order of the Most Worshipful Grand Master, and by authority of the Most Worshipful Grand Lodge of Free and Accepted Masons of the State of ......, I proclaim that its Grand Officers are now duly installed in ample form.

Response.—So mote it be!

The Grand Lodge is called down.

LAYING FOUNDATION-STONES
OF
PUBLIC STRUCTURES.

THIS CEREMONY is conducted by the Grand Master and his officers, assisted by the members of the Grand Lodge, and such officers and members of private Lodges as can conveniently attend.

The Chief Magistrate and other civil officers of the place where the building is to be erected, also generally attend on the occasion.

At the time appointed, the Grand Lodge is convened in some suitable place.

A band of music is provided, and the brethren appear, dressed in dark clothes, and white gloves and aprons.

The Lodge is opened by the Grand Master, and the rules for regulating the procession to and from the place where the ceremony is to be performed, are read by the Grand Secretary.

The necessary cautions are then given from the Chair, and the Grand Lodge is called from labor; after which, the procession sets out in the following order:

Tiler, with drawn sword;

Stewards, with rods;

Master Masons;

Two Deacons, with rods;

Secretary and Treasurer;

Past Wardens;

Two Wardens;

Past Masters;

Mark Masters;

Royal Arch Masons;

Knights Templar;[1]

---

[1] Whenever Knights Templar appear in a procession, they should act as an escort or guard of honor to the Grand Lodge.

Music;

Grand Tiler, with drawn sword;

Grand Stewards, with white rods;

Principal Architect, with Square, Level, and Plumb;

Grand Secretary and Grand Treasurer;

Bible, Square, and Compasses, carried by a Master of a Lodge, supported by two Stewards;

Grand Chaplains;

The Five Orders of Architecture;

Past Grand Wardens;

Past Deputy Grand Masters;

Past Grand Masters;

Chief Magistrate and Civil Officers of the place;

Junior Grand Warden, carrying the silver vessel with oil;

Senior Grand Warden, carrying the silver vessel with wine;

Deputy Grand Master, carrying the golden vessel with corn;

Master of the oldest Lodge, carrying Book of Constitutions;

GRAND MASTER,

Supported by two Deacons, with rods;

Grand Standard-Bearer;

Grand Sword-Bearer, with drawn sword.

A triumphal arch is usually erected at the place where the ceremony is to be performed.

The procession, arriving at the arch, opens to the right and left, and, uncovering, the Grand Master and his officers pass through the lines to the platform, while the rest of the brethren surround the platform, forming a hollow square.

The Grand Master commands silence, and announces the purposes of the occasion, when the following or some other appropriate ODE is sung:

Music—Rule Britannia.

When earth's foundations first was laid,
  By the Almighty Artist's hand,
'Twas then our perfect, our perfect laws were made,
Established by his strict command.
  Hail! mysterious, glorious Masonry!
    That makes us ever great and free.

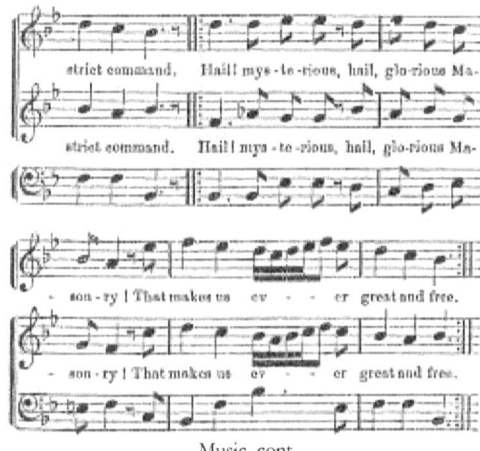

strict command. Hail! mys-te-rious, hail, glo-rious Ma-

Music, cont.

In vain mankind for shelter sought,
  In vain from place to place did roam,
Until from heaven, from heaven he was taught
  To plan, to build, to fix his home.
    Hail! mysterious, etc.

Illustrious hence we date our Art,
  Which now in beauteous piles appear,
And shall to endless, to endless time impart,
  How worthy and how great we are.
    Hail! mysterious, etc.

Nor we less famed for every tie,
  By which the human thought is bound;
Love truth and friendship, and friendship socially,
  Unite our hearts and hands around.
    Hail! mysterious, etc.

Our actions still by Virtue blest,
  And to our precepts ever true,
The world, admiring, admiring, shall request
  To learn, and our bright paths pursue.
    Hail! mysterious, etc.

The necessary preparations are now made for laying the stone, on which is engraved the year of Masonry, the name of the Grand Master, and such other particulars as may be deemed necessary.

The stone is raised up by the means of an engine, erected for that purpose.

The Grand Chaplain delivers the following or some other appropriate

171

PRAYER:

ALMIGHTY GOD, who hast given us grace at this time with one accord to make our common supplications unto thee; and dost promise that, where two or three are gathered together in thy name, thou wilt grant their requests; fulfill now, O LORD, the desires and petitions of thy servants, as may be most expedient for them; granting us in this world knowledge of thy truth, and in the world to come life everlasting.—AMEN.

Response.—So mote it be.

The Grand Treasurer, by the Grand Master's command, places under the stone various sorts of coin and medals, Masonic documents, and such other matters as may be of interest.

Solemn music is introduced, and the stone let down into its place.

The principal Architect then presents the working tools to the Grand Master, who hands the Square to the Deputy Grand Master, the Level to the Senior Grand Warden, and the Plumb to the Junior Grand Warden; when the Grand Master addresses the Grand Officers as follows:

Grand Master. R. W. DEPUTY GRAND MASTER: What is the proper jewel of your office?

Deputy Grand Master. The Square.

G. M. What are its moral and Masonic uses?

D. G. M. To square our actions by the Square of Virtue, and prove our work.

G. M. Apply the implement of your office to that portion of the foundation-stone that needs to be proved, and make report.

The Deputy applies the Square to the stone, and says:

D. G. M. MOST WORSHIPFUL: I find the stone to be square. The Craftsmen have performed their duty.

G. M. R. W. SENIOR GRAND WARDEN: What is the jewel of your office?

Senior Grand Warden. The Level.

G. M. What is its Masonic use?

S. G. W. Morally, it reminds us of equality, and its use is to lay horizontals.

G. M. Apply the implement of your office to the foundation-stone, and make report.

This is done.

S. G. W. MOST WORSHIPFUL: I find the stone to be level. The Craftsmen have performed their duty.

G. M. R. W. JUNIOR GRAND WARDEN: What is the proper jewel of your office?

Junior Grand Warden. The Plumb.

G. M. What is its Masonic use?

J. G. W. Morally, it teaches rectitude of conduct, and we use it to try perpendiculars.

G. M. Apply the implement of your office to the several edges of the foundation-stone, and make report.

This is complied with.

J. G. W. MOST WORSHIPFUL: I find the stone is plumb. The Craftsmen have performed their duty.

G. M. This corner-stone has been tested by the proper implements of Masonry. I find that the Craftsmen have skillfully and faithfully performed their duty, and I do declare the stone to be well formed, true, and trusty, and correctly laid, according to the rules of our ancient Craft.

Let the elements of Consecration now be presented.

The Deputy Grand Master comes forward with the vessel of corm, and, scattering it on the stone, says:

I scatter this corn as an emblem of plenty. May the blessings of bounteous Heaven be showered upon us and upon all like patriotic and benevolent undertakings, and inspire the hearts of the people with virtue, wisdom, and gratitude.

Response.—So mote it be.

The Senior Grand Warden then comes forward with the vessel of WINE, and pours it upon the stone; saying,

I pour this wine as an emblem of joy and gladness. May the Great Ruler of the Universe bless and prosper our national, state, and city governments, preserve the union of the States, and may it be a bond of Friendship and Brotherly Love that shall endure through all time.

Response.—So mote it be.

The Junior Grand Warden then comes forward with a vessel of OIL, which he pours upon the stone, saying,

I pour this oil as an emblem of peace. May its blessings abide with us continually, and may the Grand Master of heaven and earth shelter and protect the widow and orphan, shield and defend them from trials and vicissitudes of the world, and so bestow his mercy upon the bereaved, the afflicted, and the sorrowing, that they play know sorrowing and trouble no more.

Response.—So mote it be.

The Grand Master, standing in front of all, and extending his hands, makes the following

INVOCATION.

MAY the all-bounteous Author of Nature bless the inhabitants of this place with an abundance of the necessaries, conveniences, and comforts of life; assist in the erection and completion of this building; protect the workmen against every accident; long preserve the structure from decay; and grant to us all a supply of the CORN of *nourishment*, the WINE of *refreshment*, and the OIL of *joy*.—AMEN.

Response.—So mote it be.

The Grand Master strikes the stone three times with the gavel, and the public grand honors are given.

The Grand Master then delivers over to the Architect the implements of architecture; saying,

WORTHY SIR (or BROTHER): Having thus, as Grand Master of Masons, laid the foundation-stone of this structure, I now deliver these implements of your profession into your hands, intrusting you with the superintendence and direction of the work, having full confidence in your skill and capacity to conduct the same.

The Grand Master ascends the platform, when an appropriate ANTHEM may be sung.

The Grand Master then addresses the assembly as follows:

MEN AND BRETHREN HERE ASSEMBLED: Be it known unto you, that we be lawful Masons, true and faithful to the laws of our country, and engaged, by solemn obligations, to erect magnificent buildings, to be serviceable to the brethren, and to fear GOD, the Great Architect of the Universe. We have among us, concealed from the eyes of all men, secrets which cannot be divulged, and which have never been found out; but these secrets are lawful and honorable, and not repugnant to the laws of GOD or man. They were intrusted, in peace and honor, to the Masons of ancient times, and having been faithfully transmitted to us, it is our duty to convey them unimpaired to the latest posterity. Unless our Craft were good, and our calling honorable, we should not have lasted for so many centuries, nor should we have been honored with the patronage of so many illustrious men in all ages, who have ever shown themselves ready to promote our interests and defend us from all adversaries. We are assembled here to-day in the Pace of you all, to build a house, which we pray GOD may deserve to prosper, by becoming a place of concourse for good men, and promoting harmony and brotherly love throughout the world, till time shall be no more.—AMEN.

Response.—So mote it be!

A voluntary collection is then made by the Grand Stewards among the Brethren for the needy workmen, and the sum collected is placed upon the stone by the Grand Treasurer.

The Grand Chaplain then pronounces the following, or some other suitable

BENEDICTION.

GLORY be to GOD on high, and on earth peace, and good-will toward men! O LORD, we most heartily beseech thee with thy favor to behold and bless this assemblage; pour down thy mercy, like the dew that falls upon the mountains, upon thy servants engaged in the solemn ceremonies of this day. Bless, we pray thee, all the workmen who shall be engaged in the erection of this edifice; keep them from all forms of accidents and harm; grant them in health and prosperity to live; and finally, we hope, after this life, through thy mercy, wisdom, and forgiveness, to attain everlasting joy and felicity, in thy bright mansion—in thy holy temple—not made with hands, eternal in the heavens.—AMEN.

Response.—So mote it be.

After which, the procession returns in the same order to the place whence it set out, and the Grand Lodge is closed with the usual formalities.

DEDICATION OF MASONIC HALLS.

AT the time appointed for the celebration of the ceremony of dedication, the Grand Master and his officers, accompanied by the members of the Grand Lodge, meet in a convenient room, near to the place where the ceremony is to be performed, and the Grand Lodge is opened in ample form.

The procession is then formed, under direction of the Grand Marshal, when the Grand Lodge moves to the hall to be dedicated, in the following order:

MUSIC;

Tiler, with drawn sword;

Stewards, with white rods;

Grand Secretaries;

Grand Treasurers;

A Past Master, bearing the Holy Writings, Square and

Compasses, supported by two Stewards, with rods;

Two Burning Tapers, borne by two Past Masters;

Chaplain and Orator;

Past Grand Wardens;

176

Past Deputy Grand Masters:

Past Grand Masters

The Globes;

Junior Grand Warden, carrying a silver vessel with corn;

Senior Grand Warden, carrying a silver vessel with wine;

Deputy Grand Master, carrying a golden vessel with oil;

THE LODGE,

Covered with white linen, carried by four Brethren;

Master of the oldest Lodge, carrying Book of Constitutions;

GRAND MASTER,

Supported by two Deacons, with rods;

Grand Standard-Bearer;

Grand Sword-Bearer, with drawn sword;

Two Stewards, with white rods.

When the Grand Officers arrive at the center of the Lodge-room, the Grand honors are given.

The Grand Officers then repair to their respective stations.

The LODGE is placed in front of the altar, toward the East, and the gold and silver vessels and lights are placed around it.

These arrangements being completed, the following or some other appropriate ODE is sung:

Master Supreme! accept our praise;
  Still bless this consecrated band;
Parent of light! illume our ways,
  And guide us by thy sovereign hand.

May Faith, Hope, Charity, divine,
  Here hold their undivided reign;
Friendship and Harmony combine
  To soothe our cares—to banish pain.

May pity dwell within each breast,
  Relief attend the suffering poor;
Thousands by this, our Lodge, be blest,
  Till worth, distress'd, shall want no more.

The Master of the Lodge to which the hall to be dedicated belongs, then rises, and addresses the Grand Master as follows:

MOST WORSHIPFUL: The Brethren of .... Lodge, being animated with a desire to promote the honor and interest of the Craft, have erected a Masonic Hall, for their convenience and accommodation. They are desirous that the same should be examined by the Most Worshipful Grand Lodge; and if it should meet their approbation, that it be solemnly dedicated to Masonic purposes, agreeably to ancient form and usage.

The Architect or Brother who has had the management of the structure then addresses the Grand Master as follows:

MOST WORSHIPFUL: Having been intrusted with the superintendence and management of the workmen employed in the construction of this edifice; and having, according to the best of my ability, accomplished the task assigned me, I now return my thanks for the honor of this appointment, and beg leave to surrender up the implements which were committed to my care, when the foundation of this fabric was laid, (*presenting to the Grand Master the Square, Level, and Plumb*), humbly hoping that the exertions which have been made on this occasion will be crowned with your approbation, and that of the Most Worshipful Grand Lodge.

To which the Grand Master replies:

BROTHER ARCHITECT: The skill and fidelity displayed in the execution of the trust reposed in you at the commencement of this undertaking, have secured the entire approbation of the Grand Lodge; and they sincerely pray that this edifice may continue a lasting monument of the taste, spirit, and liberality of its founders.

The Deputy Grand Master then rises, and says:

MOST WORSHIPFUL: The hall in which we are now assembled, and the plan upon which it has been constructed, having met with your approbation, it is the desire of the Fraternity that it should be now dedicated, according to ancient form and usage.

The Lodge is then uncovered, and a procession is made around it in the following form, during which solemn music is played.

Grand Tiler, with drawn sword;

Grand Sword-Bearer, with drawn sword.

Grand Standard-Bearer;

A Past Master, with light;

A Past Master, with Bible, Square, and Compasses, on a velvet cushion;

Two Past Masters, each with a light;

Grand Secretary and Treasurer, with emblems;

Grand Junior Warden, with vessel of corn;

Grand Senior Warden, with vessel of wine;

Deputy Grand Master, with vessel of oil;

GRAND MASTER;

Two Stewards, with rods.

When the procession arrives at the East, it halts; the music ceases, and the Grand Chaplain makes the following

CONSECRATION PRAYER.

ALMIGHTY and ever-glorious and gracious LORD GOD, Creator of all things, and Governor of every thing thou hast made, mercifully look upon thy servants, now assembled in thy name and in thy presence, and bless and prosper all our works begun, continued, and ended in thee. Graciously bestow upon us *Wisdom*, in all our doings; *Strength* of mind in all our difficulties, and the *Beauty* of harmony and holiness in all our communications and work. Let Faith be the foundation of our *Hope*, and *Charity* the fruit of our obedience to thy revealed will.

May all the proper work of our institution that may be done in this house be such as thy wisdom may approve and thy goodness prosper. And, finally, graciously be pleased, O thou Sovereign Architect of the Universe, to bless the Craft, wheresoever dispersed, and make them true and faithful to thee, to their neighbor, and to themselves. And when the time of our labor is drawing near to an end, and the pillar of our strength is declining to the ground, graciously enable us to pass through the "valley of the shadow of death," supported by thy rod and thy staff, to those mansions beyond the skies where love, and peace, and joy forever reign before thy throne.—AMEN.

Response.—So mote it be!

All the other Brethren keep their places, and assist in singing the ODE, which continues during the procession, excepting only at the intervals of dedication.

ODE.

Genius of Masonry, descend,
And with thee bring thy spotless train,
Constant our sacred rites attend,
While we adore thy peaceful reign.

181

The first procession being made around the Lodge, the Grand Master having reached the East, the Grand Junior Warden presents the vessel of CORN to the G. Master; saying,

MOST WORSHIPFUL: In the dedications of Masonic Halls, it has been of immemorial custom to pour corn upon the Lodge, as an emblem of nourishment. I, therefore, present you this vessel of corn, to be employed by you according to ancient usage.

The Grand Master then, striking thrice with his mallet pours the corn upon the Lodge; saying,

In the name of the great JEHOVAH, to whom be all honor and glory, I do solemnly dedicate this hall to FREEMASONRY.

The grand honors are given.

Bring with thee VIRTUE, brightest maid!
  Bring LOVE, bring TRUTH, bring FRIENDSHIP here;
While social MIRTH shall lend her aid
  To soothe the wrinkled brow of CARE.

The second procession is then made around the Lodge, and the Grand Senior Warden presents the vessel of wine to the Grand Master; saying,

MOST WORSHIPFUL: Wine, the emblem of refreshment, having been used by our ancient brethren in the dedication and consecration of their Lodges, I present you this vessel of wine, to be used on the present occasion according to ancient Masonic form.

The Grand Master then sprinkles the wine upon the Lodge; saying,

In the name of the holy SAINTS JOHN, I do solemnly dedicate this hall to VIRTUE.

The grand honors are twice repeated.

Bring CHARITY! with goodness crowned,
  Encircled in thy heavenly robe!
Diffuse thy blessings all around,
  To every corner of the GLOBE!

The third procession is then made round the Lodge, and the Deputy Grand Master presents the vessel of oil to the Grand Master; saying,

MOST WORSHIPFUL: I present you, to be used according to ancient custom, this vessel of oil, an emblem of that joy which should animate every bosom on the completion of every important undertaking.

The Grand Master then sprinkles the oil upon the Lodge; saying,

In the name of the whole FRATERNITY, I do solemnly dedicate this hall to UNIVERSAL BENEVOLENCE.

The grand honors are thrice repeated.

To Heaven's high Architect all praise,
  All praise, all gratitude be given,
Who deigned the human soul to raise,
  By mystic secrets, sprung from Heaven.

The Grand Chaplain, standing before the LODGE, then makes the following

INVOCATION.

AND may the LORD, the giver of every good and perfect gift, bless the Brethren here assembled, in all their lawful undertakings, and grant to each one of them, in needful supply, the corn of nourishment, the wine of refreshment, and the oil of joy.—AMEN.

Response.—So mote it be.

The LODGE is then covered, and the Grand Master retires to his chair.

The following or an appropriate original oration may then be delivered, and the ceremonies conclude with music:

BRETHREN: The ceremonies we have performed are not unmeaning rites, nor the amusing pageants of an idle hour, but have a solemn and instructive import. Suffer me to point it out to you, and to impress upon your minds the ennobling sentiments they are so well adapted to convey.

This Hall, designed and built by WISDOM, supported by STRENGTH, and adorned in BEAUTY, we are first to consecrate in the name of the great JEHOVAH; which teaches us, in all our works, begun and finished, to acknowledge, adore, and magnify him. It reminds us, also, in his fear to enter the door of the Lodge, to put our trust in him while passing its trials, and to hope in him for the reward of its labors.

Let, then, its altar be devoted to his service, and its lofty arch resound with his praise! May the eye which seeth in secret witness here the sincere and unaffected piety which withdraws from the engagements of the world to silence and privacy, that it may be exercised with lese interruption and less ostentation.

Our march round the Lodge reminds us of the travels of human life, in which Masonry is an enlightened, a safe, and a pleasant path. Its tesselated pavement of Mosaic-work intimates to us the chequered diversity and uncertainty of human affairs. Our step is time; our progression, eternity.

Following our ancient Constitutions, with mystic rites we dedicate this Hall to the honor of FREEMASONRY.

Our best attachments are due to the Craft. in its prosperity, we find our joy; and, in paying it honor, we honor ourselves. But its worth transcends our encomiums, and its glory will outsound our praise.

Brethren: it is our pride that we have our names on the records of Freemasonry. May it be our high ambition that they should shed a luster on the immortal page!

The Hall is also dedicated to VIRTUE.

This worthy appropriation will always be duly regarded while the moral duties which our sublime lectures inculcate, with affecting and impressive pertinency, are cherished in our hearts . and illustrated in our lives.

As Freemasonry aims to enliven the spirit of Philanthropy, and promote the cause of Charity, so we dedicate this Hall to UNIVERSAL BENEVOLENCE; in the assurance that every brother will dedicate his affections and his abilities to the same generous purpose; that while he displays a warns and cordial affection to those who are of the Fraternity, he will extend his benevolent regards and good wishes to the whole family of mankind.

Such, my brethren, is the significant meaning of the solemn rites we have just performed, because such are the peculiar duties of every Lodge. I need not enlarge upon them now, nor show how they diverge, as rays from a center, to enlighten, to improve, and to cheer the whole circle of life. Their import and their application is familiar to you all. In their knowledge and their exercise may you fulfill the high purposes of the Masonic Institution!

How many pleasing considerations, my brethren, attend the present interview! While in almost every other association of men, political animosities, contentions, and wars interrupt the progress of Humanity and the cause of Benevolence, it is our distinguished privilege to dwell together in peace, and engage in plans to perfect individual and social happiness. While in many other nations our Order is viewed by politicians with suspicion, and by the ignorant with apprehension, in this country, its members are too much respected, and its principles too well known, to make it the object of jealousy or mistrust. Our private assemblies are unmolested; and our public celebrations attract a more general approbation of the Fraternity. Indeed, its importance, its credit, and, we trust, its usefulness, are advancing to a height unknown in any former age. The present occasion gives fresh evidence of the increasing affection of its friends; and this noble apartment, fitted up in a style of such elegance and convenience, does honor to Freemasonry, as well as reflects the highest credit on the respectable Lodge for whose accommodation and at whose expense it is erected.

We offer our best congratulations to the Worshipful Master, Wardens, Officers, and Members of ...... Lodge. We commend their zeal, and hope it will meet with the most ample recompense. May their Hall be the happy resort of Piety, Virtue, and Benevolence! May it be protected from accident, and long remain a monument of their attachment to Freemasonry! May their Lodge continue to flourish; their union to strengthen; and their happiness to abound!—And when they, and we all, shall be removed from the labors of the earthly Lodge, may we be admitted to the brotherhood of the perfect, in the building of GOD, the Hall not made with hands, eternal in the heavens!

The Grand Lodge is again formed in procession, as at first, returns to the room where it was opened, and is closed in ample form.

GRAND VISITATIONS.

THE Grand Master, accompanied by the Grand Officers, should, at least once a year, or as often as he may deem expedient, visit the Lodges under his jurisdiction, to make the customary examinations. When this laudable duty becomes impracticable, from the extent of jurisdiction and large number of Lodges, the Grand Master may appoint any one or more of his Grand Officers, who shall visit and inspect such Lodges as the Grand Master shall designate, and make report to him of the result.

The following is the ceremony observed on such occasions:

The Grand Secretary, by command of the Grand Master or Presiding Grand Officer, notifies the Lodge of the intended visit.

The Master opens his Lodge in the third degree, and places his Deacons at the sides of the door, with their staves crossed. The Brethren arrange themselves in a line from the door, on each side, to the Chair. The orders, borne by some of the most respectable private Brethren, wait near the door, to walk before the Grand Master when they enter. This being arranged in this manner, the Master deputes a Past Master to escort the Grand Officers, who enter in the following form:

Grand Marshal;

Grand Stewards;

Grand Pursuivant, with sword;

Two Grand Deacons;

Grand Treasurer and Secretary;

Grand Chaplain;

THE services herein arranged for the Burial of the Dead are adapted for all the purposes for which ceremonies of that character may be required. The arrangement is such that any portion of the service—each part being complete—may be used as occasion requires. It is not expected that the whole ceremony or can be used at any one time. If the weather should be stormy, or the body of the deceased taken, for interment, to a distance, where it would be impossible for the brethren to attend, that portion of the service set apart for the Lodge-room, or at the house of the deceased, may be performed.

MASONIC FUNERAL SERVICES:

PREPARED BY

ROBERT MACOY,

AUTHOR OF THE MASONIC MANUAL, BOOK OF THE LODGE, TRUE MASONIC GUIDE, PAST DEPUTY GRAND MASTER, GRAND RECORDER, ETC.

THE CEREMONIES which are observed on the occasion of funerals are highly appropriate; they are performed as a melancholy Masonic duty, and as a token of respect and affection to the memory of a departed brother.

GENERAL DIRECTIONS.

I. No FREEMASON can be buried with the formalities of the Fraternity, unless it be at his own request, or that of some of his family, communicated to the Master of the Lodge of which he died a member; foreigners or sojourners excepted; nor unless he has received the Master Mason's degree, and from this restriction there can be no exception.

II. Fellow-Crafts or Entered Apprentices are not entitled to these obsequies; nor can they be allowed to unite, as Masons, in the funeral of a brother.

M. No Lodge, or body of Masons, can unite in the obsequies of a person not a Mason, without permission of the Grand Master, or consent of the Grand Lodge.

IV. The Master of the Lodge, having received notice of the death of a brother, (the deceased having attained to the degree of Master Mason,) and of his request to be buried with the ceremonies of the Craft, fixes the day and hour for the funeral, (unless previously arranged by the friends or relatives of the deceased,) and issues his command to the Secretary to summon the Lodge. He may invite as many Lodges as he may think proper, and the members of those may accompany their officers in form; but the whole ceremony must be under the direction of the Master of the Lodge of which the deceased was a member.

V. Upon the death of a sojourner, who had expressed a wish to be buried with the Masonic ceremonies, the duties prescribed in Article IV. will devolve upon the Master of the Lodge within whose jurisdiction the death may occur; and if in a place where there be more than one Lodge, then upon the Master of the oldest Lodge, unless otherwise mutually arranged.

VI. Whenever civic societies, or the military, may unite with Masons in the burial of a Mason, the body of the deceased must be in charge of the Lodge having jurisdiction. The Masonic services should in all respects be conducted as if none but Masons were in attendance.

VII. If the deceased was a Grand or Past Grand officer, the officers of the Grand Lodge should be invited; when the Master of the Lodge having jurisdiction, will invite the Grand officer present who has attained the highest rank to conduct the burial service.

VIII. The pall-bearers should be Masons, selected by the Master. If the deceased was a member of a Chapter, Commandery, or Consistory, a portion of the pall-bearers should be taken from these bodies severally.

IX. The proper clothing for a Masonic funeral is a black hat, black or dark clothes, black neck-tie, white gloves, and a plain square white linen or lambskin apron, with a band of black crape around the left arm, above the elbow, and a sprig of evergreen on the left breast. The Master's gavel, the Wardens' columns, the Deacons' and Stewards' rods, the Tiler's sword, the Bible, the Book of Constitutions, and the Marshal's baton, should be trimmed with black crape, neatly tied with white ribbon. The officers of the Lodge should, and Past Masters and Grand Officers may, wear their official jewels.

X. While the body is lying in the coffin, there should be placed upon the latter a plain white lambskin apron.

XI. If a Past or Present Grand Master, Deputy Grand Master, or Grand Warden, should join the procession of a private Lodge, proper attention must be paid to them. They take place after the Master of the Lodge. Two Deacons, with white rods, should be appointed by the Master to attend a Grand Warden; and when the Grand Master or Deputy Grand Master is present, the Book of Constitutions should be borne before him, a Sword-Bearer should follow, and the Deacons, with white rods, on his right and left.

XII. When the head of the procession shall have arrived at the place of interment, or where the services are to be performed, the lines should be opened, and the highest officer in rank, preceded by the Marshal and Tiler pass through, and the others follow in order.

XIII. Upon arriving at the entrance of the cemetery, the brethren should march in open order to the tomb or grave. If the body is to be placed in the former, the Tiler should take his place in front of the open door, and the lines be spread so as to form a circle. The coffin should be deposited in the circle, and the Stewards and Deacons should cross their rods over it. The bearers should take their places on either side—the mourners at the foot of the coffin, and the Master and other officers at the head. After the coffin has been placed in the tomb, the Stewards should cross their rods over the door, and the Deacons over the Master.—If the body is to be deposited in the earth, the circle should be formed around the grave, the body being placed on rests over it; the Stewards should cross their rods over the foot, and the Deacons the head, and retain their places throughout the services.

XIV. After the clergymen shall have performed the religious services of the Church, the Masonic services should begin.

XV. When a number of Lodges join in a funeral procession, the position of the youngest Lodge is at the head or right of the procession, and the oldest at the end or left, excepting that the Lodge of which deceased was a member walks nearest the corpse.

XVI. The procession must return to the Lodge-room in the same order in which it marched to the grave.

XVII. A Lodge in procession is to be strictly under the discipline of the Lodge-room; therefore, no brother can enter the procession or leave it without express permission from the Master, conveyed through the Marshal.

SERVICE
IN THE
LODGE-ROOM.

The brethren having assembled at the Lodge-room, the Lodge will be opened briefly in the third degree; the purpose of the communication must be stated; and remarks upon the character of the deceased may be made by the Master and brethren, when the service will commence—all the brethren to stand:

Master. What man is he that liveth, and shall not see death? Shall he deliver his soul from the hand of the grave?

Sen. War. His days are as grass; as a flower of the field, so he flourisheth.

Jun. War. For the wind passeth over it, and it is gone; and the place thereof shall know it no more.

Master. Where is now our departed Brother?

Sen. War. He dwelleth in night; he sojourneth in darkness.

191

Jun. War. Man walketh in a vain shadow; he heapeth up riches, and cannot tell who shall gather them.

Master. When he dieth, he shall carry nothing away; his glory shall not descend after him.

Sen. War. For he brought nothing into the world, and it is certain he can carry nothing out.

Jun. War. The Lout gave, and the LORD hath taken away; blessed be the name of the LORD.

Master. The LORD is merciful and gracious, slow to anger, and plenteous in mercy.

Sen. War. GOD is our salvation; our glory, and the rock of our strength; and our refuge is in GOD.

Jun. War. He hath not dealt with us after our sins, nor rewarded us according to our iniquities.

Master. Can we offer any precious gift acceptable in the sight of the LORD to redeem our brother?

Sen. War. We are poor and needy. We are without gift or ransom.

Jun. War. Be merciful unto us, O LORD, be merciful unto us; for we trust in thee. Our hope and salvation are in thy patience. Where else can we look for mercy?

Master. Let us endeavor to live the life of the righteous, that our last end may be like his.

Sen. War. The LORD is gracious and righteous; yea, our GOD is merciful.

Jun. War. GOD is our GOD for ever and ever; He will be our guide, even unto death.

Master. Shall our brother's name and virtues be lost upon the earth forever?

Response by the Brethren. We will remember and cherish them in our hearts.

Master. I heard a voice from heaven, saying unto me, "Write, from henceforth blessed are the dead who die in the LORD! Even so, saith the Spirit; for they rest from their labors."

Here the Master will take the SACRED ROLL[1], on which have been inscribed the name, age, date of initiation or affiliation, date of death, and any matters that may be interesting to the brethren; and shall read the same aloud, and shall then say,

ALMIGHTY FATHER! in thy hands we leave, with humble submission, the soul of our departed brother.

Response. Amen! So mote it be!

The grand honors[2] should then be given three times; the brethren to respond each time—

The will of GOD is accomplished.—AMEN. So mote it be!

The Master should then deposit the ROLL in the archives of the Lodge.

The following or some other appropriate HYMN may be sung:

AIR—*Balerma.* C. M.

---

[1] A sheet of parchment or paper, prepared for the purpose.
[2] See note, p. 207.

Few are thy days, and full of woe,
O man, of woman born!
  Thy doom is written,
"Dust thou art,
  And to dust return."

Behold the emblem of thy state
  In flowers that bloom and die;
Or in the shadow's fleeting form,
  That mocks the gazer's eye.

Determined are the days that fly
  Successive o'er thy head;
The number'd hour is on the wing,
  That lays thee with the dead.

Great GOD, afflict not, in thy wrath,
  The short allotted span
That bounds the few and weary days
  Of pilgrimage to man.

The Master or Chaplain will repeat the following or some other appropriate PRAYER:

ALMIGHTY AND HEAVENLY FATHER—infinite in wisdom, mercy, and goodness—extend to us the riches of thy everlasting grace. Thou alone art a refuge and help in trouble and affliction. In this bereavement we look to thee for support and consolation. May we believe that death hath no power over a faithful and righteous soul! May we believe that, though the dust returneth to the dust as it was, the spirit goeth unto thyself. As we mourn the departure of a brother beloved from the circle of our Fraternity, may we trust that he hath entered into a higher brotherhood, to engage in nobler duties and in heavenly work, to find rest from earthly labor, and refreshment from earthly care. May thy peace abide within us, to keep us from all evil! Make us grateful for present benefits, and crown us with immortal life and honor.—And to thy name shall be all the glory forever.—AMEN.

Response. So mote it be.

A procession should then be formed, which will proceed to the church or the house of the deceased, in the following order:

MARSHAL.

Tiler, with drawn sword;
Stewards, with white rods;
Master Masons;
Secretary and Treasurer;
Senior and Junior Wardens;
Past Masters;
The Holy Bible,
On a cushion, covered with black cloth, carried by the oldest
member of the Lodge.
THE MASTER,
Supported by two Deacons, with white rods.

When the head of the procession arrives at the entrance of the building, it should halt and open to the right and left, forming two parallel lines, when the Marshal, with the Tiler, will pass through the lines to end, and escort the Master or Grand Officer into the house, the brethren closing in and following, thus reversing the order of procession—the brethren with heads uncovered.

SERVICE
AT THE
CHURCH OR THE HOUSE OF THE DECEASED.

After the religious services have been performed, the Master will take his station at the head of the coffin, the Senior Warden on his right, the Junior Warden on his left; the Deacons and Stewards, with white rods crossed, the former at the head and the latter at the foot of the coffin; the brethren forming a circle around all, when the Masonic service will commence by the Chaplain or Master repeating the following or some other appropriate PRAYER, in which all the brethren will join:

Our Father which art in heaven, hallowed be thy name. Thy kingdom come. Thy will be done in earth as it is in heaven. Give us this day our daily bread. And forgive us our debts, as we forgive our debtors. And lead us not into temptation, but deliver us from evil. For thine is the kingdom, and the power, and the glory, for ever.—AMEN.

Master. Brethren, we are called upon by the imperious mandate of the dread messenger Death, against whose free entrance within the circle of our Fraternity the barred doors and Tiler's weapon offer no impediment, to mourn the loss of one of our companions. The dead body of our beloved Brother A...... B...... lies in its narrow house before us, overtaken by that fate which must sooner or later overtake us all; and which no power or station, no virtue or bravery, no wealth or honor, no tears of friends or agonies of relatives can avert; teaching an impressive lesson, continually repeated, yet soon forgotten, that every one of us must ere long pass through the valley of the shadow of death, and dwell in the house of darkness.

Sen. War. In the midst of life we are in death; of whom may we seek for succor but of thee, O LORD, who for our sins art justly displeased. Thou knowest, Loan, the secrets of our hearts; shut not thy merciful ears to our prayer,

Jun. War. LORD, let me know my end, and the number of my days; that I may be certified how long I have to live.

Master. Man that is born of woman is of few days and full of trouble. He cometh forth as a flower, and is cut down; he fleeth also as a shadow, and continueth not. Seeing his days are determined, the number of his months are with thee; thou hast appointed his bounds that he cannot pass; turn from him that he may rest, till he shall accomplish his day. For there is hope of a tree, if it be cut down, that it will sprout again, and that the tender branch thereof will not cease. But man dieth and wasteth away; yea, man giveth up the ghost, and where is he? As the waters fail from the sea, and the flood decayeth and drieth up, so man lieth down, and riseth not up till the heavens shall be no more.

Sen. War. Our life is but a span long, and the days of our pilgrimage are few and full of evil.

Jun. War. So teach us to number our days, that we may apply our hearts unto wisdom.

Master. Man goeth forth to his work and to his labor until the evening of his day. The labor and work of our brother are finished. As it hath pleased Almighty GOD to take the soul of our departed brother, may he find mercy in the great day when all men shall be judged according to the deeds done in the body. We must walk in the light while we have light; for the darkness of death may come upon us, at a time when we may not be prepared. Take heed, therefore, watch and pray; for ye know not when the time is; ye know not when the Master cometh, at even; at midnight, or in the morning. We should so regulate our lives by the line of rectitude and truth, that in the evening of our days we may be found worthy to be called from labor to refreshment, and duly prepared for a translation from the terrestrial to the celestial Lodge, to join the Fraternity of the spirits of just men made perfect.

Sen. War. Behold, O LORD, we are in distress! Our hearts are turned within us; there is none to comfort us; our sky is darkened with clouds, and mourning and lamentations are heard among us.

Jun. War. Our life is a vapor that appeareth for a little while, and then vanisheth away. All flesh is as grass, and all the glory of man as the flower of grass. The grass withereth, and the flower thereof falleth away.

Master. It is better to go to the house of mourning than to go to the house of feasting; for that is the end of all men; and the living will lay it to his heart.

Response by all the Brethren. So mote it be.

Then may be sung the following or some other appropriate HYMN:

NAOMI.—C. M., DR. L. MASON.

Here Death his sacred seal hath set,
  On bright and bygone hours;
The dead we mourn are with us yet,
  And—more than ever—ours!

Ours, by the pledge of love and faith;
  By hopes of heaven on high;
By trust, triumphant over death,
  In immortality!

The dead are like the stars by day,
  Withdrawn from mortal eye;
Yet holding unperceived their way
  Through the unclouded sky.

By them, through holy hope and love,
  We feel, in hours serene,
Connected with the Lodge above,
  Immortal and unseen.

The MASTER or CHAPLAIN will repeat the following or some other appropriate PRAYER:

MOST GLORIOUS GOD! author of all good, and giver of all mercy! pour down thy blessings upon us, and strengthen our solemn engagements with the ties of sincere affection! May the present instance of mortality remind us of our approaching fate, and draw our attention toward thee, the only refuge in time of need! that when the awful moment shall arrive, that we are about to quit this transitory scene, the enlivening prospect of thy mercy may dispel the gloom of death; and after our departure hence in peace and in thy favor, we may be received into thine everlasting kingdom, to enjoy, in union with the souls of our departed friends, the just reward of a pious and virtuous life.

Response. So mote it be.

If the remains of the deceased are to be removed to a distance where the brethren cannot follow to perform the ceremonies at the grave, the procession will return to the Lodge-room or disperse, as most convenient.

SERVICE AT THE GRAVE.

When the solemn rites of the dead are to be performed at the grave, the procession should be formed, and proceed to the place of interment in the following order:

Tiler, with drawn sword;

Stewards, with white rods;

Musicians,
If they are Masons, otherwise they follow the Tiler;

MARSHAL.
Master Masons;
Secretary and Treasurer;
Senior and Junior Wardens;
Past Masters;

The Holy Writings,
On a cushion, covered with black cloth, carried by the oldest member of the Lodge;

THE MASTER,
Supported by two Deacons, with white rods;

Officiating Clergy;

The Body,

with the insignia placed thereon;

Pall-bearers; Pall-bearers;

Mourners.

If the deceased was a member of a Royal Arch Chapter and a Commandery of Knights Templar, and members of those bodies should unite in the procession, clothed as such, the former will follow the Past Masters, and the latter will act as an escort or guard of honor to the corpse, outside the Pall-bearers, marching in the form of a triangle; the officers of the Commandery forming the base of the triangle, with the Eminent Commander in the center.

When the procession has arrived at the place of interment, the members of the Lodge should form a circle around the grave; when the Master, Chaplain, and other Officers of the acting Lodge, take their position at the head of the grave, and the mourners at the foot.

After the Clergyman has performed the religious service of the Church, the Masonic service should begin.

THE Chaplain rehearses the following or some other appropriate PRAYER:

ALMIGHTY and most merciful Father, we adore thee as the God of time and eternity. As it has pleased thee to take from the light of our abode one dear to our hearts, we beseech thee to bless and sanctify unto us this dispensation of thy providence. Inspire our hearts with wisdom from on high, that we may glorify thee in all our ways. May we realize that thine all-seeing eye is upon us, and be influenced by the spirit of truth and love to perfect obedience—that we may enjoy the divine approbation here below. And when our toils on earth shall have ended, may we be raised to the enjoyment of fadeless light and immortal life in that kingdom where faith and hope shall end—and love and joy prevail through eternal ages. And thine, O righteous Father, shall be the glory forever.—AMEN.

Response.—So mote it be.

The following exhortation is then given by the Master:

BRETHREN: The solemn notes that betoken the dissolution of this earthly tabernacle, have again alarmed our outer door, and another spirit has been summoned to the land where our fathers have gone before us. Again we are called to assemble among the habitations of the dead, to behold the "narrow house appointed for all living." Here, around us, in that peace which the world cannot give or take away, sleep the unnumbered dead. The gentle breeze fans their verdant covering, they heed it not; the sunshine and the storm pass over them, and they are not disturbed; stones and lettered monuments symbolize the affection of surviving friends, yet no sound proceeds from them, save that silent but thrilling admonition, "Seek ye the narrow path and the straight gate that lead unto eternal life."

We are again called upon to consider the uncertainty of human life; the immutable certainty of death, and the vanity of all human pursuits. Decrepitude and decay are written upon every living thing. The cradle and the coffin stand in juxtaposition to each other; and it is a melancholy truth, that so soon as we begin to live, that moment also we begin to die. It is passing strange that, notwithstanding the daily mementos of mortality that cross our path; notwithstanding the funeral bell so often tolls in our ears, and the "mournful procession" go about our streets, that we will not more seriously consider our approaching fate. We go on from design to design, add hope to hope, and lay out plans for the employment of many years, until we are suddenly alarmed at the approach of the Messenger of Death, at a moment when we least expect him, and which we probably conclude to be the meridian of our existence.

What, then, are all the externals of human dignity, the power of wealth, the dreams of ambition, the pride of intellect, or the charms of beauty, when Nature has paid her just debt? Fix your eyes on the last sad scene, and view life stript of its ornaments, and exposed in its natural meanness, and you must be persuaded of the utter emptiness of these delusions. In the grave, all fallacies are detected, all ranks are leveled, all distinctions are done away. Here the scepter of the prince and the staff of the beggar are laid side by side.

While we drop the sympathetic tear over the grave of our deceased brother, let us cast around his foibles, whatever they may have been, the *broad mantle of Masonic charity*, nor withhold from his memory the commendation that his virtues claim at our hands. Perfection on earth has never yet been attained; the wisest, as well as the best of men, have gone astray. Suffer, then, the apologies of human nature to plead for him who can no longer plead for himself.

Our present meeting and procedings will have been vain and useless, if they fail to excite our serious reflections, and strengthen our resolutions of amendment.. Be then persuaded, my brethren, by this example, of the uncertainty of human life—of the unsubstantial nature of all its pursuits, and no longer postpone the all-important concern of preparing for eternity. Let us each embrace the present moment, and while time and opportunity permit, prepare with care for that great change, which we all know must come, when the pleasures of the world shall cease to delight, and be as a poison to our lips; and while we may enjoy the happy reflection of a well-spent life in the exercise of piety and virtue, will yield the only comfort and consolation. Thus shall our hopes be not frustrated, nor we hurried unprepared into the presence of that all-wise and powerful Judge, to whom the secrets of all hearts are known. Let us resolve to maintain with sincerity the dignified character of our profession. May our *faith* be evinced in a correct moral walk and deportment; may our *hope* be bright as the glorious mysteries that will be revealed hereafter; and our *charity* boundless as the wants of our fellow-creatures. And having faithfully discharged the great duties which we owe to GOD, to our neighbor, and ourselves; when at last it shall please the Grand Master of the universe to summon us into his eternal presence, may the *trestle-board* of our whole lives pass such inspection that it may be given unto each of us to "eat of the hidden manna," and to receive the "white stone with a new name," that will insure perpetual and unspeakable happiness at his right hand.

The Master then (presenting the apron) continues:

The lambskin, or white apron, is the emblem of innocence and the badge of a Mason. It is more ancient than the Golden Fleece or Roman Eagle; more honorable than the Star and Garter, when worthily worn.

The Master then deposits it in the grave.

This emblem I now deposit in the grave of our deceased brother. By it we are reminded of the universal dominion of Death. The arm of Friendship cannot interpose to prevent his coming; the wealth of the world cannot purchase our release; nor will the innocence of youth, or the charms of beauty propitiate his purpose. The mattock, the coffin, and the melancholy grave, admonish, us of our mortality, and that, sooner or later, these frail bodies must moulder in their parent dust.

The Master (holding the evergreen) continues:

This *evergreen*, which once marked the temporary resting-place of the illustrious dead, is an emblem of our faith in the immortality of the soul. By this we are reminded that we have an immortal part within us, that shall survive the grave, and which shall never, *never*, NEVER, die. By it we are admonished that, though, like our brother, whose remains lie before us, we shall soon be clothed in the habiliments of DEATH, and deposited in the silent tomb, yet, through our belief in the mercy of GOD, we may confidently hope that our souls will bloom in eternal spring. This, too, I deposit in the grave, with the exclamation, "Alas, my brother!"

The brethren then move in procession around the place of interment, and severally drop the sprig of evergreen into the grave; after which, the public grand honors[1] are given.

The Master then continues the ceremony:

From time immemorial, it has been the custom among the Fraternity of Free and Accepted Masons, at the request of a brother, to accompany his remains to the place of interment, and there to deposit them with the usual formalities.

In conformity to this usage, and at the request of our deceased brother, whose memory we revere, and whose loss we now deplore, we have assembled in the character of Masons, to offer up to his memory, before the world, the last tribute of our affection; thereby demonstrating the sincerity of our past esteem for him, and our steady attachment to the principles of the Order.

The Great Creator having been pleased, out of his infinite mercy, to remove our brother from the cares and troubles of this transitory existence, to a state of endless duration, thus severing another link from the fraternal chain that binds us together; may we, who survive him, be more strongly cemented in the ties of union and friendship; that, during the short space allotted us here, we may wisely and usefully employ our time; and in the reciprocal intercourse of kind and friendly acts, mutually promote the welfare and happiness of each other. Unto the grave we have consigned the body of our deceased brother; earth to earth (*earth being sprinkled on the coffin*), ashes to ashes, (*more earth*), dust to dust, (*more earth*); there to remain till the trump shall sound on the resurrection morn. We can cheerfully leave him in the hands of a Being, who has done all things well; who is glorious in holiness, fearful in praises, doing wonders.

---

[1] The grand honors practiced among Masons during the burial ceremonies, either in public or private, are given in the following manner: Both arms are crossed on the breast, the left uppermost, and the open palms of the hands striking the shoulders; they are then raised above the head, the palms striking each other, and then made to fall sharply on the thighs, with the head bowed. This is repeated three times. While the honors are being given the third time, the brethren audibly pronounce the following words—when the arms are crossed on the breast:—"we cherish his memory here;" when the hands are extended above the head—"We commend his spirit to Goa who gave it;" and when the hands are extended toward the ground—"And consign his body to the earth."

To those of his immediate relatives and friends, who are most heart-stricken at the loss we have all sustained, we have but little of this world's consolation to offer. We can only sincerely, deeply, and most affectionately sympathize with them in their afflictive bereavement. But we can say, that HE who tempers the wind to the shorn lamb, looks down With infinite compassion upon the widow and fatherless, in the hour of their desolation; and that the Great Architect will fold the arms of his love and protection around those who put their trust in him.

Then let us improve this solemn warning that at last, when the sheeted dead are stirring, when the great white throne is set, we shall receive from the Omniscient Judge, the thrilling invitation,

Come, ye blessed, inherit the kingdom prepared for you from the foundation of the world.

The following, or some other suitable ODE, may be sung:

SCOTLAND.
Arranged from Dr. CLARE. by Br. JAS. B. TAYLOR.

Thou art gone to the grave but we will not deplore thee,
  Tho' sorrow and darkness encompass the tomb;
The Good has pass'd on thro' its portals before thee,
  And the cassia blooms greenly to lighten the gloom,
  And the cassia blooms greenly to lighten the gloom.

Scotland, cont.

Thou art gone to the grave; we no longer behold thee,
  Nor tread the rough paths of the world by thy hand;
But the wide arms of Mercy are spread to enfold thee,
  And we'll meet thee again in the heavenly land.

Thou art gone to the grave; and its mansion forsaking,
  Perchance thy weak spirit in doubt lingered long;
But the sunshine of heaven beamed bright on thy waking,
  And the sound thou didst hear was the seraphim's song.

Thou art gone to the grave; but 'twere wrong to deplore thee,
When GOD was thy trust and thy guardian and guide;
He gave thee, he took thee, and soon will restore thee
In the blest Lodge above where the faithful abide.

Or this:

PLEYEL'S HYMN.

Solemn strikes the fun'ral chime,
Notes of our departing time;
As we journey here below,
Thro' a pilgrimage of woe.

Mortals, now indulge a tear,
For Mortality is here!
See how wide her trophies wave
O'er the slumbers of the grave!

Here another guest we bring;
Seraphs of celestial wing,
To our fun'ral altar come,
Waft our friend and brother home.

There, enlarged, thy soul shall see
What was wailed in mystery;
Heavenly glories of the place
Show his Maker face to face.

LORD of all! below—above—
Fill our hearts with truth and love;
When dissolves our earthly tie,
Take us to thy Lodge on high.

The service may be concluded with the following or some other suitable PRAYER:

MOST GLORIOUS GOD, author of all good and giver of all mercy, pour down thy blessings upon us and strengthen our solemn engagements with the ties of sincere affection. May the present instance of mortality remind us of our own approaching fate, and, by drawing our attention toward thee, the only refuge in time of need, may we be induced so to regulate our conduct here, that when the awful moment shall arrive, at which we must quit this transitory scene, the enlivening prospect of thy mercy may dispel the gloom of death; and that after our departure hence in peace and thy favor, we may be received into thine everlasting kingdom, and there join in union with our friend, and enjoy that uninterrupted and unceasing felicity which is allotted to the souls of just men made perfect.—AMEN.

Response. So mote it be.

Master. The will of God is accomplished.

Response. So mote it be.

Master. From dust we came, and unto dust we must return.

Response. May we all be recompensed at the resurrection of the just.—AMEN.

Thus the service ends, and the procession will return in form to the place whence it set out, where the necessary business of Masonry should be renewed. The insignia and ornaments of the deceased, if an officer of a Lodge, are to be returned to the Master, with the usual ceremonies, and the Lodge will be closed in form.

REGULATIONS FOR PROCESSIONS.

When the Grand Master, Deputy Grand Master, or either of the Grand Wardens, joins the procession of a private Lodge, proper respect is to be paid to the rank of that officer. His position will be immediately before the Master and Wardens of the Lodge, and two Deacons will be appointed to attend him.

When the Grand or Deputy Grand Master is present, the Book of Constitutions will be borne before him. The honor of carrying this book belongs of right to the Master of the oldest Lodge in the jurisdiction, whenever he is present. The Book of Constitutions must never be borne in a procession unless the Grand or Deputy Grand Master be present.

In entering public buildings, the Bible, Square, and Compasses, and the Book of Constitutions, are to be placed in front of the Grand Master, and the Grand Marshal and Grand Deacons must keep near him.

When a procession faces inward, the Deacons and Stewards will cross their rods, so as to form an arch for the brethren to pass beneath.

Marshals are to walk or ride on the left flank of a procession. The appropriate costume of a Marshal is a cocked hat, sword and scarf, with a baton in his hand. The color of the scarf must be blue in the procession of a Subordinate Lodge, and purple in that of the Grand Lodge.

All processions will return in the same order in which they set out.

The post of honor in a Masonic procession is always in the rear.

RITUAL
FOR A
LODGE OF SORROW.

BY JOHN W. SIMONS,

PAST GRAND MASTER OF NEW YORK.

15*

PREFACE.

IN the performance of the ceremonies of a Lodge of Sorrow, it should be understood that the ritual, although necessarily of a funereal character, differs essentially from the office for the burial of the dead.

In the latter case, we are in the actual presence of the deceased, and engaged in the last rites of affection and respect for one who has been our companion in life, and whose mortal remains we are about to consign to the last resting-place, amid the tears of surviving friends, and under the peculiar influences which attach to the rites of sepulture and the final earthly farewell to one who, but a few hours previous, could respond to our questions, and exchange with us the signs of the living. We are then called to consider the "mattock, the spade, the coffin, and the melancholy grave," in all their gloomy reality, and to reflect that the hour must soon be tolled "when we, too, shall be clothed in the habiliments of death, and deposited in the voiceless tomb."

The Lodge of Sorrow, on the contrary, is intended to celebrate the memory of our departed brethren; and while we thus recall to our recollection their virtues, and temper anew our resolutions so to live, that, when we shall have passed the silent portals, our memories may be cherished with grateful remembrance, we learn to look upon death from a more elevated point of view; to see in it the wise and necessary transition from the trials and imperfections of this world, to the perfect life for which our transient journey hero has been the school and the preparation. We thus learn "that the soul is the whole of man; that for it to be born, is really to die; that earth is but its place of exile, and heaven its native land."

In the preparation of the following ritual, it has been sought to typify the inevitable necessity of death; the gloom and sorrow that attend the "last of earth," and surround "the narrow house appointed for all living," and the consoling fact of the immortality of the soul and the resurrection to a new and true life, where sorrow and tears have no place.

Guided by these views in the accomplishment of our task, and aided by the use of rituals from Germany, France, and England, it is believed that the work now submitted will supply a want long felt by the brethren in the United States, and enable them to conduct the solemn exercises of such occasions with dignity and propriety.

Vocal and instrumental music are indispensable to the proper effect of the ceremony.

Brethren should wear dark clothing, and no insignia but the white lambskin apron and white gloves.

Finally, we desire to add, that there is no good reason for any attempt at secrecy in the ceremonies of Sorrow Lodges; but that, on the other hand, they may be held in churches or public halls, or in the presence of friends at the lodge-room, with benefit to all concerned. This, however, will necessarily be subject to the wishes of the brethren themselves.

LODGE OF SORROW.

PREPARATION OF THE HALL.

I. THE Lodge-room should be appropriately draped in black, and the several stations covered with the same emblem of mourning.

II. On the Master's pedestal is a skull and lighted taper.

III. In the center of the room is placed the catafalque, which consists of a rectangular platform, about six feet long by four wide, on which are two smaller platforms, so that three steps are represented. On the third one should be an elevation of convenient Night, on which is placed an urn. The platform should be draped in black, and a canopy of black drapery may he raised over the urn.

IV. At each corner of the platform will be placed a candlestick, bearing a lighted taper, and near it, facing the East, will be seated a brother, provided with an extinguisher, to be used at the proper time.

V. During the first part of the ceremonies the lights in the room should burn dimly.

VI. Arrangements should be made to enable the light to be increased to brilliancy at the appropriate point in the ceremony.

VII. On the catafalque will be laid a pair of white gloves, a lambskin apron, and, if the deceased brother had been an officer, the appropriate insignia of his office.

VIII. Where the Lodge is held in memory of several brethren, shields bearing their names are placed around the catafalque.

OPENING THE LODGE.

The several officers being in their places, and the brethren seated, the Master will call up the Lodge, and say,

Master. Brother Senior Warden: For what purpose are we assembled?

Senior Warden. To honor the memory of those brethren whom death hath taken from us; to contemplate our own approaching dissolution; and, by the remembrance of immortality, to raise our souls above the considerations of this transitory existence.

Master. Brother Junior Warden: What sentiments should inspire the souls of Masons on occasions like the present?

Junior Warden. Calm sorrow for the absence of our brethren who have gone before us; earnest solicitude for our own eternal welfare, and a firm faith and reliance upon the wisdom and goodness of the Great Architect of the Universe.

Master. Brethren: Commending these sentiments to your earnest consideration, and invoking your assistance in the solemn ceremonies about to take place, I declare this Lodge of Sorrow opened.

The Chaplain or Master will then offer the following or some other suitable PRAYER:

GRAND ARCHITECT OF THE UNIVERSE, in whose holy sight centuries are but as days, to whose omniscience the past and the future are but as one eternal present; look down upon thy children, who still wander among the delusions of time—who still tremble with dread of dissolution, and shudder at the mysteries of the future; look down, we beseech thee, from thy glorious and eternal day into the dark night of our error and presumption, and suffer a ray of thy divine light to penetrate into our hearts, that in them may awaken and bloom the certainty of life, reliance upon thy promises, and assurance of a place at thy right hand.—AMEN.

Response. So mote it be.

The following or some other appropriate ODE may here be sung:

Music by DE. LOWELL MASON, arranged for four voices, by T. S. NEDHAM.

Brother, thou art gone to rest;
  We will not weep for thee;
For thou art now where oft on earth
  Thy spirit longed to be.

Brother, thou art gone to rest;
  Thy toils and cares are o'er;
And sorrow, pain, and suffering, now,
  Shall ne'er distress thee more.

Brother, thou art gone to rest;
  And this shall be our prayer,
That, when we reach our journey's end,
  Thy glory we shall share.

The Master (taking the skull in his hand) will then say,

BRETHREN: In the midst of life we are in death, and the wisest cannot know what a day may bring forth. We live but to see those we love passing away into the silent land.

Behold this emblem of mortality, once the abode of a spirit like our own: beneath this mouldering canopy once shone the bright and busy eye: within this hollow cavern once played the ready, swift, and tuneful tongue; and now, sightless and mute, it is eloquent only in the lessons it teaches us.

Think of those brethren who, but a few days since, were among us in all the pride and power of life; bring to your minds the remembrance of their wisdom, their strength, and their beauty; and then reflect that "to this complexion have they come at last;" think of yourselves, thus will you be when the lamp of your brief existence has burned out. Think how soon death, for you, will be a reality. Man's life is like a flower, which blooms to-day, and to-morrow is faded, cast aside, and trodden under foot. The most of us, my brethren, are fast approaching, or have already passed the meridian of life; our sun is setting in the West; sand, oh! how much more swift is the passage of our declining years than when we started upon the journey, and believed—as the young are too apt to believe—that the roseate hues of the rising sun of our existence were always to be continued. When we look back upon the happy days of our childhood, when the dawning intellect first began to exercise its powers of thought, it seems as but yesterday, and that, by a simple effort of the will, we could put aside our manhood, and seek again the loving caresses of a mother, or be happy in the possession of a bauble; and could we now realize the idea that our last hour had come, our whole earthly life would seem but as the space of time from yesterday until to-day. Centuries upon centuries have rolled away behind us; before us stretches out an eternity of years to come; and on the narrow boundary between the past and the present flickers the puny taper we term our life. When we came into the world, we knew naught of what had been before us; but, as we grew up to manhood, we learned of the past; we saw the flowers bloom as they had bloomed for centuries; we beheld the orbs of day and night pursuing their endless course among the stars, as they had pursued it from the birth of light; we learned what men had thought, and said, and done, from the beginning of the world to our day; but only through the eye of faith can we behold what is to come hereafter, and only through a firm reliance upon the Divine promises can we satisfy the yearnings of an immortal soul. The cradle speaks to us of remembrance—the coffin of hope, of a blessed trust in a never-ending existence beyond the gloomy portals of the tomb.

Let these reflections convince us how vain are all the wranglings and bitterness engendered by the collisions of the world; how little in dignity above the puny wranglings of ants over a morsel of food or for the possession of a square inch of soil.

What shall survive us? Not, let us hope, the petty strifes and bickerings, the jealousies and heart-burnings, the small triumphs and mean advantages we have gained, but rather the noble thoughts, the words of truth, the works of mercy and justice, that ennoble and light up the existence of every honest man, however humble, and live for good when his body, like this remnant of mortality, is mouldering in its parent dust.

Let the proud and the vain consider how soon the gaps are filled that are made in society by those who die around them; and how soon time heals the wounds that death inflicts upon the loving heart; and from this let them learn humility, and that they are but drops in the great ocean of humanity.

And when God sends his angel to us with the scroll of death, let us look upon it as an act of mercy, to prevent many sins and many calamities of a longer life; and lay down our heads softly and go to sleep, without wrangling like froward children. For this at least man gets by death, that his calamities are not immortal. To bear grief honorably and temperately, and to die willingly and nobly, are the duties of a good man and true mason.

A solemn piece of music will now be performed, or the following ode may be sung:

Music—Naomi. DR. LOWELL MASON.

When those we love are snatched away,
By Death's relentless hand,
Our hearts the mournful tribute pay,
That Friendship must demand.

While pity prompts the rising sigh,
With awful power imprest;
May this dread truth, "I too must die,"
Sink deep in every breast.

Let this vain world allure no more:
Behold the opening tomb!
It bids us use the present hour;
To-morrow death may come.

The voice of this instructive scene
May every heart obey;
Nor be the faithful warning vain
Which calls to watch and pray!

At its conclusion the Chaplain will read the following passages:

Lo, He goeth by me and I see Him not. He passeth on also, but I perceive Him not. Behold He taketh away, who can hinder Him?

Man that is born of a woman is of few days, and full of trouble. He cometh forth like a flower, and is cut down; he fleeth also as a shadow, and continueth not. Seeing his days are determined, the number of his months are with Thee, Thou hast appointed his bounds that he cannot pass; turn from him that he may rest, till he shall accomplish, as an hireling, his day. For there is hope of a tree if it be cut down, that it will sprout again, and that the tender branch thereof will not cease. Though the root thereof wax old in the earth, and the stock thereof die in the ground, yet through the scent of water it will bud and bring forth boughs like a plant. But man dieth and wasteth away; yea, man giveth up the ghost, and where is he? As the waters fail from the sea and the flood decayeth and drieth up, so man lieth down, and riseth not; till the heavens be no more they shall not awake nor be raised out of their sleep.

My days are passed, my purposes are broken off, even the thoughts of my heart. If I wait, the grave is mine house, I have made my bed in the darkness. I have said to corruption, thou art my father. And where is now thy hope? as for my hope, who shall see it? They shall go down to the bars of the pit, when our rest together is in the dust.

My bone cleaveth to my skin and to my flesh. Oh, that my words were now written; oh, that they were printed in a book! That they were graven with an iron pen and lead in the rock forever! For I know that my Redeemer liveth, and that He shall stand at the latter day upon the earth. And though after my skin worms destroy this body, yet in my flesh shall I see God. Whom I shall see for myself, and mine eyes shall behold, and not another.

For Thou cast me into the deep, in the midst of the seas; and Thy floods compassed me about; all Thy billows and Thy waves passed over me Then I said, I am cast out of Thy sight; yet will I look again toward Thy holy temple. The waters compassed me about, even to the soul, the depth closed me round about, the weeds were wrapt about my head.

I said, in the cutting off of my day I shall go to the gates of the grave; I am deprived of the residue of my years; I said, I shall not see the Lord, even the Lord in the land of the living; I shall behold man no more with the inhabitants of the world. Behold, for peace I had great bitterness; but Thou hast in love to my soul delivered it from the pit of corruption. For the grave cannot praise Thee, death cannot celebrate Thee; the living, the living, he shall praise Thee as I do this day.

Are not my days few? Cease, then, and let me alone, that I may take comfort a little, before I go whence I shall not return, even to the land of darkness, and the shadow of death. A land oT darkness, as darkness itself; and of the shadow of death, without any order, and where the light is as darkness.

An interval of profound silence will be observed. The general lights of the Hall, if there be convenience, will be turned low, and the four brethren will extinguish the tapers near which they are placed.

PRAYER BY THE CHAPLAIN.

OUR FATHER WHO ART IN HEAVEN, it hath pleased thee to take from among us those who were our brethren. Let time, as it heals the wounds thus inflicted upon our hearts and on the hearts of those who were near and dear to them, not erase the salutary lessons engraved there; but let those lessons always continuing distinct and legible make us and them wiser and better. And whatever distress or trouble may hereafter come upon us, may we ever be consoled by the reflection that thy wisdom and thy love are equally infinite, And that our sorrows are not the visitations of thy wrath, but the result of the great law of harmony by which everything is being conducted to a good and perfect issue in the fullness of thy time. Let the loss of our brethren increase our affection for those who are yet spared to us, and make us more punctual in the performance of the duties that Friendship, Love, and Honor demand.

When it comes to us also to die, may a firm and abiding trust in thy mercy dispel the gloom and dread of dissolution. Be with us now, and sanctify the solemnities of this occasion to our hearts, that we may serve thee in spirit and understanding. And to thy name shall be ascribed the praise forever.—AMEN.

Response. So mote it be.

The Wardens, Deacons and Stewards, will now approach the East and form a procession, thus:

Two Stewards, with rods.

Two Wardens, with columns.

Deacon,   THE MASTER.   Deacon,
with rod.   with rod.

Which will move once round the catafalque to slow and solemn music.

On arriving in the East, the procession will halt and open to the right and left. The Junior Warden will then advance to the catafalque and placing upon it a bunch of white flowers will say:

Junior Warden. In memory of our departed brethren I deposit these white flowers, emblematical of that pure life to which they have been called, and reminding us that as these children of an hour will droop and fade away, so, too; we shall soon follow those who have gone before us, and inciting us so to fill the brief span of our existence that we may leave to our survivors a sweet savor of remembrance.

The Junior Warden will now return to his place, and ah interval of profound silence will be observed.

The procession will again be formed, and move as before, to the sound of slow music, twice around the catafalque.

They will open as before, and the Senior Warden approaching the catafalque will place upon it a wreath of white flowers and say:

Senior Warden. As the sun sets in the West, to close the day and herald the approach of night, so, one by one we lay us down in the darkness of the tomb to wait in its calm repose for the time when the heavens shall pass away as a scroll, and man, standing in the presence of the Infinite, shall realize the true end of his pilgrimage here below. Let these flowers be to us the symbol of remembrance of all the virtues of our brethren who have preceded us to the silent land, the token of that fraternal alliance which binds us while on earth and which we hope will finally unite us in heaven.

The Senior Warden returns to his place, and an interval of silence will be observed.

The procession will again be formed, and move three times around the catafalque to slow music, as before.

Arrived in the East, the Master will advance and place upon the urn a wreath of evergreen, and say:

Master. It is appointed unto all men once to die, and after death cometh the resurrection. The dust shall return to the earth and the spirit unto God who gave it. In the grave all men are equal; the good deeds, the lofty thoughts, the heroic sacrifices alone survive and bear fruit in the lives of those who strive to emulate them.

While, therefore, nature will have it's way, and our tears will fall upon the graves of our brethren, let us be reminded by the evergreen symbol of our faith in immortal life that the dead are but sleeping, and be comforted by the reflection that their memories will not be forgotten; that they will still be loved by those who are soon to follow them; that in our archives their names are written, and that in our hearts there is still a place for them. And so, trusting in the infinite love and tender mercy of him without whose knowledge not even a sparrow falls, let us prepare to meet them where there is no parting and where with them we shall enjoy eternal rest.

The Master will return to his place, and a period of silence will obtain.

The Chaplain will now be conducted to the altar, where he will read:

But some man will say: How are the dead raised up? and with what body do they come? Thou fool, that which thou sowest is not quickened except it die: and that which thou sowest thou sowest not that body that shall be, but bare grain; it may chance of wheat or of some other grain: but God giveth it a body as it hath pleased him, and to every seed his own body.

All flesh is not the same flesh; but there is one kind of flesh of men, another flesh of beasts, another of fishes, and another of birds. There are also celestial bodies, and bodies terrestrial: but the glory of the celestial is one, and the glory of the terrestrial is another.

There is one glory of the sun, and another glory of the moon, and another glory of the stars; for one star differeth from another star in glory. So also is the resurrection of the dead. It is sown in corruption; it is raised in incorruption: it is sown in dishonor; it is raised in glory: it is sown in weakness; it is raised in power: it is sown a natural body; it is raised a spiritual body. There is a natural body, and there is a spiritual body. And so it is written, The first man Adam was made a living soul, the last Adam was made a quickening spirit. Howbeit, that was not first which is spiritual, but that which is natural; and afterward that which is spiritual. The first man is of the earth, earthy: the second man is the Lord from heaven. As is the earthy, such are they also that are earthy; and as is the heavenly, such are they also that are heavenly. And as we have borne the image of the earthy, we shall also bear the image of the heavenly.

Now this I say, brethren, that flesh and blood cannot inherit the kingdom of God; neither doth corruption inherit incorruption. Behold, I shew you a mystery: we shall not all sleep, but we shall all be changed; in a moment, in the twinkling of an eye, at the last trump: for the trumpet shall sound, and the dead shall be raised incorruptible, and we shall be changed. For this corruptible must put on incorruption, and this mortal must put on immortality. So when this corruptible shall have put on incorruption, and this mortal shall have put on im-mortality, then shall be brought to pass the saying that is written, Death is swallowed up in victory. O death, where is thy sting? O grave, where is thy victory?

As the Chaplain pronounces the concluding words, "O grave where is thy victory?" the lights in the Hall will be raised to brilliancy, the four brethren seated around the catafalque will relight the tapers.

The Chaplain will return to his place in the East, and the following ode will be sung, to music of a more cheerful character:

Music—*Simons.*

Friend after friend departs:
  Who has not lost a friend?
There is no union here of hearts,
  That finds not here an end.
Where this frail world our only rest,
Living or dying, none were blest.

Music cont.

There is a world above
  Where parting is unknown—
A whole eternity of love
  And blessedness alone;
And faith beholds the dying here
Translated to that happier sphere.

The Orator will then pronounce the Eulogium.

Then follows an ode:

OLD HUNDRED. L. M.

Once more, O Lord, let grateful praise,
From every heart to thee ascend;
Thou art the guardian of our days,
Our first, our best and changeless friend.

Hear, now, our parting hymn of praise,
And bind our hearts in love divine;
O, may we walk in wisdom's ways,
And ever feel that we are thine.

CLOSING.

Master. Brother Senior Warden, our recollection of our departed friends has been refreshed, and we may now ask ourselves, were they just and perfect Masons, worthy men, unwearied toilers in the vineyard, and possessed of so many virtues as to overcome their faults and shortcomings? Answer these questions, as Masons should answer.

Sen. War. Man judgeth not of man. He whose infinite and tender mercy passeth all comprehension, whose goodness endureth forever, has called our brethren hence. Let him judge.

In ancient Egypt no one could gain admittance to the sacred asylum of the tomb until he had passed under the most solemn judgment before a grave tribunal.

Princes and peasants came there to be judged, escorted only by their virtues and their vices. A public accuser recounted the history of their lives, and threw the penetrating light of truth on all their actions. If it were adjudged that the dead man had led an evil life, his memory was condemned in the presence of the nation, and his body was denied the honors of sepulture. But Masonry has no such tribunal to sit in judgment upon her dead; with her, the good that her sons have done lives after them, and the evil is interred with their bones. She does require, however, that whatever is said concerning them shall be the truth; and should it ever happen that of a Mason, who dies, nothing good can be truthfully said she will mournfully and pityingly bury him out of her sight in silence.

Master. Brethren, let us profit by the admonitions of this solemn occasion, lay to heart the truths to which we have listened, and resolve so to walk that when we lay us down to the last sleep it may be the privilege of the brethren to strew white flowers upon our graves and keep our memories as a pleasant remembrance.

Brother Senior Warden, announce to the brethren that our labors are now concluded, and that it is my pleasure that this Lodge of Sorrow be closed.

Sen. War. Brother Junior Warden, the labors of this Lodge of Sorrow being ended, it is the pleasure of the Master that it be now closed. Make due announcement to the brethren, and invite them to assist.

Jun. War. (Calling up the Lodge.) Brethren, the labors of this Lodge of Sorrow being ended, it is the pleasure of the Master that it be now closed.

Master. Let us unite with our Chaplain in an invocation to the Throne of Grace.

*　　*　　*　　*　　*　　*　　*

Master. This Lodge of Sorrow is now closed.

SELECTIONS FOR LODGE OF SORROW.

HYMN—8's & 7's M.

Brother, rest from sin and sorrow!
Death is o'er, and life is won;
On thy slumber dawns no morrow:
Rest! thine earthly race is run.

Brother, wake! the night is waning,
Endless day is round thee poured:
Enter thou the rest remaining
For the people of the LORD.

Fare thee well! tho' woe is blending
With the tones of early love,
Triumph high and joy unending
Wait thee in the realms above!

HYMN.

Why lament our Brother's dying,
Why indulge in tears and gloom?
Calmly on the LORD relying,
He can greet the opening tomb.

Tho' for him thy soul is mourning,
Tho' with grief thy heart is riven,
While his flesh to dust is turning,
All his soul is filled with heaven.

Scenes seraphic, high and glorious,
Now forbid his longer stay:
See him die, o'er death victorious,
Angels beckon him away.

Hark! The golden harps are ringing,
Sounds angelic fill his ear:
Millions now in heaven singing
Greet his joyful entrance there

SERVICE
FOR THE
CONSECRATION OF MASONIC CEMETERIES.

IF the grounds to be consecrated are the property of a particular Lodge, this service should be conducted by the officers of that Lodge, which should be opened in due form, at the usual place of meeting, and march in procession to the Cemetery.

If several Lodges are interested, the exercises should be under the supervision of the Grand Lodge.

The brethren, having arrived at the grounds, should be arranged in such a manner as to inclose an open space, in the form of an *oblong square*. The Grand Master, his Deputy, or the Master of the Lodge—as the case may be—should stand in the East, looking toward the West.

Grand Master. Let the gates of the South and the West be guarded.

The Wardens take their respective positions.

G. M. Right Worshipful Grand Senior Warden, what is a Lodge?

G. S. W. A Lodge is the symbol of the world.

G. M. What are its dimensions?

G. S. W. It reaches from the North to the South, and from the East to the West.

G. M. Hath it any limits?

G. S. W. None; it embraceth the region of stars above, the empire of graves below, and the kingdoms of eternal silence.

G. M. You have said that the Lodge is a symbol of the world. As the world then is, in one sense, a vast Lodge, what is the last and highest duty which a Mason is called upon to discharge therein?

G. S. W. To watch by the bed of a sick and dying brother, to soothe his last hours, to console and relieve his widow, protect his orphan children, and provide a suitable resting-place for his mortal remains.

G. M. Even so; and beloved brethren, we are assembled to-day to perform the last, but not the least part of this most sacred task. We are here to consecrate these grounds, by solemn services, to a solemn use. But feeling all our weakness and blindness, and knowing that our unaided efforts must be unavailing, let us first implore the presence and aid of him from whom alone light and strength can come.

PRAYER,
BY THE CHAPLAIN.

SUPREME ARCHITECT OF THE UNIVERSE! who, in all ages, hast presided over the labors of our Fraternity, and whose benevolent and paternal care all worthy • Masons have, in all times, recognized with tears of gratitude, we approach thee now, in a spirit of filial reverence and trust, to implore Thy presence and the abundance of thy benedictions upon the solemn labors of the present hour. Knowing our weakness, we ask thee for Strength. Conscious of our ignorance, we implore of thee Light. Sensible of our frailties and imperfections, we pray that the Holy Spirit may breathe upon our hearts, that they may bloom with the flowers of Virtue and Charity, as the earth blooms beneath the genial influence of the sunshine. And, finally, O God! we beseech thee to impart to us thy Wisdom, that we may be guided into the ways of Truth, accomplish our present undertaking in a manner acceptable to thee, and be prepared for a higher service in thy Spiritual Temple above.—AMEN.

Response. So mote it be.

G. M. LORD, thou hast been our dwelling-place in all generations!

Response. And thy Mercy endureth forever.

G. M. Before the mountains were brought forth, or ever thou hadst formed the earth and the world, even from everlasting to everlasting, thou art GOD.

Response. And thy Mercy endureth forever.

G. M. Thou turnest man to destruction, and sayest, return ye children of men.

Response. Yet thy Mercy endureth forever.

G. M. For a thousand years in thy sight are but as yesterday, when it is past, and as a watch in the night.

Response. But thy Mercy endureth forever.

G. M. Thou earnest them away as a flood; they are as asleep; in the morning they are like grass that groweth up.

Response. But thy Mercy endureth forever.

G. M. In the morning it flourisheth, and groweth up; in the evening it is cut down, and withereth.

Response. But thy Mercy endureth forever.

G. M. For we are consumed by thine anger, and by thy wrath we are troubled.

Response. But thy Mercy endureth forever.

G. M. Thou hast set our iniquities before thee our secret sins in the light of thy countenance.

Response. But thy Mercy endureth forever.

G. M. For all our days are passed away in thy wrath; we spend our years as a tale that is told.

Response. But thy Mercy endureth forever.

G. M. So teach us to number our days, that we may apply our hearts unto Wisdom.

Response. For thy Mercy endureth forever.

G. M. O, satisfy us early with thy Mercy; that we may be glad and rejoice all our days.

Response. For thy Mercy endureth forever.

G. M. Make us glad according to the days wherein thou hast afflicted us, and the years wherein we have seen evil.

Response. For thy Mercy endureth forever.

G. M. Let thy work appear unto thy servants, and thy glory unto their children.

Response. For thy Mercy endureth forever.

G. M. And let the Beauty of the Lord our God be upon us; and establish thou the work of our hands upon us; yea, the work of our hands, establish thou it. And to the King, eternal, immortal, invisible, the one only living and true God, be offered worship and praise.

Response. As it was in the beginning, is now, and ever shall be, world without end. So mote it be.—AMEN.

HYMN.

O God! who, when the world was young,
  Didst walk in Eden's fragrant bowers,
Where Adam, just created, sung
  His grateful hymns 'mid trees and flowers
Thy servants here, with reverence, bend,
  As did the father of our race,
Imploring thee thy grace to send,
  And with thy glory fill this place.

O thou! who look'st with pitying eye,
  On us who dwell 'mid death's alarms,
And while we live, or when we die,
  Dost fold us in thy loving arms;
Here, where in death our loved ones sleep,
  O let thy benedictions fall,
And teach us, as their loss we weep,
  That deathless Love embraceth all.

Here, let the weary find repose,
  'Mongst fragrant flowers and waving trees—
Emblems, at once, of mortal woes,
  And everlasting sympathies—
And grant, O God! that we may see
  In Nature's swelling buds, and bloom,
The Spirit's immortality
  And final victory o'er the tomb.

G. M. Brethren: As our Masonic obligations enjoin upon us not only a tender regard for all the interests of a brother while living, but also an affectionate and honorable disposal of his remains, when the great Master of Life has summoned him to his rest, these grounds have been secured and set apart for that sacred purpose. And as Freemasonry is an institution of symbols, and communicates its instructions through a sublime system of emblems, it is eminently proper that a Masonic Cemetery should be consecrated by ceremonies of a symbolical character. It should also be adorned with trees and shrubs and flowers, which have a symbolical meaning connected with such solemn uses. No artificial monuments of iron, or brass, or stone, which we erect to preserve the remembrance of the departed, can compare in efficiency or beauty with those that Nature produces, and which, though subject to decay, are perpetually renewed.

All parts of the universe are symbolic, each one of which was, no doubt, designed by the Creator to reveal, and impress upon the mind, some special idea or sentiment. The visible world is but the shadow or reflex of the verities of the invisible, and between the seen and the unseen there is a mysterious relationship. The Spiritual is mourned in every visible thing, underlies all forms, and reveals itself in every tree and flower. Through all time, and among all peoples, have the prominent features of the universe revealed the same thoughts to all earnest hearts. Ever has the mountain been the symbol of power and durability; the oak of firmness and confidence; the various evergreens of immortality; the cypress of death; and the drooping elm, and weeping willow, of a profound sorrow and an eternal sympathy. These emblems of Hope, and Faith, and Immortality, of undying affection, and tender sympathy, and everlasting love, are the appropriate decorations of a Masonic burial-place:

Types, Truth selects, appropriate
  Fair fading creatures of a day,
Of human life to indicate
  The fragile state and swift decay;
Now in prosperity elate,
  And then forever passed away;
Bedecking thus the mortal cell,
Our tale impressively they tell.
And when the Spring's reviving breath
  Wakes latent energies below,
Leaves, buds and blossoms bursting forth,
  With graceful life and beauty glow,
Symbols of triumph over death,
  The Resurrection hope they show;
  The Grave her tenants shall restore,
And Death of victory boast no more.

One reason why we have been accustomed to look with so much terror on the grave is the dreadful gloom in which human inventions have shrouded it. The funereal emblems and rites of the olden times, and of the earlier periods of the Christian Church, were exceedingly beautiful and hopeful. But for several centuries we appear to have lost much of the deep and earnest faith of their ancestors—they have seemed to doubt whether the idea of immortality be, indeed, a verity, and, under the influence of a withering skepticism, have declared that the departed are henceforth nothing to us, and we are nothing to them. Freemasonry rebukes and repudiates such gloomy theories, so repulsive to the warm affections of the heart. The Lodge has no limitations. It reaches through all worlds. It embraces the visible world of men, and the invisible world of spirits. It proclaims that friendship survives the grave, that love is immortal, and that the Masonic ties of our great Brotherhood are as perpetual as eternity. Freemasonry, therefore, would throw no gloom around man's supreme hour, nor marshal an army of hideous spectres around the beds of the dying, or the graves of the honored dead. It would rather remove every gloomy token—take from the grave's brink the briers and thorns of fear—and plant, in their place, the flowers of hope, and trust, and love. It would rend from the sculptured monuments which cover the dead the grim and spectral images of despair, and engrave thereon the symbols of a Hope that burns more and more brightly through the ages, and of a Love which even death cannot destroy. It would quiet the fears of its children, and bring to their hearts a calm and enduring Faith in the invisible, and an imperishable trust in the Father of the world. It would so quicken that faith, that it would penetrate the veil of eternity, and see the assembly of the wise and good, who have illuminated the world by their labors, reyouthed and clothed in immortal beauty, renewing and continuing the sweet communions that commenced on earth.

To such a Faith and Hope, and under the inspiration of such a Love, let this place be consecrated. Hither let us bear our brethren, who have been stricken by the hand of death, and lay them to rest among the trees and flowers. Here may they sleep in peace, where the murmurs of the winds and trees will chant their eternal requiem, and the fairest flowers affection's hand can plant will cover their graves with perpetual bloom. And hither may we, who are yet permitted to dwell amid the sorrows of mortality, come to meditate on the brevity of life, and the vanity of all its pomp, and show, and pride—on our great obligations and duties, and the glorious reward that awaits us when we are admitted to the "Middle Chamber" of the Celestial Temple. There let us come to hold communion with the spirits of our departed brothers who may be slumbering in these solemn shades. There is nothing more salutary, more humanizing to the heart, or more strengthening to our virtue, than this frequent communion with, and invocation of, the spirit of the dead. For we should never forget that the bond of Freemasonry is a three-fold cord, over which death even has no power—that our deceased brethren yet live; are still working in the heavenly Lodges, and that they are yet bound to us, and we to them, in the ties of an eternal friendship. "After life's fitful fever, they, indeed, sleep well;" but the lives they have lived, and the examples they have given to the world, can never perish. Let us pray that by their virtue we may become more virtuous, and by their wisdom more wise; that they may watch over as guardian geniuses, and preserve us from all selfishness, irreverence, and injustice in thought, word, and deed. Standing here, the awful and silent stars over our heads; the solemn and silent graves beneath our feet, let us listen to that warning voice which resounds from the regions beyond the stars, and swells up from the realms of eternal silence. "Children of mortality," yet heirs to an endless life! remember that the great Destiny Book is placed in your hands! Beware what you write therein; for every pencil stroke, be it bright or dark, will be a beam of light, bearing into your souls an exceeding peace, or a grim shadow, waving darkly through your thoughts forever!

And, finally, let us labor faithfully and reverently in our several vocations, true to all our duties to GOD and man, so that when we are, called to close our labors on earth we may be prepared for admission to the grand and solemn mysteries of the Land of Light.

PRAYER OF CONSECRATION,
BY THE CHAPLAIN.

O thou, who art the Creator, and Father, and Preserver of all men; who, although clothed with immortal splendor, and dwelling in the high and holy place, dost condescend to abide in the hearts of the humble and contrite, we, thy servants, now draw near to thee, to supplicate thy grace, and those benedictions which thou hast promised unto all such as approach thee in a spirit of loving reverence, and child-like confidence.

When we consider thy grandeur, and our own feebleness; when we cast our eyes upward, to survey the shining heavens, where mighty constellations are sweeping in brightness through their everlasting circles, and turn our thoughts upon ourselves—frail worms of the dust—we are oppressed with a deep sense of our insignificance and unworthiness, and in our humility we exclaim, "What is man that thou art mindful of him? and the sons of men that thou regardest them?" Yet, thanks to thee, Almighty God, that notwithstanding our apparent nothingness, thou hast given us minds which can soar to thee, and invested us with the attributes of an immortal nature. Thou hast also made us capable of acquiring that divine wisdom "which is brighter than the sun, and above all the order of the stars," by which the soul is expanded to angelic perfection, and imbued with the Life and Beauty of the heavenly world.

Almighty GOD, our Heavenly Father, who lookest with benignant eye upon all men; who seest every tear of misery, and hearest the mourners cry, we implore thee to impart thy grace, and the efficient consolations of thy Spirit, to all such as are called to mourn. Soothe and comfort all the bereaved, with that Faith which hath power to pierce the dark mystery of the grave, and look upon the immortal glories beyond; and that sublime Hope which with joyful tears contemplates a future reunion of all who have been separated on earth, in a circle that death can never more invade.

O thou, who art the GOD of the dead as well as of the living, we ask thy blessing to rest upon us, who are here assembled, and upon the solemn services in which we are engaged. This quiet spot, which we consecrate to the departed, we commend to thy protection and care. May it be sanctified by thy presence. May we recognize in this murmuring foliage thy paternal voice, speaking to our hearts, in accents of tenderness and love. And, grant, O God, that thy holy angels, who watched by an ancient tomb, where suffering Virtue found repose in death, may be permitted to spread their radiant wings over this place of graves, and make it bright with the Light of an immortal Hope. Here, guarded thus by heavenly watchers, may our loved ones rest in peace, until the great day when, together with us, they shall be called to the grand Convocation to receive the recompense for faithful labors.

"Now unto Him who is able to keep us from falling and to present us before the throne of his glory, with exceeding joy, be ascribed honor, dominion, and power through all ages."—AMEN.

Response. As it was in the beginning, is now, and ever shall be, world without end.—AMEN. So mote it be.

Here an appropriate piece of music should be played by a band, during which the brethren should move in procession around the Cemetery, the Grand Master in the meanwhile sprinkling the grounds with pure water. The public grand honors are then given, which closes the ceremony.

MASONIC CALENDAR.

THE ordinary calendar, or vulgar era, is not generally used by Freemasons in dating their official documents. They have one peculiar to themselves, differing according to their various rites. The Masons in all parts of the world working in the York and French rites add 4000 years to the Christian era, calling it ANNO LUCIS—*Year of Light*; abbreviated A∴ L∴; thus the year 1865 would be A∴ L∴ 5865.[1]

Masons practicing in the ANCIENT AND ACCEPTED RITE use the Jewish Calendar, which adds 3760 to the vulgar era, styled ANNO MUNDI—A∴ M∴— *year of the world*. Or they sometimes use the Hebrew year, which begins on the 17th of September, or 1st of Tisri, using the initials A∴ H∴—ANNO HEBRAICO— *Hebrew year*.

ROYAL ARCH MASONS date from the building of the second temple—530 B.C. Their style is therefore ANNO INVENTIONIS—A∴ Inv∴—*in the year of the Discovery*.

ROYAL AND SELECT MASTERS should date from the Completion of Solomon's Temple, which would add 1000 to the Christian era. Their style is ANNO DEPOSITIONIS—A∴ Dep∴—*in the year of the Deposit*.

KNIGHTS TEMPLAR date from the organization of the Order-1118. Their style is therefore ANNO ORDINIS—A∴ O∴—*in the year of the Order*.

Those of the rite of MIZRAIM add four years to the usual computation of the age of the world: thus the year 1865 would stand A∴ L∴ 5869.

MASONS OF THE YORK RITE begin the year on the first of January; but in the FRENCH RITE it commences on the first of March.

---

[1] This fact has a symbolic reference, not because they believe Freemasonry is, but that the principles and light of the institution are, coeval with the creation.

APPENDIX.

FORM OF PETITION FOR A NEW LODGE.

To the M. W. Grand Master of Masons of the State of

THE undersigned petitioners, being Ancient Free and Accepted Master Masons, having the prosperity of the fraternity at heart, and willing to exert their best endeavors to promote and diffuse the genuine principles of Masonry, respectfully represent—That they are desirous of forming a new Lodge in the ...... of .... to be named ...... No. .... They therefore pray for letters of dispensation, to empower them to assemble as a regular Lodge, to discharge the duties of Masonry, in a regular and constitutional manner, according to the original forms of the Order, and the regulations of the Grand Lodge. They have nominated and do recommend Brother A. B. to be the first Master; Brother C. D. to be the first Senior Warden, and Brother E. F. to be the first Junior Warden, of said Lodge. If the prayer of this petition shall be granted, they promise a strict conformity to the edicts of the Grand Master, and the constitution, laws and regulations of the Grand Lodge.

FORM OF DISPENSATION FOR A NEW LODGE.

To all whom it may concern:

KNOW YE, That we, A. B., Most Worshipful Grand Master of Ancient, Free and Accepted Masons of ......, having received a petition from a constitutional number of brethren, who have been properly vouched for as Master Masons in good standing, setting forth that, having the honor and prosperity of the Craft at heart, they are desirous of establishing a new Lodge at ...... under our masonic jurisdiction, and requesting a Dispensation for the same:

And whereas there appears to us good and sufficient cause for granting the prayer of the said petition; we, by virtue of the powers in us vested by the ancient Constitutions of the Order, do grant this our DISPENSATION, empowering Brother A. B. to act as Worshipful Master, Brother C. D. to act as Senior Warden, and Brother E. F. to act as Junior Warden of a Lodge to be held under our jurisdiction at ...... by the name of ...... And we further authorize the said brethren to *Enter, Pass,* and *Raise* Freemasons, according to the Ancient Constitutions of the Order, the customs and usages of the Craft, and the Rules and Regulations of the Most Worshipful Grand Lodge of ......, and not otherwise. And this our DISPENSATION shall continue of force until the Grand Lodge aforesaid shall grant a Warrant of Constitution for the same, or this DISPENSATION be revoked by us, or the authority of the aforesaid Grand Lodge.

[L. S.]   Given under our hand, and the seal [L. S.] of the
                           Grand Lodge, at ..... this .... day of ......,A∴L∴
                                   58 .

Y...... Z......,   Q...... R.....,
  Grand Secretary.   *Grand Master.*

FORM OF WARRANT FOR A LODGE.

GRAND MASTER.
DEP. G. MASTER.
SEN. G. WARDEN.
JUN. G. WARDEN.

WE, the Grand Lodge of the Most Ancient and Honorable Fraternity of Free and Accepted Masons, of the State of ......, in Ample Form assembled, according to the Old Constitutions, regularly and solemnly established under the auspices of Prince Edwin, at the city of York, in Great Britain, in the year of Masonry 4926, viz.:

The Most Worshipful	Grand Master,
The Right Worshipful	Dep. G. Master,
The Right Worshipful	Sen. G. Warden,

do, by these presents, appoint, authorize, and empower our worthy brother .... to be the Master; our worthy brother .... to be the Senior Warden; and our worthy brother .... to be the Junior Warden, of a Lodge of Free and Accepted Masons, to be, by virtue hereof, constituted, formed, and held in .... which Lodge shall be distinguished by the name or style of ...... and the said Master and Wardens, and their successors in office, are hereby respectively authorized and directed, by and with the consent and assistance of a majority of the members of the said Lodge, duly to be summoned and present upon such occasions, to elect and install the officers of the said Lodge as vacancies happen, in manner and form as is, or may be, prescribed by the Constitution of this Grand Lodge.

And further, the said Lodge is hereby invested with full power and authority to assemble upon proper and lawful occasions, to make Masons, and to admit members, as also to do and perform all and every such acts and things appertaining to the Craft as have been and ought to be done, for the honor and advantage thereof, conforming in all their proceedings to the Constitution of this Grand Lodge, otherwise this Warrant, and the powers thereby granted, to cease and be of no further effect.

Given under our hands and the seal of our Grand Lodge, at the city of ......, in the United States of America, this .... day of ......, in the year of our Lord one thousand eight hundred and ......, and in the year of Masonry five thousand eight hundred and ......

....
Grand Secretary.

Registered in the Book of the Grand Lodge,
    Page ....

FORM OF A LODGE CERTIFICATE.

TO ALL FREE AND ACCEPTED MASONS ON THE FACE OF THE GLOBE—GREETING:

We, the Master and Wardens of ...... Lodge No. .... Free and Accepted Masons, constituted under a charter from the M. W. Grand Lodge of the State of ......, do certify that our worthy brother ...... has been regularly initiated as an Entered Apprentice, passed to the degree of Fellow Craft, and raised to the sublime degree of Master Mason, and is distinguished for his zeal and fidelity to the Craft. We do therefore recommend that he be received and acknowledged as such by all true and accepted Freemasons wheresoever dispersed.

In testimony whereof we have granted him this certificate under our hands and the seal of the Lodge (having first caused our worthy brother to sign his name in the margin), this .... day of .... A. D. 18.., A. L. 58..

W. M.   S. W.

Sec'y.   J. W.

This is to certify that ...... Lodge No. .. is a legally constituted Lodge, working under the jurisdiction of the M. W. Grand Lodge of ......

     ...... 585.

        .... Grand Sec'y.

FORM OF A GRAND LODGE DIPLOMA.

We, the Grand Lodge of the State of New York, by these presents testify and declare to all whom it may concern, that our brother ......, who has signed his name in the margin hereof, is a regular Master Mason of ...... Lodge No. .., as appears to us by the certificate of the said Lodge held under our jurisdiction in the ...... county of ...... State of New York, in the United States of America. In testimony whereof we have caused our seal to be hereunto affixed, and our Grand Secretary to subscribe the same, at the city of New York, this .. day of .... A. D. 18.. A. L. 58..

.... Grand Secretary.

FORM OF A DIMIT.

FREE AND ACCEPTED MASONS.

....   Lodge No. ....

Acknowledging the jurisdiction of the Grand Lodge of the State of ......, to all whom it may concern, erecting: This certifies that brother ......, whose name appears in the margin of this dimit, is a Master Mason, and was a member of this Lodge in good standing and clear of the books, and as such we do cordially commend him to the fraternal guard of all true Free and Accepted Masons, wherever dispersed around the globe.

In testimony whereof we have caused this dimit to be signed by the Master, and the seal of the Lodge to be attached, this .... day of A. D. 18.., A. L. 68..

.... Secretary.   .... Master.

FORM OF TRIALS AND APPEALS.

THE first step to be taken toward a Masonic trial is, of course, to prefer charges, or make a complaint. The important requisites of a complaint are, that it should be brief, and yet comprehensive, clearly defining the nature of the offense charged, with an accurate specifying of the time, place and circumstances of its commission. This, when the transaction took place out of the Lodge, may be preferred by any brother, but should properly be presented by the Junior Warden. It may be in this form:

1.—Complaint.

To the W. Master, Wardens and Brethren of Triluminar Lodge, No. 800: Brother A. B. is hereby charged with *immoral and unmasonic conduct:*

First Specification.—That the said A. B., on the first day of April 1859, in the public street, at Freetown, in the county of ......, was in a state of intoxication from the use of strong and spirituous liquors, in violation of his duty as a Mason, and to the scandal and disgrace of the Masonic Fraternity.

Second Specification.—That the said A. B., on the first day of April, 1859, at Freetown aforesaid, and at various other times and places, in the year 1859, was intoxicated with strong and spirituous liquors, although admonished therefor by the Master and Wardens of this Lodge, in violation of his duty as a Mason, to the great scandal and disgrace of the Fraternity; and it is hereby demanded, that the said A. B. be dealt with therefor, according to Masonic law and usage.

Dated April 9, 1859.   R. L., Junior Warden.

2.—Complaint (in another form.)

To the W. Master, Wardens and Brethren of Triluminar Lodge, No. 800: Brother C. D. is hereby charged with *immoral and unmasonic conduct:*

First Specification.—That the said C. D., on the first day of April, 1859, at Freetown, in the county of ......, in the presence and hearing of Bro. E. F., and others, spoke and declared of Bro. G. H., of Anchor Lodge, No. 801, these words in substance: that the said G. H. was a dishonest man; that he was a knave and a cheat; and that he was a liar, to the great injury of the said G. H., and to the common scandal and disgrace of the Masonic Fraternity.

Second Specification.—That the said C. D., on the first day of April, 1859, at Freetown aforesaid, in the presence and hearing of Mr. Y. Z., and others, publicly spoke and declared of the said G. H., who was not present, that he, the said G. H., was a dishonest man, a knave, a cheat and a liar, in violation of the duties of the said C. D. as a Master Mason, to the great injury of the said G. H., and to the common scandal and disgrace of the said Anchor Lodge, No. 801, and of the Masonic Fraternity; and it is therefore hereby demanded, that the said C. D. be put upon trial therefor.

S. L., *Junior Warden.*

Dated April 9, 1859.

These forms might be indefinitely multiplied, but these will be sufficient to show the manner and importance of specifying time, place and circumstances constituting the offense.

This charge (and that contained in the first form will hereafter he followed) having been presented in open Lodge, and received, the Master thereupon appoints commissioners to hear and try the same, pursuant to the provisions of the constitution, which is entered upon the minutes. The charges need not be entered, but the nature of them should be. It is then the duty of the Secretary immediately to serve upon the accused a copy of the charges, with the following notice annexed:

3.—Notice of Charges.

Bro. A. B. Take notice, that the within (or foregoing) is a copy of the charges preferred against you, at a stated communication of Triluminar Lodge, No. 800, held on the 9th of April, inst., and that Bros. R. S., T. U. and V. N. were appointed commissioners to hear and try the same.

P. Q., Secretary.

Dated, April 10, 1859.

Should the commissioners determine, at the time the charges are preferred (and it is recommended that they should in all cases, if possible), when and where they will meet for trial, the Secretary may add to the above notice the following: "and that they will meet for that purpose on the 20th instant, at 7 o'clock P.M., at Triluminar Lodge room, at Freetown, at or before which time you are required to answer said charges."

In case the accused absent himself, so that the charges cannot he personally served, the copy may be transmitted by mail, if his residence be known; if not, after a reasonable time, and after diligent inquiry, the Secretary should report the fact to the Lodge for their further action. In all cases the prosecutor or Secretary should take care that the accused be served with notice of the time and place of meeting of the commissioners for trial, at the time of service of the charges.

The charges being served, it is the first duty of the accused, if he has an objection to any of the commissioners, to make his challenge, that the master, if satisfied that there is ground for it, may supply the vacant place by another appointment. If there be doubts as to its foundation, the master, or other commissionors, may act as triers; but it is recommended that if there be reasonable objection, or probable cause therefor be manifest, that the commissioner challenged remove all question by resignation.

The tribunal being properly constituted, it is next the duty of the accused to answer the charges. As this must be in every case equivalent to the well-known plea of "Not Guilty," it is scarcely necessary to furnish a form, yet, for the sake of making up a complete record, in cases of appeal, one is subjoined:

4.—Answer.

C. D., in person, denies the charges made against him, and every matter and thing contained in the several specifications of the same, and demands trial thereon.

Of course this answer will vary according to the facts of each case. One specification may be admitted and another denied.

The charge and specifications may be admitted, and matters set up in extenuation or excuse. Assuming the answer to be a denial the issued is formed, and the parties proceed to trial. To procure the attendance of witnesses on either side, some process may be necessary. If the witness be not a Mason, his attendance must, of course, be voluntary; but a Mason is bound to obey a summons. This may be issued by any master of a Lodge (Constitution § 56), and in the following form:

5.—Summons for Witness.

To Bro. I. J.: You are hereby summoned and required to at-. tend as a witness before the commissioners appointed for the trial of A. B., on certain charges preferred against him, on the 20th day of April, instant, at 7 o'clock P.M., at the Lodge room of Triluminar Lodge, No. 800, in Freetown, and there to testify the truth, according to your knowledge.

K. L., *Master.*

Dated, April 16, 1859.

This may be made to answer for several witnesses, by inserting their names and adding the words "and each of you" after the word "you." The brother disobeying such a summons may be proceeded against as in case of disobedience to any other summons. For this purpose the person serving it should note upon it when and how it is served.

The commissioners, having met for trial, should organize; that is to say, one of their number (and usually the first named) should preside, though they may choose another for that purpose; and another of them should be chosen to act as their clerk, and keep the minutes of their proceedings. A copy of the resolution under which they were appointed, together with their appointment, should be furnished them by the Secretary. They should keep minutes of their proceedings, which may be in this form:

6.—Minutes of Commissioners.

The commissioners appointed for the trial of A. B., on the charges a copy of which is hereto annexed (marked A) pursuant to the following resolution (copy resolution), assembled at the Lodge room of Triluminar Lodge, No. 800, on Wednesday evening, the 20th of April, 1859:

Present: R. S., T. U. and V. N., commissioners. R. S. officiated as chairman, and V. N. was chosen clerk.

A. B. appeared before them and objected to T. U., one of the commissioners, on the ground that he was present at the meeting of the Lodge when the charges were preferred, and voted for their reference.

Bro. T. U. stated that he had formed no opinion on the subject, and the other commissioners decided that he was competent to act as commissioner, to which Bro. B. took an exception.

The charges were then read by Bro. S. L., Junior Warden, together with the answer of Bro. A. B.

Bro. B. requested that P. S., Esq., an attorney and not a Mason, should examine the witnesses on his behalf and assist him in his defense. The commissioners decided against the request, but further decided that he might employ the services of any brother to assist him in defense; to which Bro. B. took an exception. He then employed Bro. N. O. to assist him as counsel. Bro. O. objected to the form of the charges as being vague and uncertain, but the commissioners decided them to be sufficient; to which Bro. O. took an exception.

Bro. E. F. was then introduced as a witness by the Junior Warden, and testified as a Master Mason as follows: I am acquainted with Bro. A. B.; I saw him on Main street, in Freetown, on the first day of April last; I was on the opposite side of the street; he appeared to be much intoxicated (objection was made to the appearance of accused, but it was overruled and an exception taken) he was there for about half an hour; he reeled as he walked, &c.

On cross-examination Bro. E. F. further testified: I know that Bro. B. had been sick, &c.

The commissioners then adjourned to meet at the same place on Thursday evening, the 21st April 1859, at 7 o'clock Y. M.

Thursday evening, April 21, 1859.

The commissioners met pursuant to adjournment: present all the commissioners and also Bro. L. the Junior Warden and Bro. A. B. and his counsel Bro. O.

Bro. U. officiated as chairman.

Mr. H. C. was then introduced as a witness by the Junior Warden, and stated as follows:

I was in Freetown on the first day of April instant, &e.

The proofs on the part of the complainant here rested.

Bro. O., on behalf of Bro. A. B., then produced the sworn affil. davit of Mr. J. B., to which the Junior Warden objected, on the ground that Mr. B. should be produced for cross-examination.

The commissioners sustained the objection on that ground, and Bro. O. took an exception.

Mr. B. was then produced, and the Junior Warden then consented that his affidavit might be read, which was read accordingly, and is hereto annexted (marked B).

The Junior Warden then cross-examined Mr. B., who stated as follows, dc.

The proofs being closed, after hearing both parties, the commissioners decided to meet again on the 23d day of April instant, to determine on their report.

Saturday, April 23, 1859.

The commissioners again met by themselves, and after consultation decided upon their report, a copy of which is hereto annexed (marked C), and notified the parties thereof.

Signed by the Commissioners.

These minutes have been given in this extended form because hey present a convenient way of stating certain facts and proceedings on trial. Thus, the statement of formal objections and the grounds of them, together with the decision thereon of the commissioners (which should always be stated), are here set forth; also, that the Junior Warden acted as prosecutor; that the employment of an attorney not being a Mason was not permitted, but that the accused was permitted to have counsel; that the first witness testified in his character as a Master Mason, and that the second witness, not being a Mason, made his statement merely, no oath being administered to either; that the testimony is taken down in the words of the witness, and of course in the first person as be spoke; that the precise point objected to is stated; that the time and place of each adjournment are noted; that a sworn affidavit was not admitted because no opportunity was given for cross-examination; and, finally, that the commissioners met alone and decided upon their report, and then gave notice to the parties; all of which may furnish useful hints to those engaged in such trials, without further comment; it being presumed that the usual forms of such proceedings and the ordinary rules of evidence are understood and will be observed. It is at the option of the commissioners whether they will admit any one to be present but the parties and the witnesses testifying, but on all such occasions none but Masons should be admitted, except the witness not a Mason, and while testifying.

As the form of the notice given to the parties by the commissioners (Constitution, § 57) may be desired, it is here given, and may be as follows.

7.—Notice of Decision.

To Bro. S., Junior Warden, and Bro. A. B.

You will each take notice that we have agreed upon and signed our report in the matter of charges against Bro. A. B., referred to us, by which we have found the charges sustained, and Brother B. guilty thereof, and that the expenses of the proceedings be paid by him; and that we shall present the report to Triluminar Lodge at its stated communication, on the 30th April instant.

(Signed by the Commissioners.)

Dated April 23d, 1859.

The trial being concluded and the report thus agreed upon, the commissioners will have it drawn up in form for the action of the Lodge. This report need not, in the first place, contain anything but the facts found and the conclusions arrived at thereon by the commissioners. These conclusions, like those of any other committee, should be in the form of resolutions, for the definite action of the Lodge. Should the Lodge, on the report coming in, desire to hear the testimony read or any of the decisions stated, it will be the duty of the commissioners to comply.

The report may be in the following form:

8.—Report of Commissioners.

To the W. Master, Wardens and Brethren of Triluminar Lodge, No. 800.

The commissioners appointed for the trial of Bro. A. B., on charges of intoxication heretofore preferred in this Lodge, respectfully report:

That they met at the Lodge room of this Lodge on Wednesday evening, the 20th of April last past, and proceeded to hear and try the matters referred to them.

That objections were presented to Bro. U., one of their number, which they overruled, and also refused to permit Bro. B. to appear by counsel, not being a Mason, and thereupon Bro. N. O. appeared for him. That objections were made to the charges, which were overruled.

That they proceeded to take testimony (in the course of which they decided not to admit a sworn affidavit), and Bro E. F. and Mr. H. C. and Mr. J. B. were examined as witnesses.

That they held three meetings, the last of which was for the purpose of agreeing upon and preparing their report.

That from the testimony before them they find the following facts:

1. That Bro. A. B. was intoxicated with strong and spirituous liquors, in a public place, at Freetown, on the first day of April, 1859.

2. That Bro. A. B. has been at least twice intoxicated in a public place, in Freetown aforesaid, within two weeks previous to the said first day of April, 1859.

They therefore recommend the adoption of the following resolutions:

Resolved, That the charges of intoxication against Bro. A. B., made and presented to this Lodge on the 9th day of April, 1859, are sustained, and that he is guilty of the said charges.

Resolved, That Bro. A. B. be and he is hereby suspended from this Lodge, and from the rights and privileges of Masonry, for the space of three months from this date.

The charges and expenses of the commissioners amount to the sum of three dollars, which they adjudge that Bro. A. B. should pay, of all which they have notified the Junior Warden and Bro. A. B. All of which is respectfully submitted,

R. S.
T. U. *Commissioners.*
V. W.

Dated, April 23, 1859.

If the resolutions be adopted, the Secretary of the Lodge should transcribe them on his minutes, together with the adjudication as to charges and expenses. The resolutions, however, are subject to the action of the Lodge, who may reverse the decision of the commissioners, or, if sustained, may amend the resolution as to the penalty by increasing or diminishing it; the decision of the commissioners, however, as to expenses is final (Cons. § 61.) Should the resolutions be adopted (and for this purpose a majority vote is sufficient, unless the by-laws provide differently,) and the accused be absent from the Lodge, it is the duty of the Secretary to furnish him immediately with a copy of the resolutions and of the award as to expenses, with a notice, which may be in this form:

9.—Notice of Judgment.

To Bro. A. B.:

Take notice, that the foregoing is a copy of resolutions adopted by Triluminar Lodge, No. 800, at their communication held at their Lodge room in Freetown, on the 30th day of April instant, together with a copy of the award made by the commissioners as to expenses.

P. Q. *Secretary.*

Dated, April 30th, 1859.

Thus have been presented the ordinary proceedings from complaint to judgment on a Masonic trial on charges preferred in a Lodge. Some of them may be found practically unnecessary, but the complaint, minutes and report are deemed important, and should be substantially followed in every case. Other proceedings, under the title of the Constitution, entitled "Of Trial and Its Incidents," may be adapted to them, varying the allegations to suit the case, and bearing in mind that in all the cases mentioned in section 54 the decision of the commissioners is final, unless an appeal be taken from it. (§ 58.) In these cases the report will be made to the Grand Lodge, and the minutes, with the report annexed, filed in the office of the Grand Secretary, and notice given to the parties by the commissioners. Their report, in such cases, need not conclude with resolutions, but with an award of judgment in the nature of both a verdict and sentence. It may be in this form, in place of the recommendation of resolutions:

10.—Report of Commissioners (*another form*).

The said commissioners do therefore adjudge and determine as follows:

1. That the charges of intoxication against Bro. A. B., of Triluminar Lodge, No. 800, preferred by Bro. C. D., of Anchor Lodge, No. 801, on the 9th day of April, 1859, are sustained, and that he is guilty of the said chargers.

2. That the said Bro. A. B. be and he is hereby suspended from said Triluminar Lodge, and from the rights and privileges of Masonry, for the space of three months from this date.

3. That the said A. B. be adjudged to pay the charges and expenses of the proceedings on this trial.

The charges and expenses, &c., (as in the preceding report, except as to parties notified, and add) and our report has been duly filed with the R. W. Grand Secretary (dated and signed by the commissioners).

The following may be the form of their notice:

11.—Notice of Judgment by Commissioners.

To .... and ....

Take notice that we have this day made and signed our report to the Grand Lodge, by which we have adjudged and determined that Bro. A. B. is guilty of the charges preferred against him, and that he is suspended from Triluminar Lodge, No. 800, and from the rights and privileges of Masonry, for the space of three months, and that he do pay the costs and expenses of the proceedings before us; amounting to the sum of three dollars.

Signed by the Commissioners.

Dated, April 23, 1859.

The subject of Appeals next claims our attention, and we shall still follow the form of proceedings after trial on charges preferred in a Lodge against a member.

The time limited in every case for bringing an appeal is six months (§ 58); but where a party is intending to appeal it is advisable that he give notice of it immediately, which may be in the following form:

12.—Notice of Appeal.

To P. Q., Secretary of Triluminar Lodge, No. 800:

Take notice, that I shall bring an appeal from the action of said Lodge on the 30th day of April, 1859, in passing sentence of suspension on me for three months, to the M. W. Grand Lodge of the State of New York (or the M. W. Grand Master, R. W. Deputy Grand Master, or R. W. District Deputy Grand Master of this district, as he may choose,) on the grounds to be stated in my appeal.

A. B.

Dated, May 4. 1859.

On receiving this notice, the Secretary of the Lodge—or, in all cases not under section 60, the commissioners—will transmit to the Grand Lodge, or Grand officer, as the case may be, a copy of the minutes of proceedings embracing the evidence, with n copy of the report, to the Lodge—marked C and numbered 8—annexed, all duly attested and certified; and by carefully observing these directions it may always be done promptly. This, if filed with the Grand Secretary, may be furnished to the Grand Lodge, or its Committee on Appeals, or to the Grand officer appealed to, when desired. When the appeal is to a Grand officer, the report may be transmitted to him directly, to be by him afterwards filed with the Grand Secretary. The appellant should next prepare his appeal, which may be in this form:

13.—Appeal.

To the M. W. Grand Lodge of the State of New York (or M. W. Grand Master):

The undersigned hereby appeals to you from the decision of Triluminar Lodge, No. 800, made April 30, 1859, in passing sentence of suspension on him for three months, and he specifies the following as the ground of his appeal:

1. That F. U., one of the commissioners on his trial, was incompetent to act, having been present at the meeting of said Lodge when the charges were preferred, and voted for their reference.

2. That the commissioners erred in deciding that P. S., Esq., should not be allowed to assist the undersigned in his defense.

3. That the second specification of the charges is vague and uncertain.

4. That the commissioners erred in receiving testimony as to appearances of intoxication.

5. That they erred in rejecting the sworn affidavit of J. R.

6. That the proofs in the case were not sufficient to warrant the finding of the commissioners.

7. That the Lodge erred in passing the resolution of suspension by a majority vote.

All of which appears by the papers, proceedings and evidence in the case.

A. B.

Dated, May 11, 1859.

A copy of this appeal should be served on the Secretary of the Lodge; and it is best, also, to serve a copy on the appellate tribunal or officer. Within ten days (this is suggested as an admirable time, there being no regulation on the subject,) an answer should be made to the appeal by the Lodge. As in most cases this is merely taking issue, the form of an answer on appeal may be unnecessary; yet one is subjoined, as follows:

14.—Answer to Appeal.

Triluminar Lodge, No. 800, answers the appeal of A. B. and says:

That the said Lodge denies that there is any error in the proceedings of said Lodge, or of the commissioners appointed for the trial of the said A. B., and further says that the decision of said Lodge in said case is sustained both by the law and evidence therein applicable thereto.

S. L., *Junior Warden.*

Dated, May 21, 1859.

This is very general, and if a specific denial is deemed necessary—taking issue upon each of the grounds of appeal and assigning reasons therefor—it may be made after the foregoing form in commencement, and adding thereto as follows:

Because the said Lodge says as to the first ground of appeal, &c.

And because the said Lodge says as to the second ground of appeal, &c.

The case being thus fairly brought up on appeal, the Grand Lodge or Grand officer may hear the same, either by oral argument, or the appeal and answer thereto may be made sufficiently full to call attention to all the points in the case and the reasons therefor. If the Secretary of the Lodge shall have omitted a transcript of the proceedings of the Lodge, and the same be required to make the case perfectly understood, the Grand Master, Deputy Grand Master, or District Deputy Grand Master may make an order in this form:

15.—Order on Appeal.

OFFICE OF THE GRAND MASTER OF MASONS,
May 28, 18..

To the W. Master, Warden and Brethren of Triluminar Lodge, No. 800:

Bro. A. B. having duly appealed from the decision of your Lodge made on the 30th April, 1859, suspending him for three months, you are hereby required to transmit, by the hand of your Secretary and seal of your Lodge, a transcript of all the proceedings of your Lodge, in the case of the said A. B., from the time of the presentation of the charges against him until the final action of your Lodge thereon, with the several dates thereof, together with all papers and documents relating thereto not heretofore returned, within .... days from the receipt of this order by you.

Given under my hand and private seal on the day
and year first above written.

...., *Grand Master.*

After argument the appellate tribunal will, with all convenient dispatch, pronounce the decision. If made by a Grand officer, it should be filed, together with the appeal papers, in the office of the Grand Secretary, and may be in this form:

16.—Decision on Appeal.

OFFICE OF THE GRAND MASTER OF MASONS, &c., June 4, 1859.

<table>
<tr><td>In the Matter of the Appeal
of
Brother A. B.</td><td>Brother A. B. having appealed from the decision of Triluminar Lodge, No. 800, made on the 30th day of April, 1859, by which he was suspended from the rights</td></tr>
</table>

and privileges of Masonry for three months, on charges of intoxication; and having heard the case, I have carefully considered the facts appearing on said appeal, and the grounds of error alleged by him. There does not seem to be any error or irregularity in the proceedings, or in the several decisions of the commissioners on the trial, and the facts of the case warrant the conclusions of the commissioners and the decision of the Lodge.

[If the officers desire to review the facts or comment upon any of the points taken, he may here insert his remarks and reasons.]

My judgment and decision, therefore, is, that the proceedings and decisions of Triluminar Lodge, No. 800, in the case of Bro. A. B., be and the same are hereby affirmed.

...., *Grand Master.*

If the decision be reversed, the appellate officer will vary the second paragraph and give his reasons for dissenting from the conclusions of the commissioners and Lodge, and use the word "reversed" in the last paragraph, instead of "affirmed." Should he desire to make any special order in the case, it may be added at the end.

When an appeal is taken from the decision of a Grand officer, on appeal to the Grand Lodge the case will be heard on the papers which were before him, and it will only need the following and final form of an appeal to bring up the matter, which should be served on the Lodge through its proper officer, a reasonable time (say twenty days) before the annual communication of the Grand Lodge, and a copy transmitted to the Grand Secretary forthwith.

17.—Final Appeal to Grand Lodge.

To the M. W. Grand Master (or R. W. Deputy Grand Master) and the W. Master Wardens and Brethren of Triluminar Lodge, No. 800:

The undersigned, A. B., hereby appeals to the M. W. Grand Lodge of the State of New York, from the decision of the M. W. Grand Master, made in and by his order of June 4th, 1859, in the case of this appellant, affirming the decision of said Lodge on the 30th April, 1859, in the same case, on the grounds particularly stated and set forth in his appeal to the M. W. Grand Master, dated May 11, 1859, and respectfully prays your consideration thereof and judgment thereon.

Dated, June 6, 1859.   A. B.

In the nature of the case, no answer to this appeal is required; and when the appeal comes before the Grand Lodge it will take the direction prescribed by its rules and usages.

From the foregoing general forms and directions, sufficient may be gathered to apply to every case of Masonic discipline and trial, between any parties and whatever may be the decision. To have extended the forms, or adapted those given to every varying change, would be great labor without adequate benefit, and especially in the great variety of charges. It should be remarked that, when the charges are based upon a section of the constitution, or of the Lodge by-laws, it should be plainly and distinctly referred to.

Should the accused admit the charges when served upon him, proof of such admission or confession will be all that the commissioners are required to have made, and they will make up their minutes, and report accordingly, adopting the foregoing forms.

If the accused fails to appear and answer the charges after personal service, the Commissioners may proceed, after taking proof of such service, to take proof of the charges, and in such case the Master should appoint some brother to appear for him. The minutes and report in such cases should be full, and the forms given can readily be modified to snit such a state of facts.

DISPENSATION TO A LODGE TO CONTINUE ITS LABORS, AFTER THE DESTRUCTION OR LOSS OF ITS WARRANT.

WE, ..., Most Worshipful Grand Master of Masons, in and for the State of ...., to the Worshipful Master, Wardens, and members of .... Lodge, No ...., held in .... GREETING: WHEREAS, our Right Worshipful Grand Lodge, by warrant under the hands of the then R. W Grand Officers, and seal of the Grand Lodge, bearing date ...... the ...... day of in the year of our LORD one thousand ...... hundred and ......, and of Masonry five thousand ...... hundred and ......, and recorded in the book of warrants ......, page ..., authorized the holding of a Lodge under their jurisdiction, in ...., or within five miles thereof, to be called .... No. .., which Lodge was duly constituted on the ...., and the labors thereof carried on agreeably to the Ancient Landmarks, so far as our Grand Lodge has information respecting the same:

And, WHEREAS, it has been represented to us that the said warrant has been lost or mislaid: Now, therefore, by virtue of the powers and authorities in us vested, we do hereby authorize, empower, and request you, the present, and succeeding Worshipful Master, Wardens, and members of the said Lodge, No. ..., to continue your Masonic labors, in the same full and complete manner, to all intents and purposes, as you could, or might legally have done, if your said warrant had not been ...... and was still in existence, agreeably to all the usages, rules and regulations of the ancient craft, and especially to those of our Grand Lodge, and not contrarywise.

Given under our hand and seal, at the city of .., in the State of .., this ... day of ...., in the year of our LORD one thousand eight hundred and. ...., and of Masonry five thousand eight hundred and ....

[L. S.]

Attest,

...., *Grand Master.*

.... *Grand Secretary.*

CERTIFICATE OF ELECTION.

The certificate of the election of officers in a Subordinate Lodge should be in the following form, and said officers cannot be recognized as members of the Grand Lodge until a proper certificate of election is filed in the Grand Secretary's office:

Be it known, that on the .... day of .... A. L. 58.., at a regular meeting of .... Lodge, No. ... held in the ...., county of .... in the State of ...., our worthy Brother .... was elected Master; our worthy Brother .... Senior Warden, and our worthy Brother .... Junior Warden of the said Lodge, for the ensuing year, and that said Master and Wardens have been duly installed.

In testimony whereof we, the members of the said Lodge, have caused the seal thereof to be hereunto affixed, and our Secretary to sign the same.

[L. S.]   ....Secretary.

FORM OF A PROXY.

The Proxy of the Subordinate Lodges should be in the following form, viz:

At a meeting of .... Lodge, No. ...., held at ...., in the county of ...., in the State of ...., on the ... day of ... A. L. 58..

Resolved, That our Worshipful Brother ...., Past Master (or Master, as the case may be,) of   Lodge, No. ..., be and he is hereby appointed Proxy, to represent this Lodge in the Grand Lodge of the State of ...., and he is fully empowered to act in our behalf, in all the transactions of the Grand Lodge, as effectually as if we ourselves were personally present.

All which we have caused to be certified by our Master and Wardens, and the seal of our Lodge to be affixed.

[L. S.]   ...., Master.
                                        ...., Senior Warden.
                                        ...., Junior Warden.

...., Secretary.

www.ingramcontent.com/pod-product-compliance
Lightning Source LLC
Chambersburg PA
CBHW050437290526
45786CB00006B/2061